1.95

W9-AXI-837

JOURNEY INTO CRIME

By the Same Author **THE FBI STORY**

JOURNEY

INTO

CRIME

Don Whitehead

RANDOM HOUSE

HV 6245
W59 j

To the Littlest Bandits—

Gene Donald, 10, Eddie, 6, and Marie, 3.

CONTENTS

JOURNEY INTO CRIME

INTRODUCTION

Crime in Any Language

The late afternoon sun threw long August shadows across the streets of West Berlin. The workday was ending for most Berliners. People streamed from office buildings heading for home or perhaps for a stroll along Kurfürstendamm, the glittering show window of the West, which contrasts so oddly with the drabness of the central streets in Communist East Berlin.

The shops along Kurfürstendamm, their display windows crammed with merchandise of all kinds, were doing a brisk trade. Hardly a table was vacant at any of the sidewalk cafés or in the restaurants where trays were piled with frosted cakes, sugar cookies and pastry creations topped with frothy blobs of whipped cream. There was no rationing and, best of all, the people had money with which to treat themselves to some of the luxuries.

The streets mirrored the economic and spiritual resurgence of West Germany since the war. The display of prosperity was an open taunt to the lords of communism. It was a magnet, drawing people from all parts of the city. East Berliners slipped across the dividing line to feast their eyes on consumer goods, like children turned loose in a toy shop, and then they smuggled small purchases past the East German guards. To these people, the line dividing the city was a hateful barrier. But the criminals and Communist agents who operated out of East Berlin often found the border a useful, protective shield.

On this August day, as the crowds thickened on Kurfürstendamm, a battered black Mercedes-Benz sedan cruised slowly through the streets of West Berlin. Police Detective Hans Wardetski sat behind the driver scanning each face that passed. For months the police had been seeking an elusive Communist courier, a much wanted criminal, who had been slipping in and out of West Berlin. He was wanted as the "finger man" in the kidnapping of several refugees by Communist agents. The police had a tip that he had entered West Berlin that morning.

The police car was halfway along a block of apartment buildings when Wardetski spotted his man. He signaled the driver to stop and stepped out of the car no more than twenty feet from his quarry. But the Red agent recognized the detective. He wheeled and ran, dodging among the startled pedestrians with Wardetski in close pursuit. The detective could not shoot for fear of hitting a pedestrian. The hunted man sprinted to an alleyway and ducked around the corner. Then he stopped and calmly fished a cigarette from a crumpled pack.

Wardetski raced to the corner and halted as if he had run head on into a glass barrier. The two men faced each other with no more than ten feet separating them. The fugitive lit his cigarette, flipped the burned match toward the detective insolently, and then laughed.

"Why don't you step over here and get me?" he taunted. "It's only a few feet. Are you frightened?"

Wardetski could only glare at the man, and inwardly curse his luck. He could not step across that line. The corner of the building was on the dividing line between East and West Berlin. If he crossed, and his chief learned about it, he probably would be summarily fired from the force. And so he had to stand and watch one of the most wanted Red agents walk away.

The West Berlin police have perhaps the most unusual problems of any police force in the free world. Ringed by Communist East Germany, they battle not only the criminals, but also Communist agents. Berlin authorities take extraordinary precautions to prevent Communist or Red sympathizers from infiltrating the police force—and for this reason, no policeman is allowed to cross into East Berlin.

Not long ago, a West Berlin policeman completed his tour of duty and entered the subway, bound for home. It had been a long, hard day and he was tired. He dozed for a few minutes and then awoke with the chilling realization that the train had crossed the border and was pulling into an East Berlin station. He got off, hoping to catch the next train back without being noticed. But even though he was not in uniform, the East German police spotted him. He was taken to police headquarters for questioning.

The police searched their prisoner and found his police

identification card and badge. The police chief was summoned. He arrived and jovially ordered beer. He talked of everything but politics and police work. At last he told an aide to return the prisoner's personal effects.

"You may go now," he said. "You see, it hasn't been unpleasant. We aren't as bad as our enemies claim."

The relieved policeman stammered his thanks, eager to get back across the border as quickly as possible. As he started toward the door, the police chief said, "This has been so pleasant, I would like you to pay us another visit . . . say Friday of next week?"

"Thanks. I'll be glad to," the policeman said.

The policeman was escorted to the subway and soon was safely in the Western sector shaking with relief. He knew his job was in jeopardy if his superiors learned he had been in East Berlin fraternizing with the Communist police. Would anyone believe his story of falling asleep on the subway and being taken to their headquarters against his will? Perhaps, but his carelessness would not go unpunished and the chances were that he would be dismissed from the force.

He decided to keep the incident to himself. He began to feel easier as the days passed and no one at headquarters asked any questions. When Friday came, he said to himself, To hell with them. I'm not going back.

Two days later a messenger left a note at his home which said: "Dear Comrade: I waited all day Friday for you to visit us as you promised. I assume you were ill, so I shall expect you next Friday." The note was signed by the East Berlin police chief.

The policeman burned the letter and again ignored the invitation. After the next Friday a messenger left another envelope at his home. When he opened it, he was horrified to find several photographs enclosed. One photo was a close-up shot of his police identification card and personal belongings. The others showed him drinking beer and shaking hands with the chief of the East Berlin police. He realized a hidden camera had recorded every move he made while at the Red headquarters.

A note enclosed with the photographs said: "Dear Comrade: You have failed to keep two appointments. You will appear at our headquarters next Friday evening or else these photographs will be sent to your superior officers."

This was the crudest kind of blackmail. The policeman knew that if he returned to East Berlin he was lost. The Reds would force him to become their agent, to spy on his own government and his own friends. To his everlasting credit, the policeman took his story to his superiors. He was suspended and for years will suffer for this one moment of carelessness. But he saved his own honor and denied the Communists a valuable agent.

Such revealing incidents as these were gathered on an eight months' trip around the world, during which I visited more than twenty countries to collect unusual crime stories and to have a look at police operations. The journey began at the headquarters of the Federal Bureau of Investigation in Washington. It led me to Scotland Yard in London, to the Sûreté in Paris, to Belgium, Germany, Liechtenstein, Austria, Italy, Spain and Greece. The journey continued through Turkey, Thailand, Indonesia, Malaya, Hong Kong, Vietnam, the Philippines, and Japan.

Perhaps the most significant thing that I found on this entire journey was the tremendous influence which the FBI and Scotland Yard are having on the police of other countries. The FBI and Scotland Yard are regarded around the world as the two outstanding police agencies in existence today. Police come from all over the world to these headquarters to study their methods of fighting crime and their organization.

The FBI has become a symbol of efficiency and integrity for many professional police officers who hope that, with time, they can achieve the same results. But I found police officials, too, particularly in some Asian countries, who despaired of ever lifting their profession above the level of corruption, cynicism and oppression that exists in their governments.

Looking into the background of Scotland Yard and the FBI, one finds a curious parallel in their early histories. Scotland Yard came into being under the same sort of distrust and bitter opposition that marked the beginning of the FBI.

When President Theodore Roosevelt authorized the formation of the first FBI within the Department of Justice in 1908, there was an uproar in Congress. Some members of Congress predicted this Federal investigative force would become an espionage system within the government and a corrupting influence. They accused Roosevelt of organizing a personal espionage force to spy on members of Congress who were unfriendly to him. It was under this sort of cloud that the FBI came into being.

Scotland Yard—or more correctly the Metropolitan Police Force—traces its history back to 1749 when Magistrate Henry Fielding organized a police force known as the Bow Street Runners. The Runners were organized to protect citizens from thieves, footpads, and cutthroats who roamed the dark streets of London at night virtually unchecked by any authority.

Earlier, the merchants who imported goods from the West Indies had organized their own river police to combat the thievery of gangs working in league with ship's crews. The merchants were frantic because about half the merchandise brought into the Thames River never did reach the merchants' warehouses. The organized looting of the ships was one of the biggest black-market operations in London's history.

These privately financed organizations spread and for years constituted London's police force. But in 1782 the government organized a police force known as the Patroles which was placed under direction of the Bow Street Magistrates—but with the Home Office having a measure of authority.

However, the Patroles became little more than a private detective agency. An investigation by Parliament described them as "private speculators in the detection of crime, rather than efficient officers for the ends of justice." Crime went almost unchecked. The great city had no means of dealing with riots or controlling large crowds except by the use of troops.

As the situation grew progressively worse, the British Government studied the problem. Committee after committee made recommendations. But nothing came of them because opponents of an organized police force cried that their liberties were at stake. It was better, they argued, for a few criminals to be free than for the people to have their liberties taken away from them by an oppressive police system.

However, in 1828, a committee headed by Sir Robert Peel led a reform movement that exposed the crime situation thoroughly to public view. The opposition was beaten down. The following year an act was passed establishing the Metropolitan Police Force.

The opponents, however, won one concession. They succeeded in exempting the old City of London from the act. This inner city within the boundaries of Greater London is now mainly the city's financial district. To this day it has an independent police force. Scotland Yard's only jurisdiction in the old city is in cases of fraud.

The Metropolitan Police Force was organized by two Irishmen, Colonel Charles Rowan and Sir Richard Mayne, who had their office at No. 4 Whitehall Place. The back of their office and police headquarters opened onto a courtyard of an ancient house which had once been the London residence of the kings of Scotland. Before long, Londoners referred to the Metropolitan Police Headquarters as Scotland Yard.

Rowan and Mayne realized that the newly organized police force would never last or have any effectiveness without the support of the public. They drilled into carefully selected recruits the necessity for helpfulness, courtesy and service—and they set a high standard of conduct that has continued throughout the years. Just as J. Edgar Hoover insisted on a high standard for his agents from the time he became FBI director, so Rowan and Mayne, almost a century earlier, demanded the best from their men.

Sir Richard Mayne defined the duties of his police in this fashion: "The primary object of an efficient police is the prevention of crime; the next that of detection and punishment of offenders if crime is committed. To these ends all the efforts of police must be directed. The protection of life and property, the preservation of public tranquillity, and the absence of crime will alone prove whether those efforts have been successful, and whether the objects for which the police were appointed have been obtained."

The headquarters of Scotland Yard was moved in 1890 into quarters near the House of Commons, which is now known as New Scotland Yard.

The Yard, as most Londoners call it, is controlled by the office of the Home Secretary and not the city fathers of London.

All other police forces throughout the country answer to local authorities at the county, borough or city level. However, the British Government pays half the operating cost of the police forces outside London and in this way maintains a measure of control over them. Each police force, to collect the government funds, must satisfy the Home Secretary that it is efficiently operated.

Frequently, efforts are made to compare the FBI and Scotland Yard, when in fact the two organizations are hardly comparable either in organization or the duties they perform. The FBI is authorized to act only against violations of Federal law and it has no jurisdiction in local crime. The Yard is more like the New York City police force in its duties and operations.

However, Scotland Yard almost always directs the investigations of major crimes such as murder, regardless of where they happen throughout the country. This comes about in this way: each local government outside of London must pay the cost of investigating a murder, unless within forty-eight hours of the crime, a request is made for Scotland Yard to handle the case. When such a request is made within forty-eight hours, then Scotland Yard takes over and the expense of the investigation is borne by the Home Office. In actual practice, the local police almost always ask for Scotland Yard's help—not only to protect their own budget but to get the experienced investigators and services which the Yard can give. In this sense, Scotland Yard is a "national" police force.

The Yard has a total force of about 20,000, of which some 1,500 are in the Criminal Investigation Department. Those in the CID are regarded as the elite of the Yard. There are about 500 women on the force, who get the same training as the men, but they specialize primarily in problems involving women and children.

The Yard has found that trained police dogs are useful in helping patrolmen on their beats. Most of the dogs are Alsatians and Labradors. They are used in areas where rowdyism prevails and in searching premises at night. About 700 arrests a year are made with the help of dogs.

The CID is divided into six sections, as follows: C1, or the Central Office, handles serious crime inside and outside the city, such as extradition and fugitive cases, international crime, forgery, fraud on banks, etc.; C2, reports and correspondence; C3, fingerprints; C4, crime records, such as methods of committing crimes, indexes of aliases, nicknames of criminals, etc.; C5, information, publications; C6, administrative duties and recommendations for promotions, etc. A special branch is detailed to handle internal security, protection of royalty, protection of ministers, naturalization and passport matters.

This grouping of special powers within the hands of Scotland Yard (the same powers that are distributed among several Federal agencies in the United States) doesn't seem to bother the Britisher. There is no outcry today in Britain that Scotland Yard has "sinister" powers or that it may become a "Gestapo."

Only on special occasions does a British policeman ever carry a weapon of any kind. Neither is the British policeman subject to the political pressures which can be brought to bear on the lawmen in American towns and counties, since his job is protected by civil service rules and not dependent on any particular administration being in power. And I have the strong impression, in reading British crime cases, that the courts give more support to their law-enforcement officers and are more sympathetic to them in their work than most American courts. The great strength of the British system is in this attitude of the courts and in a people who recognize there could be no government by law without the police. In turn, the police are careful not to overstep legal bounds.

One of the most interesting developments in the European police systems has been the effort of such countries as West Germany to overcome the memory of the Gestapo, which operated by direction of Hitler. Under their new government, the West German police have become "democratized" and are operating under stringent rules which did not apply in the days when the Nazis used their police as a virtual espionage net and individual liberties were ignored. Their greatest job, German police officials admit privately, is to merit public confidence. No police force in a democratic country can operate effectively unless it has the support of the public. And the West German police force is working hard to achieve that end.

The same situation exists also in Austria, Italy and Japan.

The police systems and the laws controlling them have been overhauled since World War II, and each country faces the difficult task of living down the reputation gained during the years in which the states corrupted the systems.

For those who seek a refuge from crime, there is the beautiful, secluded, and peaceful little postage-stamp country of Liechtenstein. Tucked between the towering Alps of Switzerland and Austria, this principality has perhaps the smallest police force of any free country in the world. Its police force numbers twelve—and most of the duties are concerned with handling the tourist traffic which rolls through the little village of Vaduz beneath the gray old castle which sits on the mountainside.

The Liechtenstein police were in a dither a few years ago as they worked on a great mystery. For several days they noticed a bicycle parked in front of the police station. No one knew to whom it belonged, and a bicycle standing day and night on the main street of Vaduz had an ominous look to it. A policeman was assigned to watch the bicycle and question the owner when he finally claimed his transportation. After hours and hours of patient watching the owner did appear. The policeman questioned him and the mystery was solved. The owner had been in jail for a minor infraction of the law.

During the last fifty-nine years, Liechtenstein has had only three violent crimes. In 1905, a butcher was working late in his shop when a German entered and made a small purchase. The customer paid for his purchase with a 1,000-franc note, but the butcher did not have the change at hand for a note of that size. He went upstairs to get the change and when he returned, the German bashed him in the head and ran away with all the money. The blow was fatal. The next violent crime came forty-seven years later when an ex-policeman, mentally deranged, shot his mother and father. Then four years later a postman in the village of Schaan was distressed to find a man on his route beating his wife. The postman warned the husband that if he caught him at this again, he would thrash him. The angry husband followed the postman, shot him fatally, and then went home and shot himself to death.

In violent contrast to the police of tiny Liechtenstein is the chilling police system that exists behind the Iron Curtain. After the death of Stalin, the political power of the Red-controlled police was reduced, but not their activities, and their methods remain the same.

The police of Hungary are typical. The political police— those who deal with the so-called crimes against the state— wear a blue insignia. The border guards, formerly a part of the army but now under control of the Budapest police headquarters, wear a green insignia. Both are called the AVH and take orders from a ministerial committee at cabinet level, under the Ministry of Interior. The army, in which Russians have "advisory" positions, trains and supplies the border guards but has no control over its operations.

In addition to the uniformed AVH, there are the plain-clothes police, the most dreaded in the AVH. They have help from an estimated 20,000 part-time police workers throughout Hungary. The latter work in pairs, visiting families and turning in reports on how many children are in each family, how many religious crosses are in each room, the type of clothing that is worn, the type food that is eaten, the political attitudes of individuals, and their daily habits. The reports become a part of the central AVH file and when the secret police find anything suspicious in the actions or attitudes of an individual, he or she is hauled in for a questioning.

The porters and janitors in apartment buildings and business houses form an effective espionage net. After the Hungarian Revolution, the Communist government fired sixty percent of the porters and janitors, and replaced them with their own informers. They are required to report every move made by inhabitants in their buildings so far as possible. They make written reports weekly on who visited whom, when they left, the movements of each occupant, and what they were overheard to say. When more than two people stop on the street for a conversation, AVH men may very well break up the gathering and take each person aside separately to question him on what the conversation was about. Unless the stories of all jibe completely, they are taken to the police station for questioning as suspicious characters.

Hungarian refugees say that the supreme commander of the

AVH is a Russian MVD (secret police) officer whose name is a well-kept secret. The so-called Soviet advisers formerly had controlling positions only in Budapest. But since the revolution the Russians reportedly occupy strategic offices throughout the AVH.

No one hears of ordinary crimes behind the Iron Curtain because virtually all such stories are suppressed in the Communist-controlled press. The only crimes publicized are the "political crimes"—which are the ones of major importance to the Reds. To read the Red-controlled press, one would get the impression that the countries are marvelously free of ordinary crimes of violence. But this, of course, is not true. It is simply that the Reds do not publicize their crimes, in order that they may boast about the superior morality in Communist countries as contrasted to capitalist states.

During the Hungarian Revolution there was a split within the police force. The blue AVH joined in the effort to suppress the revolt. But the green border guard, almost to a man, joined the revolutionary forces. The people's hatred boiled over against the blue AVH. They were the first sought out by the people for revenge in bloody battles throughout Budapest.

Police terror is an organized part of the Communist regimes. And the police control the movements of the people by means of "passports" for travel within each country. The system used in Soviet Russia is identical to the system used in the satellite states. For example, a No. 1 passport in the Soviet Union is valid for travel throughout the entire country. The No. 2 passport is valid for all Russia except seven major cities. The No. 3 passport is good only for travel in one specific Soviet Republic. These three types of passport are for those people who are "free"—the trusted political leaders and those of the managerial class. The No. 1 passport is a very rare document. The No. 3 is rather general, but if a person wishes to go from one Soviet Republic to another, he must apply for permission.

There is a fourth document that ties the holder to a specific locality. He can travel no more than twenty kilometers from a given town or city. After World War II, the Soviet government did not wish the troops who had been in Western Europe to travel around telling others what they had seen in the West.

Virtually all these troops, refugees say, were given the No. 4 document, which tied them to one spot when they returned home.

Since 1954, Hungary has issued an identity card which serves as a passport. It contains vital statistics concerning the holder. This card, when properly stamped, is valid for all Hungary except border areas, which require a special pass. There are seven cities where special permission is needed for travel. Another special permit is required if one wishes to stay in these seven cities for longer than forty-eight hours.

There are permits also to get into factories, offices, apartments, and buildings. The average citizen must fill out all sorts of information as though he were going for a visit to the atomic plant in Los Alamos—and a record is kept of each visit made to these specified places. There is one police organization which handles "reports in the general interest." It does nothing else but check on the reports from informers. Each business office has its own confidential-information section manned by trusted informants.

One Hungarian refugee said to me bitterly, "In most of the Western world, the purpose of the police is to fight criminals. But over there, the police are the State . . . and *they* are the criminals."

Refugee centers in the West, such as Marienfels in Berlin, and those in Austria, are reflections of police terror and repression behind the Iron Curtain. The refugees still come by the hundreds each week—men, women, and children. An increasing number of the adults are doctors, engineers, scientists, school teachers, and those in the upper echelon of managerial work. They are turning their backs on their old homes to seek a new life in the West, free from the police system which leaves so little hope for them or their children.

In Istanbul I crossed the Bosporus and walked through the streets of the old city to the police headquarters near the towering dome of the ancient mosque of San Sophia. I asked for an interview with someone who could give me the files on a murder which had occurred only a short time before. "You should see Inspector Huriser," a police official said. He pointed to a doorway at the end of the hall. "You will find the inspector in there."

I entered the office and a young woman, looking as trim and efficient as any American secretary, glanced up from her desk. I was glad Turkey had banished veils for the women because it would have been a crime to have hidden such a lovely face as this young lady turned to me.

"I would like to speak to your boss, Inspector Huriser," I said.

She smiled. "I am Inspector Huriser."

And so she was. I was to learn that Turkey has several women police officials and that Miss Huriser was not occupying that position just because of her looks. She had been graduated with honors from Scotland Yard's Police Training School. And this in a country which only a few years ago gave women virtually no rights.

But then there were surprises also in Bangkok, Djakarta, Singapore, Saigon, Manila, Hong Kong, and Tokyo.

I found sometimes to my surprise, that the police in almost every country were co-operative and eager to discuss their problems and the crimes which had intrigued them most. Also at times they were embarrassingly emotional about their work.

I remember vividly one evening in an exotic Asian city when a young police officer suddenly burst into tears of frustration because he wanted to be proud of his profession—and couldn't. This is his story told in his own words as nearly as I can recall them:

"I was chosen to study your Western police methods and my government sent me to Scotland Yard and then to your FBI Academy. It was a wonderful experience, you must understand. I met many fine men and they became my friends. I was taught the very latest techniques in fighting criminals and I worked with the best equipment.

"Most important, I learned that these were honest men with an honorable code and they were not asked to do dishonorable things. It made me very proud to be with them and I was determined to bring their practices back to my country.

"But when I returned, I found we do not have the modern equipment and no one cares about the fine techniques I learned.

Worst of all, who are the biggest criminals? The politicians. They are the grafters, the cheaters, and the robbers. They are robbing the people of millions—much of it your money given to us in the aid program—and I am helpless. What can I do about it?"

A retired Philadelphia detective, serving in one of the U. S. missions, was in the automobile with us. After an awkward silence, he put his hand on the young man's shoulder and said, "Don't give up, son. All of us have had to go through the same fight. Maybe you can't change things overnight, but don't stop trying. The day will come when you can help change them. And you'll be surprised how many people will be on your side."

Unless the politicians corrupt him, that young man may one day be proud of his profession.

The reason for this young man's despair can be found in such cases as the one which happened during one of the revolutionary coups in Thailand: The Ping River has its source in the mountains of northwest Thailand near the Burmese border. It flows through canyons and jungle-like mountains eastward into the Chao Phraya River, and is one of the highways through that rough country. Among other things, it is a highway for the transportation of illegal opium from the Shan states of Burma and the Yunnan region of Red China. The poppies are grown by hill tribes in these mountain regions. The tribesmen burn off entire hillsides in preparing the soil for the poppy crop. After the poppy heads are harvested and the seeds are cooked to a gummy state, the raw opium is packed in tins.

In December, 1958, a band of men carried seven tons of opium over secret mountain trails to the headwaters of the Ping River. They loaded the tins of opium onto barges and floated downstream to a rendezvous with a launch-drawn barge. The tins were transferred to the round-hulled barge and covered with rice.

Every move was made with military precision. This was not surprising because those handling the opium were army and police officials acting under orders from a high authority in Bangkok.

The seven tons of opium moved down the Ping and then the

Chao Phraya as uneventfully as any of the ordinary rice cargoes. It was en route to the Gulf of Siam to rendezvous with junks, sampans, and strange-looking craft waiting to take the opium to other ports to be refined into narcotics.

But somewhere in the deal there was a double cross. As the paddy barge neared Bangkok, a special task force of soldiers and policemen moved out of the city to intercept the barge. At 5 P.M. the task force closed in with such swiftness that the group in the barge had no chance to resist even though armed. They gave up without a fight. The inventory showed seven tons of opium and 139 pounds of morphine in the shipment. But the seizure was not a sudden case of morality. It was merely the interplay between two strong men fighting for power and wealth.

In another country in Southeast Asia, a young police officer called for me at the Western-style hotel where I was living. Men and women in dinner clothes strolled through the plush lobby and into the brilliantly lit garden, where colored lights made a rainbow of water spurting up from a fountain.

The young man said, "Come with me and I'll show you the real city. This is only the façade."

We walked through the hot night. The rains were late and the countryside had been parched by the brassy sun. The concrete and the asphalt of the city stored up the heat during the day and poured it out in waves at night. Soon we turned from the bright main street into shadowy side streets and alleyways. Old men squatted in doorways smoking their pipes. Sidewalk venders hawked rice and vegetables and meats. Brown-skinned children played at the curbs. Over it all were the odors of the East, the strong pungent sweet-sour odor of sweat and dung and garlic and spices and oils and hundreds of mingled odors no Westerner could identify.

We reached an old building where children were playing at the entrance. As we stepped up to the doorway, a big man came forward to greet us, his bare chest glistening with sweat. He waved us inside. We stepped through a wide entrance into a room hazy with smoke which had a sweetish odor. On a platform almost within sight of the street sat a huge, pot-bellied

Chinese man methodically cleaning opium pipes. On either side of him were racks of bamboo pipes, stained black with sweat from hundreds of hands.

We walked past the pipe cleaner into a room where perhaps a hundred men lounged on opium "beds" with small lamps burning beside them. A wizened man, his body hardly more than a skeleton, lay on a bamboo bed with his head on a ceramic block. His scrawny fingers held a thin metal rod that looked like a knitting needle. He opened a tin of gum opium. He lifted the lamp and trimmed the wick with a small pair of scissors. A big cockroach raced across the bed and over his shoulder but he was too intent on the opium ritual to notice.

The old man dipped the end of the rod into the brown sticky opium and carefully twirled the metal rod until he formed a small ball of opium. Then he quickly heated it over the flame of the lamp. The opium sizzled and bubbled for a minute. He picked up a small piece of cardboard, holding it above the lamp just to the side of the flame point. He began kneading the opium ball against the cardboard with quick, expert twirls until it reached the proper consistency. Then he picked up the pipe and deftly inserted the ball of opium into the narrow bowl of the pipe. He pushed the lamp back, rested his head on the hard block, and turned the pipe bowl down until the heat touched the opium. He sucked on the long stem, drawing the smoke deeply into his lungs in swallowing gulps.

Then he began the process all over again, dipping the gummy substance, twirling it into a ball, once more the sucking, gulping drafts from the pipe. When the tin was almost empty, the old man was going through the ritual mechanically, with eyes glazed and half closed. There was an other-world look on his old wrinkled face. When the last bit of opium had been smoked, his eyes closed.

The bare-chested man smiled and said, "Now he is dreaming."

Beside the old man sat a young man perhaps eighteen. His arms and legs were well muscled. I asked him how long he had been smoking opium. He replied, "For five years."

Within a few years this young man probably will have the bony, starved look of the older one. Each day he spends about two-thirds of his earnings for opium. After a long day at work, he comes to the opium divan to join his friends and to talk, laugh, enjoy a cup of tea, and a bite to eat—and then to light the pipe that will bring forgetfulness for a time.

"Why did you begin smoking opium?" I asked.

The young man grinned idiotically. "My friends say if I smoke opium I find sex better." Then he shook his head. "But soon I find I have no need for woman. The opium is better."

Human wrecks sprawled on these opium beds by the scores on the two floors of the building. The house was one of the government-licensed opium divans.

As we walked away from this opium den, the young policeman said, "What you see is not good—but it is here. And it is here because there is graft, much graft. It should not be. We have so far to go."

Obtaining a crime story in some countries was often extremely frustrating. In Djakarta, Indonesia, I visited police several times seeking their co-operation in obtaining from their files a story of one of their unusual crimes. After a few days a young police officer sat down with me to tell me the details of a murder which had aroused considerable interest in the city.

He told me this story: An Indonesian named Arnas, age thirty-five, lived in a small house at the edge of the city with his wife and four children. The children ranged in age from one year to six. Arnas worked in a bottle factory and one of the workers was a young and pretty girl named Dahlia. Arnas fell in love with Dahlia. Frequently he slipped away from his home at night to be beside Dahlia. But finally the girl said to him, "If you love me, you must prove it."

"But what can I do to prove my love?" he asked.

Dahlia replied, "Kill your wife and children. Then I will know you love me."

On a rainy evening in 1956, Arnas slipped from Dahlia's room and returned to his home. He knocked on the door and when his wife answered the knock, he bashed in her skull with a hatchet. Then he crept into the bedroom and killed the four children as they slept.

About an hour later a neighborhood watchman stumbled on the body of the woman. He called police who questioned neighbors. None had heard anything unusual during the night, but then the rain had been beating hard on the roofs and would have deadened any sound. Police sought Arnas for questioning and found he was out of the city. But in their questioning they learned of his secret life with Dahlia. A search of her home revealed a bloodstained shirt and sarong. An examination showed it to be human blood.

Police found the hatchet, which they believed to be the murder weapon, in an open well about ten feet from Arnas' home. But the blood had been washed from the weapon by the water.

Dahlia professed ignorance of the crime. She denied having seen Arnas on the night of the murders. It was Dahlia's mother who told police of the girl's demands that Arnas kill his wife and children to prove his love.

When the policeman finished telling me this story, I said: "This murder was committed two years ago. Was Arnas convicted?"

The policeman replied blandly, "Oh, no. He is in jail. We are still investigating the case."

There is no underworld anywhere to match the weird underworlds to be found in Singapore and in Hong Kong. They are composed of Chinese secret societies, which are the best organized crime rings to be found outside the United States. The members are sworn to protect each other from the police authorities, and they extort a tribute from the lowliest coolies. They are bound together in ritualistic ceremonies with secret codes, secret passwords and oaths which make them a virtual state within a state.

These societies, also called Triads, are a menace not only in crime but in the political life of the communities, where the Chinese population forms the overwhelming majority and its loyalties are divided between Nationalist China and Red China.

Hong Kong's Kowloon riots of 1956 underlined the explosive danger. In this outburst of frenzied violence, sparked by members of a secret society, mob rule for a time threatened to overwhelm the Colony.

The riots began on October 10 when pro-Nationalist members of a secret society raised the flag of Nationalist China throughout a densely packed refugee center. The flag display

was a political act in defiance of a British police order against
flying the flag of either Chinese government in a community
which is forced by geographical circumstances to walk a political tightrope of official neutrality.

Police tore down the flags. Triad gangs poured into the
streets, wearing white arm bands for identification, and battled
the police. Gangs became a screaming, pillaging mob. They
smashed shop windows, ransacked stores, and threw up barricades in the streets. This terror continued through the night,
with growing overtones of anti-Western feeling. Police warned
the small Western colony to stay away from the riot-torn
Kowloon area and remain in their homes.

But Chancellor Fritz Ernst of the Swiss Consulate decided to
drive his wife, Ursula Marguerita, to the Shatin Heights Hotel
for lunch. He was confident that his diplomatic status was protection enough, and there was no reason why they should be
in danger. Perhaps Ernst had never seen a mob. Certainly he
did not realize that mobs do not recognize diplomatic immunity
because when he turned down Tai Po Road and ran into the
rioting he did not try to turn back. He tried to drive through
the screaming crowd.

"Turn the foreign devil's car over!" a Chinese rioter shouted.

The mob seized the car and tipped it on its side. One of
them unscrewed the cap from the gasoline tank and tossed a
lighted match. Within seconds, the car was a roaring mass of
flames and Mr. and Mrs. Ernst were human torches. He managed to drag her from the car and she ran screaming through
the crowd, the flames burning the clothing from her body. Mrs.
Ernst was burned fatally and he was badly hurt.

Four Triad members were convicted and sentenced to death
for this outrage. The riots lasted for forty-eight hours before
tank-led police were able to gain control and restore the rule of
law to Hong Kong. Since then, the police campaign against the
Triads has been intensified but the societies remain the gravest
political and crime problem in the Colony.

The greatest personal difficulty in assembling these stories
from police files around the world was not in traveling some
30,000 miles by plane, train, and automobile through more than

a score of countries. It wasn't the nagging interruption of schedules, the food poisoning in Turkey, the hotels that stuffed their pillows with concrete, or the stifling heat of Saigon, Djakarta, and Bangkok. It was the barrier of language. Fortunately, this toughest of all barriers was overcome with the help of American legal attachés, Embassy security officers, and newspaper friends, who generously arranged introductions and acted as interpreters when necessary.

Before reaching Tokyo, I was warned: "You can't get to the files of the Japanese police. They're too suspicious. And worst of all, you don't speak the language. You might as well write Japan off your list." I took my problem to U. S. Legal Attaché William Child and his assistant, Robert Kunkel, both of whom speak fluent Japanese. One telephone call from Child to the Japanese police headquarters removed all the barriers.

The next day, an English-speaking aide to the Japanese chief of police called for me at my hotel. I was taken to the Metropolitan Police Headquarters to meet the superintendent general of police, Hisato Kawai, a handsome, strong-faced, young-looking man. He listened courteously to my request for help in piecing together the full story of the most monstrous murderer to appear in Japan in many years.

Kawai told his aides to see that I got full co-operation. Then he wanted to hear all that I could tell him of the FBI and its director, J. Edgar Hoover. He was most intrigued by the fact that Hoover was only twenty-nine when he was given responsibility in 1924 for directing the bureau, and had been continuously in office since.

"I wish he would come over here," he said with a grin, "and tell me how he did it."

I was conducted on a tour of the headquarters and, finally, taken to the top floor of the building where we stopped outside a door, removed our shoes, and put on felt slippers. Then I was shown into the central communications room—the heart of the Tokyo police network from which the city's 20,000 police are directed in their work.

No one would suspect that in the grimy, drab old building there would be such an electronics center. On both sides were banked radio equipment and rows of teleprinters and telephones from which wires fanned out to district and precinct headquarters throughout Tokyo. On one wall hung a huge map of Tokyo with red pins marking the locations of head-quarters and areas where radio cars were operating. Any segment of the great city map could be enlarged by flashing a slide on a screen, showing each house, street and alleyway. The enlargements were used when a major crime was committed and the police wished to seal off the area for a search. With this map, they could follow or direct the movements of the police from house to house.

After this honor of being one of the first Americans ever permitted into this inner sanctum of Tokyo law enforcement, I was taken to meet Inspector Ohori, a slight little man with owlish eyes who is perhaps the top detective in all Japan. Several days later, Inspector Ohori found a break in his work schedule and he came to see me. He brought along voluminous police and court files. We sat down together, with an interpreter, and for hours I took notes and questioned the inspector about details of the spectacular murder and bank-robbery case which Ohori and his men had solved after months of investigation that hinged on a single clue—a calling card.

And so it went in country after country. Luckily, in most of the cases in which I was interested, I was able to interview the detectives or police officers who had solved the crimes. This enabled me to get many details which did not appear in the official records.

In this gallery of crime, I believe my favorite criminal is little Karl Peglow, artist, counterfeiter, and lover extraordinary. The most gruesome character was the Englishman who dumped his victims into vats of acid. And perhaps the wildest scheme was Hitler's effort to wreck the British economy with a flood of counterfeit bank notes. There is no doubt that the most vicious police system in the world belongs to the Communists.

But it is time to get on with the stories.

ENGLAND

THE TIME: *1949*

THE PLACE: *London*

THE CRIME: *Murder*

England was recovering slowly from the war which had been such a terrible burden spiritually, physically, and financially. London was gaunt, and pocked by the bomb damage and fires left raging by Hitler's Luftwaffe. But the ancient city had hidden its scars behind wooden fences. The debris of shattered buildings was being carted away. New buildings were already beginning to rise on the foundations of the old.

Even though the war had ended almost four years earlier, the people still gathered in queues to wait patiently for their rations of meat, butter and other scarce foodstuffs. They had not yet thrown off the torpor that came with victory in Europe. The Empire was at its lowest ebb. And the United States was pumping dollar credits into London to help the struggling giant back to its feet.

Workmen picking through the ruins during and after the war often found bodies entombed beneath brick, stone and timber. And when they were found, Scotland Yard's police began the slow and difficult task of identifying the victims and determin-

ing the cause of death. They could not assume that each died as a victim of the Nazis, because the suspicion arose, and sometimes was verified, that a murderer had stalked the streets even while the sirens wailed and the bombs crashed. And under cover of fear and confusion, the killer had struck down his victim. No one will ever know how many of those found in the wreckage were murder victims—or how many of the "missing" were victims of a perfect crime.

The English are among the most law-abiding people in the world. But the English also produce perhaps the most bizarre murders to be found in any civilized country. England's famous murders have a startling quality to them because they happen in unlikely places and to the wrong people. Such was the case in the year 1949 when a killer turned up in the quiet, shabbily respectable area of South Kensington—a killer who reasoned that if the police could not find the body of his victim, then he could not be convicted of murder.

1. The Disappearing Bodies

The nightmare always began with a vision of a dense, forbidding forest rising before him, a forest of crucifixes. The crosses slowly changed into trees. The dark, leafless branches seemed to be dripping rain or drops of heavy dew. He drew nearer to the trees and saw then that the glistening drops were neither rain nor dew—but blood.

Suddenly the trees began to writhe as though in torture and blood oozed from their trunks. A blurred figure dashed from tree to tree, catching the fluid in a cup. And when the cup was brimming, the dream figure came close and said in a commanding voice: "Drink!" He strained to step forward and raise his hand to the cup. But he could not move his limbs. He knew that before he could reach out and take a draught from the cup to find release from this nightmare . . . he must kill.

Such was the dream which John George Haigh related to a psychiatrist.

But long before he told anyone of his dream, Haigh was confronted in his London bedroom by a woman who was no part of a dream world. She was stern, starched Mrs. Hilda Kirkwood, head bookkeeper of the Onslow Court Hotel, holding in her hand a non-dreamlike hotel bill totaling £49, 15s, 1d ($140.16).

Haigh had resided at the hotel for five years. It was a quiet, faded little retreat in South Kensington favored by elderly widows, retired colonials, pensioners and businessmen, who wanted companionship, a respectable address and solid if uninspiring food at a decent price. Haigh was thirty-seven years old and lowered the age average at the hostelry considerably. Being darkly handsome as well as polite and unobtrusive, he was a favorite of some of the women.

But five years residence at the Onslow Court Hotel, and having a title of director of an engineering firm, did not entitle Haigh to overlook prompt settlement of bills for bed and board. Mrs. Kirkwood's appearance at this time was particularly embarrassing to Haigh because he was overdrawn by £83 at his bank.

"It was a nuisance having my check returned, Mrs. Kirkwood," Haigh said. "I shall demand an apology from my bank, you may be sure. Now, how much did you say is due?"

"This bill totals thirty-two pounds, five shillings and five pence," Mrs. Kirkwood said, "and this one seventeen pounds, nine shillings and eight pence."

"Do you prefer cash or a check?"

"Cash, if you please," she replied firmly.

Haigh waved to an open desk drawer. "Take what you need from there."

Mrs. Kirkwood counted out the amount due. There were four shillings, eleven pennies left for Haigh. He held the coins in his palm for a moment and then snapped shut his hand. He had reached a decision.

The next day at lunchtime, Haigh entered the dining room and took his usual seat. Soon he was chatting with his neighbor, Mrs. Olive Durand-Deacon, an elderly widow whose husband had left her a comfortable estate. After five years under the same roof, she and "that nice Mr. Haigh" were on amiable terms. Her dearest friend was Mrs. Constance Lane, with whom she had tea each afternoon in the Tudor Room. But Mrs. Lane, a resident at the Onslow Court Hotel for nine years, permitted herself only a formal, nodding acquaintanceship with the younger man. Mrs. Lane often chided her friend for being too friendly with "strangers."

Mrs. Durand-Deacon and Haigh bent their heads together at the table as she showed him a box of artificial fingernails which she had made from paper. She wondered aloud if there were any commercial possibilities in artificial fingernails made of plastic. Haigh said he thought the idea extremely clever. He said he believed his firm, Hurstlea Products, Limited, might be interested in manufacturing them. At least, it would do no harm for them to run down to Crawley, where the firm was, on Friday and discuss the possibility with his managing director. Would Mrs. Durand-Deacon be interested?

"Oh, yes," she exclaimed. "It's very exciting."

Haigh immediately made preparations for Mrs. Durand-Deacon's visit to Crawley. He first went to Victor Blagden & Co. at Gascoigne Wharf, Barking, and purchased a steel drum which

had been specially treated to resist corrosive acids. Then he arranged to have another firm deliver a ten-gallon jug of commercial sulphuric acid to a storehouse on Leopold Road in
Crawley where he already had stored twenty gallons of acid.
When someone asked Haigh about the work he was doing at the
storehouse, he said, "I'm engaged in a conversion project."

After lunch on Friday, February 28, 1949, Mrs. Durand-Deacon left the Onslow Court Hotel wearing her best jewelry and a
smart black Persian lamb coat. Haigh left a few minutes later,
carrying a brief case in one hand and a square leather box in
the other. About two hours later, the bookkeeper at the George
Hotel in Crawley saw Haigh, whom he knew well, enter the
hotel with an elderly woman who wore a black coat. They
visited the hotel restrooms and immediately left. He saw them
enter Haigh's automobile.

The car drove away—taking Mrs. Durand-Deacon to a rendezvous with horror.

Haigh returned to the Onslow Court Hotel that night about
10:30 P.M. He walked through the empty lobby and went upstairs—alone.

The following day, Haigh came into the Onslow Court Hotel
dining room for breakfast, freshly shaved and looking fit and
rested. When he saw Mrs. Durand-Deacon's place unoccupied,
there was a distressed look on his face.

The waitress noticed his expression and said, "Mrs. Durand-
Deacon wasn't down for dinner last night. Is she sick?"

"I don't know," Haigh said. "I'll ask Mrs. Lane. She should
know."

Haigh found Mrs. Lane in the Tudor Room. "Mrs. Durand-
Deacon wasn't down for dinner last evening and I haven't seen
her this morning. Is she ill?"

"I don't think so," Mrs. Lane said. "I haven't seen her but she
must be about."

"I thought you might know where she is."

"I do remember now," Mrs. Lane said. "Why, she told me
yesterday you wanted to take her to your factory at Crawley."

"Yes, I did," Haigh said. "But I was late having lunch and she
asked me to pick her up later at the Army and Navy store. I

waited an hour for her but she didn't show up and I had to leave."

"Well, I must do something about it," Mrs. Lane said. She went directly upstairs to Mrs. Durand-Deacon's room. Her bed had not been slept in. But then perhaps she had spent the night with a friend and forgotten to call. That must be it, Mrs. Lane thought.

At Sunday breakfast, Haigh again asked Mrs. Lane if she had any news of their friend.

"No, I haven't . . . and I've made up my mind that after lunch I'm going to the Chelsea police station and ask them to find her. This is not like Olive and I'm very upset about it."

Haigh said it was most disturbing. Later, he suggested to Mrs. Lane, "I think we had better go together to the police station. You shouldn't be going there alone."

Mrs. Lane agreed gratefully and together they told police of the strange absence of Mrs. Durand-Deacon from the hotel. Haigh repeated to the police, in more detail, the story he had told Mrs. Lane. After Mrs. Durand-Deacon had failed to show up for their appointment, he said, he drove to Crawley alone, concluded his business, dined at the Ancient Prior's Café, and left there just before seven o'clock; he returned to the Onslow Court Hotel about eight and went directly to his room.

With this report, Scotland Yard began the hunt. The name of Mrs. Durand-Deacon was listed with those hundreds who disappear mysteriously each year in the great city. After long and patient searching by police, most of them are found hiding under a new name for one reason or another. But Mrs. Durand-Deacon wasn't the type to hide herself deliberately from her friends.

Chief Inspector Shelley Symes and Detective Inspector Albert Webb of Scotland Yard called at the Onslow Court Hotel to question Haigh for further details. He didn't add much to what he already had told.

Haigh showed no sign of nervousness over the questioning, but then he wasn't aware that Scotland Yard already was looking at him with suspicion. Something about the first report he gave at the Chelsea station caused Chief Symes to pick up a telephone and call Superintendent Jim Duncan, head of the criminal records office. Duncan called back a few minutes later. "From the description you give," he said, "your man is identical with CRO 86522—Haigh, John George, sentenced to four years at Surrey Assizes in November, 1937, for obtaining money by false pretenses, and to twenty-one months at London Assizes in June, 1941, for theft." (Haigh had committed the theft while on parole for the first crime.)

Symes gave a low whistle. "Thanks, Jim," he said, "this looks like trouble."

At this point there was nothing to suggest foul play and no evidence that Haigh was connected with the widow's disappearance. Perhaps Mrs. Durand-Deacon would show up at any time. Still, the man Haigh did have a shady background and Symes thought it best to have his men make some discreet inquiries.

At Crawley, Detective Sergeant Patrick Joseph Heslin questioned Directing Manager Edward Jones of Hurstlea Products, Limited. Jones denied that Haigh, as he claimed, was a director of the company, which engaged in light engineering and tool work. Jones said he had known Haigh for about twelve years and Haigh had acted from time to time as his unpaid London representative. In return for his help, Jones permitted him the use of a company storehouse on Leopold Road where Haigh said he was working on a conversion job. Haigh had taken the keys to the storehouse only a few days ago—but that wasn't unusual.

Sergeant Heslin went with Jones to the storehouse and they forced open the door. In the center of the floor were three ten-gallon acid jugs. A rubber apron and rubber gloves had been tossed to one side. On a table in one corner was a large, square leather box, containing a .38 Webley automatic that apparently had been fired recently. In the box, also, was a Horsham dry cleaner's receipt for a Persian lamb coat valued at £50. On the whitewashed walls were splashes that looked suspiciously like blood.

Information began to pour into Scotland Yard. The coat described by the receipt had been left at the cleaner's the day following Mrs. Durand-Deacon's disappearance. The man who left

it was identified from a picture as Haigh. An officer also reported that a man meeting Haigh's description had obtained an
appraisal on some "family jewelry" from a Horsham jeweler.
Another officer found the same jewelry had been sold in Horsham for £100—jewelry which was identified by Mrs. Durand-
Deacon's sister as the small treasures belonging to the missing
woman.

Scotland Yard had no doubts at this point that a crime had
been committed—but where was the woman, missing now for
ten days? Was she dead or alive?

Chief Inspector Symes ordered Haigh brought to the Chelsea
headquarters. Inspector Webb found him entering his car outside the Onslow Court Hotel and asked him to come at once to
the police station.

"Certainly," Haigh said. "I'll do anything to help you, as you
know."

Symes wasted no time. He told Haigh that his men had found
the black Persian lamb coat left at the cleaner's in Horsham.
"How many times recently have you been to Horsham?"

Haigh replied, "Oh, I used to go to Horsham a lot, but lately
I have been there once in the evening, to the pictures."

Symes said, "You have been there in the morning recently on
no less than four occasions. I want you to tell me about that."

Haigh looked at his interrogator and realization came that he
was trapped.

"I can see you know what you are talking about," he said. "I
admit the coat belonged to Mrs. Durand-Deacon and that I sold
her jewelry . . ."

Symes held out the dry cleaner's receipt found in the storehouse at Crawley.

"Yes," Haigh said, "I wondered if you had got it when you
started talking."

"How did you come by this property," Symes demanded,
"and where is Mrs. Durand-Deacon? I must tell you anything
you say may be used in evidence."

Haigh squirmed in his seat. He said finally, "It is a long story
of blackmail and I shall have to implicate others. How do I
stand about that?"

Symes retorted, "What you have to say is entirely a matter for you." And the chief left the room to let Haigh think things over. Only Inspector Webb was left in the room with him.

After a time, Haigh said to Webb, "Tell me, frankly, what are the chances of anyone being released from a hospital for the criminally insane?"

The detective said, "I can't discuss that sort of thing with you."

"If I told you the truth," Haigh said, "you wouldn't believe me; it sounds too fantastic for belief . . ."

The officer interrupted. "Remember, what you say . . ."

"I understand all that," Haigh said impatiently. "I'll tell you all about it. She has disappeared completely and no trace of her can ever be found again." He looked at Webb to see the effect of his statement.

Webb said evenly, "What has happened to her?"

"What has happened to her?" Haigh said. "I have destroyed her with acid . . . every trace has gone . . . and how can you prove murder if there is no body? How can you?"

Detective Webb summoned Chief Symes to hear Haigh repeat his statement. And once his tongue was loosened, Haigh went on and on with a story that made the police officers shudder inside because of its horror . . .

"I shot her in the back of the head while she was looking at some paper for use as artificial fingernails. Then I went out to the car and fetched in a drinking glass. I took a penknife and made an incision on one side of her throat and collected a glass of blood . . . and I drank it.

"After that, I took off the coat and jewelry she was wearing and put her in a forty-five-gallon tank. I filled the tank up with sulphuric acid . . . and left it to react. In between shoving her in the tank and pumping in the acid, I went around to the Ancient Prior's for a cup of tea.

"I went to the George Hotel for dinner and I remember I was late, about nineish. I then came back to town and returned to the hotel about half past ten . . ."

The room was silent except for the voice of Haigh. "On Monday, I returned to Crawley to find the reaction [of the acid] almost complete, but a piece of fat and bone was still floating on the sludge. I emptied off the sludge with a bucket and tipped it on the ground opposite the shed. I pumped more acid into the tank . . . On Tuesday, I returned and found that the body had dissolved completely. I emptied the tank and left it outside in the yard . . ."

The police officers pressed Haigh to tell them why it was he had in his possession ration books and coupons bearing the names of a Donald and Amy McSwan and their son, William, and also the names of Dr. Archie Henderson and his wife, Rose, who had been missing for more than a year.

Haigh said he became friendly with the McSwans during the war and finally chose them as his victims. He said he met the son, William, in a pub in Kensington in 1944. "We went to Number Seventy-nine Gloucester Road into a basement which I had rented. I hit him on the head with an iron bar. I took a glass of blood from his throat and drank it. He was dead within five minutes or so. I put him in a forty-gallon tank and disposed of him with acid . . . [pouring] the sludge down a manhole in the basement . . . The following year, I took the father, Donald, and the mother, Amy, into the basement and killed them in exactly the same way as the son . . ."

It seems incredible that it could happen in England, but the McSwans had disappeared from the face of the earth without a whisper of suspicion until Haigh told his story. He said he told the elder McSwans their son was hiding out to escape the military call-up and didn't want to involve them. Later, Haigh wrote letters to the parents, giving them news purporting to come from their son.

Haigh also told the officers of events leading up to the murder of Archie and Rose Henderson. This is how he described the crimes later in his prison diary: ". . . by now I was seized with an awful urge. Once more I saw the forest of crucifixes which changed to trees dripping with blood. Once more I wakened with the desire which demanded fulfillment . . . Archie was to be the next victim . . . I drove him to Crawley, and in the storeroom at Leopold Road I shot him in the head with his own revolver . . .

"I then returned to Brighton and told Rose that Archie had been taken ill very suddenly and needed her. I said I would take her to him. She accompanied me to the storehouse at

Crawley, and there I shot her. From each of them I took my draught of blood."

After each of these murders, Haigh forged powers of attorney and other documents which enabled him to dispose of their real estate, automobiles, and personal effects. His bank account rose by some £6,800 after the McSwans' deaths and by about £7,771 after the Hendersons' deaths.

Without doubt, John George Haigh was one of the most monstrous criminals ever trapped by Scotland Yard—a monster who thought he could not be condemned to death for murder if the police could find no body. But the sludge in the storehouse yard at Crawley contained human fat, pieces of undissolved bone identified as that of an elderly female, a denture positively identified by a dentist as the one he had made for Mrs. Durand-Deacon, and the victim's red plastic purse, which had not dissolved in the acid. This evidence helped convict Haigh; but even if no part of the body had been found, he was doomed by circumstantial evidence and his own confession. Haigh didn't know it, but police are not required by law to produce a dead body to prove murder.

When he came to trial in the ancient courtroom at Lewes in July, 1949, Haigh assumed the role of a madman. The defense relied heavily on his unsupported story of the blood dreams, and the ritual of blood-drinking as proof of insanity.

The prosecution scoffed at his stories. The attorney general said they were nonsense, dreams deliberately manufactured by Haigh, after he was trapped, in the hope that even if convicted, his worst possible punishment would be imprisonment in Broadmoor.

The jury required only seventeen minutes to reach a unanimous verdict of guilty, and, in so doing, they brushed aside Haigh's defense of insanity. The condemned man was hanged at Wandsworth prison on August 6, 1949.

THE TIME: *1955*

THE PLACE: *An English Golf Course*

THE CRIME: *Murder*

The pulse of England was quickening with the postwar economic recovery. Across all of England, the talk in the month of April was of Winston Churchill's resignation as prime minister, the succession of Anthony Eden to the old war hero's post, and the coming May elections (which the Tories would win).

The talk of politics was the same in the pubs of Potter's Bar, a small town in Middlesex, as in the clubs of London. The talk was the same until the morning of May 1, when the shadow of murder fell across Potter's Bar, and then no one in the town could talk of anything but this terrible crime. It was a savage murder that spread fear throughout the community and made every male who was over sixteen a potential suspect.

A killer at large in a great city causes hardly a ripple of personal concern among the people because the threat seems so remote. But in a small community men look at each other and wonder if a familiar face hides a murderer. Danger lurks in every dark street and shadow.

36

A *sex-mad killer had chosen the golf course at the edge of the town as the scene of his crime. And he left only one small clue behind him. Finding the killer posed a problem for Scotland Yard which demanded some of the most painstaking detective work it had ever done.*

There is no case on record, to my knowledge, in which an entire town co-operated so willingly to hunt down a murderer. The Englishman's sensitivity to any invasion of his privacy by the police, or anyone else, is well known—but in this case the citizens of Potter's Bar were willing to waive their rights in the interest of justice.

The case illustrates vividly the real strength of Scotland Yard. It is a strength which comes from the Englishman's deep-seated respect for government by law, and from Scotland Yard's own sensitivity to the individual rights of the people.

2. Murder at the Seventeenth Tee

Mrs. Elizabeth Currell was forty-six years old but she looked about thirty-five. She was a petite thing, only five feet tall, with large dark eyes, wavy brown hair, a peaches-and-cream complexion typical of many English women, and a figure that was the envy of many younger women.

It is little wonder that admiring males watched her progress as she walked down the main street of Potter's Bar in Middlesex County, North London, on the last day of April, 1955. A warm breeze pressed her cotton dress tightly against her thighs. Perhaps it was the feeling of spring come to England that caused so many heads to turn as she passed. But she paid no attention to the glances while she hurried to the grocery shop where she worked.

Among those who noticed Elizabeth Currell was one who watched her with more than casual interest. He looked at her not merely with pleasure, but with a desire for possession.

In that moment, a crime began to unfold.

After her day's work was done, Mrs. Currell left the shop and walked briskly to the comfortable, two-story brick home on Cranbourne Road at the edge of town to prepare supper for her husband, Alfred, a bus driver. She and Alfred were a happy couple, still very much in love.

This night they had supper and, as usual, cleaned up the dishes together. While she washed and he dried them, they continued their talk about the day's happenings and their plans for tomorrow. Their Corgi dog, Tina, lay quietly in a corner of the kitchen.

When the dishes were put away, Alfred Currell went upstairs to put on a lounging robe and slippers. Mrs. Currell pulled on a light red topcoat and called to her husband, "I'm going out with Tina, dear." When he came downstairs she was gone. He switched on the television set and settled into a comfortable chair. It was eight P.M.

Mrs. Currell, the dog trotting ahead of her, walked briskly to the dead end of Cranbourne Road and followed a path under the nearby railroad tracks. The path turned and ran along the railroad embankment, past an old World War II brick pillbox built for the ground defense of Britain. Then it angled across the Potter's Bar golf course toward the village of Little Heath.

Each evening when the weather permitted, Mrs. Currell brought Tina along the path to the seventeenth tee to give her a run. Rarely did she meet anyone and tonight the golf course seemed as deserted as usual at this hour.

But Elizabeth Currell was not alone. As she was turning down the path from the railway underpass, a pair of eyes was peering at her through a slit in the old pillbox. A man crouched there in the darkness, remembering the outlines of her body when the afternoon breeze had pressed the dress against it.

After she had passed the pillbox, the dark figure slipped out and merged into the shadows of a hedge. The grass deadened the sound of his footsteps. He moved swiftly toward the woman. The Corgi dog growled and Elizabeth Currell turned. Even in the dimming light she saw the menace in the face she recognized.

"You?" she exclaimed. And then his arms closed roughly around her. "No . . . no . . . you'll only get into trouble! . . . no . . . please!"

She struggled out of his arms. A scream formed in her throat. but the man's fist crashed into her jaw. His fingers closed around her throat and her scream was only a gasping rattle. She clawed at the fingers. Then darkness overwhelmed her and her body was limp. Her attacker dragged her into the tall grass beside the seventeenth tee nearby and in a frenzy ripped at her clothing . . .

Elizabeth Currell moaned as consciousness began to return. The man yanked off one of her stockings. He looped it around her neck to choke her, but it tore apart. His hand reached out and closed on an iron tee marker. The heavy marker crashed against her skull again and again until there was no life left in her. Then the attacker pushed himself to his feet and ran into the darkness.

Alfred Currell, sitting at the television set, glanced at the clock on the wall and saw that it was 9:30. It wasn't like his wife to stay out this long with Tina. He went to the kitchen door and when he opened it, he saw the dog standing there, whimpering.

Currell knew something was wrong. He walked to the path under the railroad, past the pillbox and onto the golf course, shouting his wife's name. There was no answer. He searched for two hours and then, with growing fright, called the police. Within a short time a search was under way.

About 7:30 the following morning, Mrs. Irene Queripel carried a steaming pot of tea to the bedroom of her son, Michael, a tall, husky young man who looked older than his eighteen years. He spent most of his spare time alone, tinkering with a motorcycle or sitting for hours listening to classical music. He didn't care much for girls, or at least he didn't seem to. He often took long walks alone at night because, he said, they helped his migraine headaches.

Mrs. Queripel enjoyed bringing tea to Michael each morning. It gave her a chance to talk to him before he left home for the town hall, where he worked as a clerk in the tax office. This morning she opened his bedroom door and said, "Here's your tea, Mick. It's nice and hot." She put the tray beside the bed as her son roused himself.

And then Mrs. Queripel saw there were stains that looked like blood on the clothing strewn on the floor. "Why, Mick," she exclaimed, "have you had an accident?"

"I cut myself working on the motorcycle over at the garage," he said. He showed her a cut on his arm, a slice so thin that it might have been done with a razor blade.

"Goodness, you must have bled a great deal," Mrs. Queripel said after a closer look at the clothing.

"I always do," he said.

"Should I send for a doctor, Mick?"

"Oh, Mother," he snapped impatiently, "don't make such a fuss."

When he had gone to work, Mrs. Queripel tried to wash the

blood from the clothing. But when the stains wouldn't wash away, the clothes were tossed onto a fire in the back yard.

It was daybreak when a member of the searching party saw the bruised and battered body sprawled like a discarded doll in the high grass beside the seventeenth tee. Police roped off the area and began a careful search for clues. The blood-smeared tee marker, with strands of brown hair clinging to it, was found beside the body. The police wrapped the marker in paper and took it to headquarters for a closer examination.

Potter's Bar was shocked by the murder of pretty, vivacious Mrs. Currell, who was known by sight to so many in the town of 19,000 population. Now a killer was loose and women were warned not to walk on lonely streets at night or outside the town, without a male escort known to them.

Chief Inspector Leonard Crawford and Detective Inspector Denis Hawkins of Scotland Yard hurried to Potter's Bar to take charge of the investigation. They examined the murder weapon, and there they saw the clue they were seeking. Etched into the dried blood on the marker was a fragment of someone's palm print. It was only a square inch in size but the impression was clear. Apparently the killer, in pushing himself to his feet, had placed his palm against the marker.

The officers were certain this clue could lead them to the killer if the print could be matched with the proper palm. They reasoned the killer very likely would be found somewhere in Potter's Bar or Little Heath because it was improbable that the path leading through the golf course would be used by someone who was a stranger to the area.

But how could they find a matching square inch of a palm among the thousands of men living in Potter's Bar and Little Heath? And they had to admit the possibility that the killer, while familiar with the path through the golf course, lived somewhere else and had only been visiting in the town on the night of the murder. Nevertheless, the police decided to take the palm prints of every male citizen over sixteen who was known to have been in the area that night.

Perhaps never before had the taking of prints on such a huge scale been undertaken in seeking a solution to a crime. The police could not order citizens to have their palm prints taken. The procedure would have to be entirely voluntary, with the citizens sympathetic to the idea.

Scotland Yard Commissioner R. L. Jackson approved the immense task of palm-printing thousands of men. Crawford and Hawkins obtained the co-operation of town officials and community leaders, who publicly permitted their palm prints to be taken. They urged all the male citizens over sixteen to come forward to do the same.

Scotland Yard sent a squad of thirty detectives to Potter's Bar to work under the direct command of Detective Inspector Hawkins, with Chief Inspector Crawford in overall charge.

A special "murder investigation center" was established in the town. Before Hawkins sent the detectives out on the job, he lectured them on the necessity of being tactful in this operation, which moved so near the point of invading the citizens' jealously guarded right of privacy.

"Remember," Hawkins told his men, "you are a guest in these people's homes. The vast majority are decent, law-abiding, self-respecting citizens. Their home is their castle . . . and all that. There must be a good reason for us to go into their homes—and we have a good reason. The murdered woman was a respected woman. We cannot take the palm prints by force of law. We must approach each person as a law-abiding citizen and try to get his voluntary co-operation. If there are any complaints, we must assume the fault is ours and that we have not been as tactful as we should have been. If there is any trouble, leave it to me to smooth over."

The detectives went from door to door in the methodical task of taking statements and prints from all the menfolk, and checking as best they could on their whereabouts on the night of April 30. Within a short time they were amazed to discover that approximately eight hundred men who had been in Potter's Bar on the night of the murder had left the area—gone on vacation, moved to another city, left the country for new jobs, or returned to homes around the world after a brief visit with relatives. None could be automatically eliminated as a suspect.

The hunt extended to the United States, Ireland, Canada, Chile, Eritrea, Malaya and the African Gold Coast. In each of these places, men who had been in Potter's Bar that night were asked to give police a print of their palms . . . and they did.

When police finally reached the home of Michael Queripel, he refused at first to have his palms printed, saying it was against his principles. Young Queripel's brother, Robert, exclaimed, "That's bloody silly, Mick. Come on—it can't hurt anything." And so Michael Queripel's palm prints were added to the thousands of others now piling up in the records room at Scotland Yard headquarters in London.

Teams of fingerprint experts, under the direction of Chief Superintendent Jack Livings, worked in relays, seven days a week, trying to find that square inch of palm among thousands of prints. It was a tedious, painfully slow task.

In mid-August, one of the fingerprint specialists began a careful examination of the 4,605th card among the 8,889 which had accumulated over the weeks. After a short time he cried out, "Here it is!" The others in the room dropped their work and crowded around to examine the print. To these men, there was no doubt about it—the lines on the card were identical with those left on the tee marker.

The card was rushed to Commissioner Jackson for his examination. He checked the prints and said to his men, "You have done a truly remarkable job. Congratulations. I think we've found a murderer."

On August 19, Chief Inspector Crawford and Detective Inspector Hawkins walked into the town hall at Potter's Bar and approached the clerk who was laughing at a joke someone had just told.

"Are you Michael Queripel?" Crawford asked.

"Yes."

"We are police officers and we wish to talk to you."

Queripel followed them from the building and climbed into the police car waiting outside.

Crawford said, "Do you know why we want to see you?"

Queripel hesitated. Finally he said, "Yes, I know what it's all about."

"What is it all about?"

Queripel sat silent for a long moment. "I found her . . . but she was dead."

Crawford said, "Your palm print was found on the tee plate. If you found her, why didn't you tell the police?"

"You wouldn't have believed me," Queripel said. The officers sat looking at him. Finally he blurted out, "I hit her. Then I tried to strangle her."

"Don't say any more now," interrupted Crawford. And Queripel was taken to the police station.

Queripel sat at a desk and Hawkins handed him a pen and placed a sheaf of paper before him and he began to write. He wrote:

". . . I saw her walking toward me with her dog. She walked along the path and I waited until she was out of sight. I walked over to the green and waited behind the trees. She came back. I walked through the hedge and ran up behind her and tried to knock her out. She turned just as I was going to hit her. She struggled until I managed to hit her on the jaw . . . I put my hands around her throat and tried to strangle her. Then I dragged her over to the hedge where I undressed her. Her coat and blouse were torn in the struggle. I ripped off most of her underclothes. She started to come round and I pulled off one of her stockings and tied it round her neck. It broke straight-away . . . so I hit her with the tee iron. I had to hit her several times before I was sure she was dead . . ."

On October 12, 1955, Michael Queripel was brought into Old Bailey court in London where he pleaded guilty to the murder of Elizabeth Currell. His trial lasted just five minutes. He was sentenced to be "detained during Her Majesty's pleasure"—meaning life imprisonment.

And Scotland Yard closed the book on another case of murder.

FRANCE

THE TIME: *1947–1950*

THE PLACE: *Paris*

THE CRIME: *Robbery and Murder*

Crime and criminals flourished throughout France in the hungry years that followed World War II, as they do after every war. Respect for law and order did not return automatically to the country when the heel of the dictator was removed by the Allied liberation.

During the Nazi occupation, a Frenchman's revolt against German authority was not necessarily a criminal act in the eyes of his own countrymen. More often than not, the Frenchman looked upon such lawbreaking with passive unconcern, if not approval. At such times the difference between a criminal act and an act of patriotism depends on who does the judging.

The postwar years were made to order for France's criminals, who no longer could cloak their acts in patriotism. Weapons were easy to obtain and almost impossible to trace. Automobiles were available once more. American tourists had returned to pour millions of dollars into shop tills. The political chaos in the government inevitably lowered the efficiency of the police and the Sûreté Nationale, which is France's equivalent of the FBI.

In this climate, crime increased. To some men crime is a way of life whether the government is that of an invader or that of their own country. And such a man was serpent-eyed Émile Buisson, who came closer to organizing an American-style gang operation in Paris than any French criminal before him. Success depended on cunning and absolute ruthlessness, two qualities which Buisson possessed in abundance.

The story of Buisson is in reality the story of postwar crime in France—and the Gallic flair with which a master detective went about the task of hunting down his old enemy, not only for personal pride but for the honor of the Sûreté.

3. M. Chenevier Stalks a Killer

Emile Buisson lived by theft, fraud and violence from the time he was eight years old. For forty years he knew no other way of life and, he conceded cheerfully, he did not want to know another. Crime was his business and his pleasure. Criminals were his friends. The police were his enemies.

He was a nondescript little man. He merged into the background of Paris as though he were a part of the brick and mortar which one sees and yet doesn't see. He was secretive and suspicious and he hid himself even from his gang until the time came for another raid. He was generous in sharing the spoils of his crimes with his confederates, but if one of them made a mistake or lost his trust, then Buisson became judge and executioner.

There was one thing about Buisson that people did remember —the terrifying look in his eyes when he became enraged. One man who saw him at such a moment said later, "His eyes suddenly looked like the eyes of a serpent. They were evil and cruel . . ."

What the police remembered was that he had robbed Parisians and tourists of a multimillion-franc fortune, left a bloody trail of dead men behind in his sudden outbursts of violence, and then disappeared as if by magic. In all of France, he had no peer as a criminal.

The last chapters in Buisson's crime career really began in 1947 while he was serving time in Paris' Santé prison for the 1,800,000-franc robbery of the Crédit Lyonnais in Troyes. His cell mate was a thief named Roger Dekker and together they made plans for escape.

Buisson decided his best chance for escape was to convince prison officials that he was mentally unbalanced. If successful, he knew he would be transferred to L'Asile Psychiatrique de Villejuif, where supervision over the patients was relaxed.

Gradually, he began acting the role of a prisoner whose mind had slipped its moorings. His guards first noticed that he paced back and forth in his cell like a caged animal night after night.

He never slept more than two hours out of any twenty-four. Then he began to cry and shout and beat the walls until his fists were bloody. He kept the other prisoners in a tempest of unrest.

Prison officials became convinced that only a madman could act as Buisson acted. He was taken to the prison hospital and given painful electric shock treatments—treatments which most mental patients dreaded and fought to escape. Buisson begged for the treatments, cursing the doctors if they did not listen to him.

At last he was transferred to the asylum at Villejuif on the southern outskirts of Paris. His outbursts of violent rage subsided. He was permitted to roam the prison yard with more and more freedom, seemingly a docile, broken man with the brain of an idiot.

One day in August, 1947, a woman came to the asylum to visit Buisson. She was the mistress of his brother, Jean. While he pretended only vague recognition, she whispered, "Dekker has escaped. He and Jean are at the place on Rue Bichat. They want to know if you can be at the south wall of the asylum just before daybreak on September 3. Can you do it?"

Buisson said, "Tell them I'll be there."

In the early morning hours on the agreed date, Buisson slipped from his room into the asylum yard and crouched in the deep shadows of the stone wall. There were whispers from atop the wall and a ladder was lowered. Within a few seconds, Buisson had clambered to freedom. By the time his absence was discovered, he was safely in hiding in a house on Rue Bichat, celebrating his freedom with Dekker, André Leonard, Henri Russac, François Guillo, and his brother, Jean, all of them ex-convicts.

That night five armed men entered a small, crowded bar in Montmartre while a sixth waited outside behind the wheel of a stolen car. A nondescript man with fierce eyes cowed the crowd with a machine gun and gave the orders while his men stripped the men and women of jewels and cash worth a small fortune. As quickly as they came, the bandits were gone. Later, the robbery victims looked at photographs and pointed to pictures of Emile Buisson as the little man who held the machine gun.

A week later, Buisson and his men entered a restaurant on Rue Le Sueur. He fired two shots over the heads of the terrified customers. "Give us your jewelry and money," he demanded. Again he menaced the room with the machine gun until the booty was collected. He gave the signal to leave, and one of the bandits said, "Let's go, Guillo." They ran to the car where Dekker waited.

Police threw up barricades within minutes in an effort to seal off the entire area. Dekker raced into Rue de Clichy and headed straight into a barricade. He crashed the car through the barrier in a hail of gunfire, and kept going. Two motorcycle policemen gave chase in a wild running gun battle. The police were gaining when Buisson snapped, "Stop the car."

The bandit car skidded to a halt. Buisson stepped out and opened fire with the machine gun. One shot tore into a policeman's chin, knocking him out. The other policeman was forced into retreat before the heavy fire. When police reinforcements arrived, there was no trace of the bandits.

Back at the hideout, Buisson exploded in fury. He grabbed Russac and threw him into a chair. "You fool," he said. "I should kill you. You put us all in danger."

"What did I do?" stammered Russac.

"Do? You stupid dog, you called out Guillo's name at the restaurant." Then he mimicked Russac's voice. "'Let's go, Guillo.'"

The terrified Russac said, "I was excited . . . I am sorry . . ."

Buisson ordered Russac to leave Paris with his wife that same night and to stay in hiding until he was told to return. Russac bolted out of the door and as it closed behind him Buisson said to Dekker, "We can do without that one. He is too stupid."

Two weeks later, Buisson sent word to Russac that the danger was past. The fugitive returned to Paris and met Buisson and Dekker to celebrate his homecoming. He was full of apologies for the slip he had made during the robbery. "Forget it," Buisson said. "The police know nothing." He poured Russac another glass of wine and then another. Many glasses of wine later, Russac weaved his way into the night with his companions. His body was found next morning, his skull punctured by a bullet.

But the police did know something. A few days after Russac's body was found, they closed in on the hide-out at Rue Bichat, where Buisson had called a conference. Dekker was there with Jean Buisson, Pierre Pailley, and their mistresses, Suzanne and Yvette.

Police battered in the front door but while the others milled about in confusion, Buisson raced upstairs, slipped through a window, pulled himself onto the roof of the house, and ran across the rooftops. Police gave chase and Buisson darted into the shadow of a chimney. He held his breath as his pursuers brushed by his hiding place and went on across the roofs.

Buisson remained behind the chimney for several hours until the neighborhood was quiet again. Then he crawled across the roofs and cautiously made his way to the street to join the early risers on their way to work.

In that narrow escape, Buisson realized he had been too careless. From that time on, he did not permit even his most trusted friends or his mistress to know where he lived. He moved periodically from place to place, but always into a room rented from a respectable couple living in a quiet neighborhood. He contacted his gang members by telephone and before joining them for a conference he always scouted the area himself to be sure none had been followed. Each night he slipped from his room to prowl the neighborhood and be sure nothing was amiss. Except on rare occasions he dined alone, always armed and sitting near an exit where he could watch everyone who entered.

After the police raid on Rue Bichat, Buisson went into hiding from October, 1947, until February, 1948. Then he began reorganizing his gang. Guillo put him in touch with Henri Ribot, Désiré Polledri, Maurice Yves, and Jean-Baptiste Orsoni, as tough a crew of cutthroats as Paris ever saw.

This gang, with others occasionally drifting in and out, struck time after time in swift raids so carefully planned by Buisson that the bandits were safely away from the scene before police arrived. Their loot in jewelry, ration coupons and cash was running into millions of francs.

In May, 1949, Buisson again became the judge and execu-

tioner as he had so many times before. It came about in this
way: Polledri and Yves were driving to a rendezvous with Buisson and Orsoni. Yves was driving and Polledri sat beside him,
tinkering with a machine pistol. The gun fired accidentally and
the shot plowed through Yves' heart. The car careened across
the curb and crashed into a building, with Yves slumped
across the wheel. Polledri darted from the car and ran. He went
directly to the rendezvous where Buisson and Orsoni were
waiting.

"Where is Maurice?" Buisson asked. He had become extremely fond of the tough little man known to the underworld
as the Fishmonger.

"He's dead." Polledri said.

"What do you mean 'dead'?" exclaimed Buisson. "What happened?"

"He shot himself," Polledri said. "He was fooling around with
a machine pistol." He told them he was at the wheel of the car
when the accident happened.

That night Buisson left Paris to hide for a time with his mistress, who lived in a quiet suburb. He wanted to see if the police
would be able to link Yves' death with Polledri before he made
another move. He couldn't take any chances, because if the police arrested Polledri he might talk.

Buisson pondered Polledri's story of Yves killing himself. The
newspapers said Yves had been found slumped over the wheel
of the car. Obviously he had been driving—so he wouldn't have
been toying with the pistol as Polledri said. Polledri was lying.
He had killed the Fishmonger himself.

When the police search for Yves' killer died down, Buisson returned to Paris. He called Polledri. "Meet me for dinner," he
said. "I've got something good lined up."

Buisson met Polledri and Orsoni at a restaurant near the Hô-
tel des Invalides. It was ten o'clock when they left the restaurant
and strolled toward the Quai d'Orsay. An automobile parked a
block away moved into the street and rolled along behind them,
slowly.

Buisson said, "There is a little bar down this way where we can
talk." He steered Polledri into a side street. They had walked a
short distance when an automobile's lights behind them blinked

and its horn sounded. Polledri turned and at that moment Buisson pulled his pistol and fired seven shots into him at point-blank range. Polledri fell, mortally wounded. Buisson and Orsoni jumped into the waiting car, which sped away.

Polledri lived for two hours. When police asked who shot him, he whispered, "Buisson . . . Buisson did it." And then he died. Ironically, the last shot fired by Buisson had pierced his tongue.

In the early months of 1950, the Préfecture de Police (the Paris metropolitan police) and the Sûreté Nationale (France's FBI) opened an all-out drive to break up Buisson's gang operations. One by one, police and detectives picked off his confederates, but Buisson always managed to escape. But the pressure was becoming so great that he was forced to move into a suburban hide-out.

At his headquarters at the Sûreté Nationale, Monsieur Charles Chenevier, Directeur aux Affaires Criminelles, pondered the case of Emile Buisson. The search for Buisson had become a grim contest between this master detective and the master criminal.

Usually the search for a criminal is a coldly impersonal business with law enforcement officers. But occasionally such a hunt becomes an intensely personal affair—such as the time when the FBI's J. Edgar Hoover was goaded into leaving his Washington office to track down the killer Alvin Karpis. In this case, a United States Senator was publicly sarcastic in his remarks that Hoover had not personally made the arrests in the FBI's drive against hoodlums. Smarting from these comments, Hoover sent word to his agents that Karpis was "his man." When Karpis' hiding place was discovered, Hoover flew into New Orleans, surprised Karpis before he could reach for a gun, and arrested him.

Chenevier, too, was goaded by personal pride. People had begun to make sly jokes about the police failure to cope with the outlaw. The police had orders from the Préfecture to shoot Buisson on sight. But Chenevier was determined to capture him alive. He was certain that Buisson alone knew the stories behind many of Paris' unsolved crimes. And he wanted to hear those stories.

That is why, in the spring of 1950, Charles Chenevier was seen night after night strolling through the streets of Paris, a thick-shouldered, powerful, impeccably groomed man who seemed to have no thought other than to enjoy the sounds, sights and smells of the city he knew so well. Occasionally he paused to say a few words to a shabby figure lounging in a doorway, or to ask a question of an acquaintance at a bar. Then he would move on again in the search that would not end until he faced Emile Buisson.

When a friend questioned him about his seeming obsession with the Buisson search, Chenevier said, "Have you ever played the game of cards called stud poker? No? Well, it's a game I learned from the Americans during the war. In this game, you constantly conceal your own strength while trying to force your opponent to expose his position."

Chenevier paused to light a cigarette. "You see, this is a game of poker between me and Buisson. He is clever but one day I shall trick him into a mistake, and when I do—I am the winner."

Now the time had come to force Buisson into making the vital mistake. As he considered the problem, Chenevier said to an aide, "I am one of the few men in Paris who knows Buisson by sight. I arrested him before. He will avoid me at all costs."

"Why not send informants out to contact Buisson?" his aide suggested. "One of them may reach him."

Chenevier shook his head. "No. That is not the way. He will be suspicious of anyone who is seeking him. He is no fool. Consider his position. His old pals are dead or in jail. He is in hiding. But he cannot hide forever. One day he must have money . . . and when this time comes, what will he do? He will look for someone to help him in another robbery. We must force him to come into the open—and then I want his contact to be someone who is friendly to me."

Chenevier could afford to wait. But, just as he predicted, Buisson couldn't. His cash was running low and he was becoming desperate. Finally, late in May, Buisson made his first mistake in his poker game with Chenevier. He approached an ex-convict he had known in prison and promised him a handsome payment if he would deliver a gun and automobile.

"I'll see what I can do," his contact said.

Within a few minutes after this meeting, Chenevier knew
Buisson had been flushed from hiding. The ex-convict ap-
proached by Buisson was one who owed Chenevier a favor.
Now he was paying off the debt.

An excited aide said, "Will you send a squad to arrest Buisson when the car and gun are delivered?"

Again Chenevier shook his head. "No," he said. "Buisson
won't fall for a trap like that. Right now he's suspicious of our
man. He won't show himself until he's certain that it's safe. Even
if he did, he would try to shoot his way out of any trap. We
might have two or three of our men killed."

Chenevier arranged to have the car and gun delivered to
Buisson. He gave no orders for his men to shadow the informer.
But within a few hours, Chenevier learned what he wanted to
know. Buisson was hiding in a small inn at the edge of Paris on
the road to Deauville.

On the morning of June 3, Chenevier called a conference at
the Sûreté headquarters. When his men had assembled, he told
them: "Gentlemen, I merely wanted to announce to you that at
one forty-five P.M. on June tenth—seven days from today—
Emile Buisson will be under arrest."

The announcement brought on a barrage of questions, but
Chenevier, relishing the moment of drama, quieted the ques-
tioners. "That's all you need to know. You are not to discuss this
with anyone—but remember . . . at one forty-five P.M. on
June tenth."

Chenevier did not mention the fact that he knew Buisson's
hiding place or that he was receiving a daily report on the
fugitive's habits at the inn. The thing that interested him most
was that Buisson habitually appeared for lunch at 1 P.M., and
remained at his table for never less than an hour. He always sat
at the same table, from which he could see anyone driving up to
the inn, or entering the small dining room adjoining the one
where he ate.

Chenevier was in no hurry. He wanted Buisson to feel more
and more secure in his hide-out.

Early in the morning of June 10, Chenevier left his office and
drove to a point about three miles from the inn. He left his car
and cautiously made his way on foot through a forest until he

reached a dense clump of bushes directly across the road from the inn. And there he waited.

Shortly after noon, two Sûreté inspectors and their wives—all dressed in sports clothes—left the Sûreté headquarters and climbed into a big, shiny Delahaye limousine, the kind driven around Paris by the rich playboys.

A short time later, the Delahaye pulled up before the inn where Buisson was having lunch. He watched the shirt-sleeved men—obviously unarmed—and two attractive women pile out of the car and head for the inn. When they entered the small dining room next to the main room where he sat, he could hear them chatting and laughing about the holiday ahead. He heard them order lunch and then one of the men said to the waiter, "Would you please call the reception desk at the Normandie Hotel in Deauville? I want to ask about my reservations."

The waiter came to the telephone near Buisson and placed the call for Deauville. In a short time he called to the guest in the next room, "Monsieur, here is your party."

The man left his table and walked past Buisson without a glance. He picked up the telephone and said, "Reception desk? This is Monsieur Jacques Durand. I would like to confirm my reservation with you for myself and my wife. We will arrive this evening for one week's stay."

The clerk said, "Just a moment, Monsieur."

"Very good, very good," Durand said. "What is your rate for a room with twin beds and bath—breakfast only?"

The clerk said, "I'm sorry but I cannot find a reservation made for you, Monsieur Durand. Are you . . . ?"

Durand interrupted. "That is satisfactory. We are bringing friends with us, Monsieur and Madame Pierre Duclos—D-u-c-l-o-s. Can you give them a room, also?"

The bewildered clerk said, "Monsieur, please, there is no . . ."

"Yes, a double room also—and adjoining my room if possible."

"Monsieur Duclos" sauntered to the doorway and said, "Jacques, were you able to arrange a room for us?"

And then the two men leaped for Buisson. They pinned his arms to his sides before he could claw the pistol from his belt. One of the detectives got an arm free and blew a blast on a whistle. There was a pounding of feet and Chenevier burst into the room, pistol in hand. When he saw Buisson in the arms of the detectives, he relaxed.

Buisson snarled, "You, again?"

Chenevier smiled. "Yes, Buisson, it is I again." He looked at his watch. "It is one forty-seven P.M. I regret that I am two minutes late."

He handed his pistol to a detective. "Gentlemen, take Monsieur Buisson's pistol from beneath his coat. He won't be needing it."

Chenevier seated himself and picked up a menu. "That was quite a tramp through the woods," he said, "and I'm hungry. I generally have lunch at one o'clock." He waved to a chair. "Sit down, Buisson. You have time for coffee."

Buisson glared as Chenevier ate a hearty lunch and then ordered fresh strawberries. Buisson said, "Do you know where those strawberries came from? I picked them myself this morning from the garden."

"Really?" Chenevier said. He tasted one of the berries. "They are magnificent."

Buisson's lips formed a thin smile. "If I had known you were going to eat them, believe me, I would have sprinkled poison on them."

Chenevier laughed. "Tell me, Buisson," he said, "what was it about our little act that fooled you?"

Buisson thought it over for a moment and then said, "I think it was the automobile. You don't expect cops to be riding around in a Delahaye limousine."

Chenevier nodded. "I thought that was a nice touch myself. Well, if you have finished your coffee, shall we go?"

A few weeks later, as the gray dawn chased the shadows from the Paris prison courtyard, the blade of the guillotine chopped off the head of Emile Buisson.

BELGIUM

THE TIME: *1872–1881*

THE PLACE: *Antwerp*

THE CRIME: *Murder*

Mrs. O'Leary's cow had kicked over a lantern in the O'Leary barn at 558 De Koven Street in Chicago, and the fire had spread in billowing, terrifying waves to consume the heart of the city in one of the greatest disasters of the day.

Reporter Henry M. Stanley had made his way from the office of the New York Herald into the "dark continent" of Africa, searching for the missing missionary, Dr. David Livingstone. He had found his man in Tanganyika and uttered the famous greeting: "Dr. Livingstone, I presume?"

The United States was recovering from the Civil War, and the great westward march was picking up momentum, while lawlessness was rampant along the frontier.

In Europe, Germany had emerged victorious in the Franco-Prussian war, and France, as usual, was in political turmoil. On the sidelines of this conflict, Belgium was prospering and the port of Antwerp was a major center of commerce, art, culture and finance.

In this gaslit era, Belgium was shocked by one of the most sensational murders in the history of the country—a murder that remains among the classic cases of European crime because it involved wealth, society, jealousy, intrigue, deception, and a beautiful woman.

This murder story has long been buried in musty files and almost forgotten with time. But the police, court, and newspaper records of the time reveal that the Belgian police of almost a century ago could piece together a puzzling murder with perhaps as much efficiency as their modern counterparts—even though fingerprinting had not been invented and there were no laboratories to give scientific aids in searching for clues.

Belgium today has one of the most modern and efficient police forces on the continent of Europe. But it is revealing to look back almost a century, to see a murder unfold and to see how the lawmen went about solving the case.

4. Brotherly Love Meant Murder

The tall, bony old man stood on the windswept Belgian sand dunes and peered across the waters of the North Sea to where the horizon dissolved into the gray mists. He rubbed a clawlike hand across his balding head and his lips moved over toothless gums as though he were talking to someone. But there was no sound.

A fisherman saw him standing there, the gaunt scarecrow of a man whose clothing flapped about his thin body. The fisherman scanned the water to see what it was the old fellow was watching so intently, but he saw nothing except a few gulls wheeling in graceful circles. He shrugged and continued on down the beach. Once he looked back, but the tall figure was lost in the dunes.

Alone with the gulls and the wind once more, the old man began walking slowly toward the sea as though someone were beckoning from out there in the mists. He walked from the dunes onto the flat, hard-packed sand and into the froth of the tiny waves which came dancing onto the beach in long rows like chorus girls dressed in billowy, lacy costumes. His steps slowed when the water reached his knees and dragged against his feet. But still he moved forward. The water came to his waist and climbed to his shoulders and finally his head disappeared beneath the surface. The wind and the gulls had the beach and the sea to themselves.

Two days later, on July 3, 1922, the sea gave back the old man's body to the shore. A coastal policeman patrolling the beach saw it lying in the shallow water. He dragged the body to the dunes and searched the pockets for identification. Then he hurried to a nearby farm home to get help.

He found farmer Vander Stickelen working in his barnyard and told him of finding the body. "Could you bring your cart and help me take the body to the mortuary?"

"Of course," the farmer said. "Is it anyone we know?"

The policeman shook his head. "I did not recognize him. There was nothing in his pockets giving a name."

The farmer hitched his horse to a two-wheeled cart and with the policeman soon came to the beach where the body lay sprawled in the sand. He reached into the cart and pulled out a shabby, faded carpet which he sometimes bundled about his shoulders on cold or rainy days. It was a curious thing he should have the carpet on this day and at this place. It had been given to him years before by a wealthy publisher who owned a nearby coastal villa. The carpet had once been a fine one gracing a fine room in Brussels. But that was long ago.

The farmer spread the carpet on the sand and said, "We'll use this." They wrapped the carpet about the body, lifted it into the cart, and set out for the mortuary in the nearby hamlet of Klemskerke—totally unaware that they were actors in a strange aftermath to one of the most sensational crimes in the history of Belgium.

It was strange, you see, because a murderer once had stood on this carpet watching his victim die of a bullet in the back of his neck. And now, forty years later, the carpet was wrapped about the body of the murderer.

But the aftermath was hardly more bizarre than the story of passion, intrigue and murder which had its beginning with a fashionable wedding in Antwerp in 1872 . . .

A buxom society matron stepped from her carriage on a fashionable street in Antwerp and hurried into a brownstone mansion, bearing an exciting piece of news for her friend. "Louise!" she exclaimed after embracing her friend, "have you heard? Julie Pecher is engaged—and you can't imagine to whom! To Guillaume Bernays!"

Such scenes were taking place throughout Antwerp and Brussels. The buzz of astonishment spread across the little country through drawing rooms and servants' quarters. For months there had been a guessing game over who would win the hand of beautiful, auburn-haired Julie, whose green eyes sparkled with laughter as she danced with a succession of ardent beaux at glittering balls. She enjoyed wide popularity among young men in business, diplomatic and society circles not only because of her beauty, but because her family was from highest society and her father, M. Edouard Pecher, was political leader

of the very conservative Liberal Party and an influential businessman as well.

Julie had not taken a serious interest in any of her admirers
until the day her father invited three business acquaintances to
the Pecher home for dinner. Two of the guests were well known
to Julie, Leon and James Peltzer. The third was a stranger,
Guillaume Bernays, a dark, intense man whom Julie found fasci-
nating. Bernays was a Jewish lawyer with a good standing in
conservative Antwerp circles. An intensely ambitious man, he
had accumulated a personal fortune as counsel for some of
Antwerp's largest business firms and had moved into the fringe
of society at the time he met Julie. His wit and charm captured
Julie that evening, and before many weeks had passed he had
her promise to marry him. The announcement set off a chain of
parties for the couple and their marriage was one of the brilliant
events in Antwerp society in 1872. In the gaiety there was no
hint of the dark clouds that were gathering for both of them.

The first shadow came for Julie a few weeks after she and
Guillaume were settled in their new home. At first she had been
pleased when Guillaume told her he had decided to convert to
the Catholic faith. But then she heard, by chance, that her husband still held his membership in a secret society actively opposed to Catholicism.

Julie told him what she had heard and asked if it were true.

Bernays was evasive. "Don't worry your pretty head over my
business affairs, my dear," he said.

"Business?" she exclaimed. "But you can't do this, Guillaume.
It's . . . it's immoral."

"I do not wish to discuss it," Bernays said coldly.

Julie realized the gossip was true and at that moment the
suspicion was born that even their marriage perhaps was a "business affair" to her husband. The shock came at the worst possible
time because she was pregnant.

Julie gave birth to a son, Ende, a year after the marriage. He
was a handsome child to whom she devoted herself. Outwardly,
the household was a happy one but at night Julie locked her
bedroom door and slept alone. When Bernays protested, she explained that in giving birth to their son something had gone

wrong and she could not risk another pregnancy. She refused to give herself to her husband.

They lived almost as strangers, tortured but willing to suffer anything to avoid open scandal even though the servants smirked and gossiped among themselves. The servants smirked because they knew that Bernays, rebuffed by his wife, had found comfort in the arms of pretty Marie Thérèse, one of the housemaids.

This was the state of affairs in the Bernays household when Leon and James Peltzer—who were with Bernays when he first met Julie—found themselves bankrupt and threatened with being sued for fraud because of Leon's careless management of their commercial firm. They turned to Bernays for legal help.

"There is only one way out," Bernays told them, "and that is to raise enough money to satisfy the creditors. Is there no one to whom you can turn?"

"Our brother, Armand, has a successful import-export business in Buenos Aires," Leon said, "but I doubt that he can raise the money."

"It is the only way," Bernays said.

Armand Peltzer was a man proud of his family background. One of his Peltzer forebears had been a prime minister of the Hannover kingdom, one a mayor of the city of Onasbruck, and another a member of the Prussian House of Lords. He had gone to Buenos Aires with his young daughter in 1870, soon after the death of his wife, and his business had prospered.

When Armand learned of his older brothers' plight, he rushed to Antwerp and pledged his entire fortune to cover most of the debts. He promised the creditors he would pay every cent due them from his future earnings—on the condition that his family's name would not be dragged through the dishonor of a trial for fraud. His impassioned plea won agreement from the creditors. Armand was ruined financially, but he had saved his brothers. James settled down to work in Brussels. Leon wandered to England, Argentina and then to New York, leaving a trail of shady deals behind him. Before he left Antwerp, Leon embraced Armand and said, "If ever I can do anything to repay you—you have only to ask."

Bernays was tremendously impressed by the handsome, brilliant Armand Peltzer. He brought him into his business and soon Armand was a frequent visitor at the Bernays home. Often when Guillaume was in Brussels on business or detained at the office, Armand came to see Julie, who seemed to be happiest when he was around. The servants, hearing them laughing together behind the closed doors of the drawing room, were certain that Julie had secretly taken Armand as her lover. They even resorted to organized spying on the two, but never found them in a compromising situation.

Armand often acted as peacemaker between Julie and Guillaume and both of them confided in him. Once Guillaume received anonymous letters saying that Armand and Julie were lovers, but he refused to believe it.

The three friends continued in this fashion for eight years, but one day Guillaume and Julie had a violent quarrel because Julie's parents, learning of his indiscretions, were urging her to sue for divorce. "Don't bring your parents into this house again," Bernays shouted. "I don't want to see them again."

The angry voices reached the ears of the servants who already had chosen sides in the husband-wife conflict. One of them was Amelie Pfister, the governess, who followed Bernays when he stamped angrily into his study.

"What is it, Amelie?" he asked.

"I couldn't help hearing what was said, sir. I do think you should know that if anybody gets a divorce, it's you who deserves it, not Mrs. Bernays."

"What do you mean? What are you saying?" Bernays demanded.

The governess poured out her mean story of suspicion and backstairs gossip. This time Bernays was ready to listen. The woman was saying that for several years, behind his back, his wife had been the mistress of his best friend, Armand Peltzer.

Bernays selected a pistol from a case, shoved it in his belt, and ordered his carriage. He drove to Armand's home and when he saw his friend, he pulled the pistol. He told Armand what he had heard from the governess. "If this is true," he said, "I'm going to kill you."

Armand said, "Only fools believe liars—and you are not a fool,

Guillaume. Now put that pistol away and let me talk to you."
Armand convinced Bernays that the governess' story was a vicious falsehood. Not once had there ever been anything improper between him and Julie. The two men talked long into the night, and when Bernays left, he was convinced.

The following day Julie overheard the servants talking in their quarters. She learned of the governess' visit to her husband and what she had told him. Trembling with anger, she confronted her husband and told him what she had heard. "If you don't get that woman out of this house, then I'll leave," she said coldly.

Bernays called the governess into his study to dismiss her. But before the enraged woman left the room she had convinced him once more that he was a cuckold and that his wife—who would not sleep with him—had been Peltzer's mistress for years and all the servants knew it.

This time, Bernays wrote Armand Peltzer a coldly formal note, forbidding him to enter his house. The note was dated September 18, 1881. Peltzer pleaded with Bernays to listen to reason. Mutual friends tried to intercede. But the poison of suspicion had taken hold and Bernays chose to believe the backstairs gossip. His door remained closed to Peltzer.

Guillaume Bernays, having made his decision, thought he had banished Armand Peltzer from his life. But, in fact, he had only opened a door on an adventure into murder.

A month after receiving the bitter note from his old friend, Armand announced he was going to Paris to attend a meeting of engineers. But the only meetings he had were with his brother, Leon, who once had said: "If I can ever do anything to repay you you have only to ask." The brothers met often during Armand's four days in Paris.

The following month, Lawyer Bernays received an intriguing letter, written in English and posted from Hamburg, Germany, asking him to act as legal counsel for a proposed transoceanic navigation firm to be financed with American capital. The letter bore the signature "Henry Vaughan." A few days later, another letter announced that Vaughan was coming to Brussels, en route to Antwerp. But then Vaughan wrote that his daughter was too ill to travel and for this reason he was rent-

ing an apartment in Brussels. Would Bernays be kind enough
to visit him on January 7 at 159 Rue de la Loi where they could
discuss further details of the new business venture?

Bernays replied that, under the circumstances, he would
come to Brussels. Having a child himself, he well understood a
father's concern over his child's illness.

Bernays left Antwerp for Brussels on the morning of January 7,
telling his servants he would be home in time for dinner. Julie
was not unduly concerned when he did not return that evening.
But as the hours passed she became alarmed. Even with all
their bickering and fighting, Guillaume was thoughtful enough
to let her know when he would be away overnight and this silence was not like him.

Next morning Julie questioned the servants and made inquiries of friends and relatives, but none knew of Bernays'
whereabouts. Many questions went through Julie's head. Did
he have a mistress in Brussels? Had he been injured in an accident? Would he have killed himself because of their fights? She
made a hasty search of his papers, but saw nothing mentioning
a trip to Brussels.

When Bernays had not returned after four days, his disappearance was reported to the police. They questioned members
of the household. Some of the servants told of Bernays' quarrel
with Peltzer over Julie and they hinted darkly that Armand was
somehow mixed up in this business. The newspapers picked up
the story and soon all Antwerp knew about the servants' gossip.

One night Bernays' mother screamed out in her sleep and her
husband found her sitting in bed, weeping. "It was a terrible
dream," she said. "I saw Guillaume slain and his body buried
in a vacant lot in Brussels on Rue de la Loi. It was so real it
must be true." To humor her, the vacant lot she described
was dug over but no body was found.

On January 18, a startling letter was received by the Attorney
General of Belgium although it was addressed to the "Coroner
of Antwerp." It was signed by "Henry Vaughan." The letter
said: "I have been surprised to learn from the newspapers that
M. Bernays hasn't been found so far. I must conclude that my
earlier letter has gone astray, and that the terrible accident
which occurred on January 7, at No. 159 Rue de la Loi hasn't

been discovered . . ." The letter went on to say that the writer, Vaughan, had been showing Bernays an antique pistol when the weapon fired accidentally and killed the lawyer. Vaughan said he was so overcome by terror that he fled with his wife and sick child to the south of France. He had written an explanatory note to the coroner after the killing, but he must have forgotten to mail it. He promised that he would return soon and place himself at the disposal of Belgian justice. The letter had been posted from Basle, Switzerland.

The Attorney General asked a friend to show the letter to Julie Bernays, but the friend was too busy and requested Armand Peltzer to break the news. And so it was Armand who called on the widow with the killer's letter, gravely solicitous and ready to do anything possible to help her. It was Armand who comforted her and sat with her through her storm of tears.

When the emotional storm passed, Julie looked at the Vaughan letter more closely. "This handwriting is familiar," she said. "I'm sure I've seen it before among Guillaume's papers." She searched again through her husband's desk and this time found the correspondence with Vaughan which she had overlooked before. At last she knew what it was that took her husband to Brussels.

Julie Bernays accompanied the Attorney General, an investigating magistrate and a policeman to 159 Rue de la Loi. A locksmith opened the door to the Vaughan apartment and as the door swung open, Julie screamed and fainted. Bernays' body lay sprawled in an armchair. There was a blood smear on one side of his face, and blood stained the new carpet. He had been shot in the back of the neck. Apparently he had fallen on the carpet and then his body had been lifted into the armchair. There was a footprint in the blood on the carpet.

The killer had washed blood from his hands in a wash basin that stood in one corner of the room. Beside the basin was a wedding ring inscribed "Henry and Lucy 1871." On one table were several calling cards bearing the name of Henry Vaughan. They found Vaughan's unmailed letter addressed to "the coroner," describing Bernays' death as accidental and promising to return to Belgium on January 11. Several antique pistols lay on the main table, and the gaslight in the room still was burning.

The disappearance of Guillaume Bernays no longer was a mystery, but the investigating officers were puzzled by the curious manner in which Vaughan had furnished the apartment. It was a large one with several rooms, but only the main room and a small chamber used as a bedroom were furnished. The only windows which were curtained were those facing the street. The policeman looked out of an uncurtained window and saw it faced on a vacant lot which had been dug over recently. He wondered why anyone would be digging there in the dead of winter.

The police had no difficulty tracing the movements of Henry Vaughan while he was in Brussels. He had arrived at the Hotel Brittania a month before the killing, carrying his right arm in a sling. Because of his injury, a hotel porter had filled in the identification forms required by the police. The hotel employees remembered Vaughan as a swarthy, dark-haired man who always wore tinted glasses. He had gone about town letting everyone he met know that he was an Englishman representing American financial interests. He had purchased calling cards, rented the apartment on Rue de la Loi, and bought furniture, a carpet, curtains and other household furnishings. It seemed to police they were tracing a man who made a special effort to identify himself wherever he went.

There were some puzzles, too. Vaughan had told some of his acquaintances he spoke only English, but police found witnesses who had heard him speak Spanish and Flemish. His hair was dark and yet strands of fair hair were found in a comb at the Rue de la Loi apartment. The blond hair might have been from the head of Vaughan's wife or child, but no one remembered seeing a wife and child.

L'Affaire Bernays became a newspaper sensation. Here was a mystery involving wealth, beauty, high society, rumors of an illicit love affair, gossiping servants, and murder. Stories were revived about Armand saving his brothers from prison and recalling Leon's shady reputation. Gossip spread the servants' whispers that Armand and Julie were lovers. People then took sides for and against Bernays—for and against Armand and Julie. All through Antwerp, walls were chalked with anonymous inscriptions: "Find Leon . . . Find Armand."

Armand continued to call on the fair Julie, ignoring the storm of gossip. Once she asked him bluntly, "Armand, did you know Henry Vaughan?" He protested so vehemently that Julie said, "I'm sorry I asked. Forget I said it."

A month after Bernays' body was found, Judge Ketels, the investigating magistrate, called Armand into his office. "You are aware," the judge said, "that your brother, Leon, is suspected by some of being the killer."

Armand protested. "It is impossible. I have proof here that my brother was in America when Bernays was slain." He pulled several letters from his pocket. Here, he said, was a copy of a letter he had written to Leon in the United States, four months prior to the killing. Another he identified as Leon's answer which said he was going to California—a letter posted in St. Louis on December 18 at the time Henry Vaughan was writing to Bernays from Brussels.

Judge Ketels was impressed by the letters and Armand's manner. Armand had not shown him the envelopes in which the letters were posted, but then few people saved envelopes from their mail. Judge Ketels told an aide, "If he is lying, he is one of the best actors I have known." But he ordered police to keep an eye on Peltzer.

Armand was aware that he was being secretly watched by the police. Soon after his talk with the judge, he went to see his old friend, Dr. Rémy Lavise, in Brussels. "My friend, I need your help," he said. "The police are watching me day and night as if I were a criminal. There is a letter from a lady friend waiting for me at the post office. I do not dare get it myself for fear the police will learn we are having an affair, and the lady will be compromised. Will you pick up the letter for me?"

Doctor Lavise was indignant that the police should be treating his friend in this manner. He obtained the letter for Peltzer and helped him mail and receive others. The last communication Armand entrusted to him was a telegram to the unknown lady.

The day after this telegram was dispatched, Peltzer called on the doctor in a state of extreme excitement. "Something terrible has happened," he blurted. "Leon did not understand my telegram and he will arrive at Brussels' north railroad station at four thirty-eight A.M. Please, Rémy, would you go and meet his train? Could you bring him to your place?"

The doctor was stunned. He realized that Armand's story of a "lady friend" had been a subterfuge and he had been helping send messages to Leon Peltzer.

"You have betrayed our friendship," he told Armand. "Now get out. I will help you no more."

Doctor Lavise told his story to Judge Ketels who warned him to say nothing of their talk. Armand was secretly arrested and again brought before the judge. Once more Armand protested that his brother was in the United States.

Judge Ketels said quietly, "Then look behind you."

Armand turned just as a door opened and a policeman entered with Leon. Armand stared at his brother and then exclaimed, "Leon was Vaughan all the time . . . the miserable wretch!" Leon shook his head pityingly and muttered, "My poor brother . . ."

Armand immediately gave a statement that threw all the blame on Leon. He told this story: Leon came to Europe as the representative of a wealthy American named Henry Murray, to establish a transoceanic transport company. Leon discussed the deal with him in Paris and he tried to dissuade him. But Leon was determined to go through with it and wanted Bernays to handle the legal details. Armand left Leon in Paris and didn't see him again until after Bernays was slain. Then Leon wrote, asking him to meet him in Maastricht, a small Dutch town near the Belgian border. They met, and Leon told him he had arranged to meet Bernays in Brussels but, knowing of Armand's quarrel with the lawyer, he had assumed a disguise so that Bernays would not suspect his true identity. Leon admitted he killed Bernays but insisted the killing was accidental. As for himself, he was moved by brotherly love to try to protect Leon. He had dictated the letter addressed to the coroner and helped prepare the letters which he showed to Judge Ketels in the effort to prove Leon was in the United States. This was Armand's story.

Leon swore the story Armand told was true. But then the police pointed out that Bernays had been shot in the back of the neck. Powder burns indicated the muzzle of the gun had not been more than eight inches away, and Bernays could not have been killed as Leon claimed. The police urged him to think it over.

Leon changed his story. This time he said Bernays came to the apartment on Rue de la Loi, recognized him in spite of the disguise, and began insulting and threatening him; he seized a pistol to defend himself, the gun fired accidentally in a struggle, and Bernays fell dead; then, alone, he wrote the letter to the coroner which was found at the scene of the crime.

Armand and Leon Peltzer came to trial on November 27, 1882, charged with murder. The prosecution had quite a different theory about the slaying, pieced together by Attorney General van Maldeghem from the stories of witnesses and correspondence between Leon and Armand which he said was written in code. And the story was this: Armand Peltzer had fallen desperately in love with Julie Bernays. When he was forbidden to enter the Bernays home, he decided to get rid of his former friend so that he could woo Julie. He summoned his brother, Leon, from the United States and told him the time had come to repay the debt incurred when Armand saved him from going to prison. Armand was the mastermind and Leon his puppet. Daumuche, a famous hairdresser for Parisian actors, was paid to make a dark wig for Leon to be worn to a "fancy dress ball." The disguise was so successful that when Leon was at the Brittania Hotel he was not recognized even by a manservant who had waited on him often in Antwerp. The disguise had fooled Bernays who never suspected that his "client" was Leon Peltzer, brother of the man he hated. The "Henry Vaughan" calling cards and the wedding ring left at the scene of the crime were merely part of the window dressing to throw police off the trail. The brothers themselves created a fictional American financier; there was no proof that such a person ever existed. Armand had planned the crime with meticulous care. After the slaying, he had entered the apartment to arrange things as he wanted police to find them. He had left a footprint in the blood on the carpet.

People fought to get into the courtroom, particularly on the day when Julie Bernays—pale and beautiful in widow's black—came to testify. If Armand had been her lover, she gave no sign of it. The accused man watched her with an emotion he could not conceal, scarcely taking his eyes from her face. But Julie barely gave him a glance—and many people wondered why Armand had ever thought, if he truly did, that he had a chance to win her. A physician testified *in camera* that Julie actually had suffered an injury at childbirth that made sexual relations dangerous for her—and thus it was unlikely that she had ever taken a lover.

During the long trial, an attendant brought into the courtroom the bloodstained carpet on which Bernays had died. As the attendant walked down the aisle, he stumbled. Armand quickly grabbed the carpet and carried it forward himself to show to the jury. Afterward, the carpet, along with the other furnishings at No. 159 Rue de la Loi, was sold at auction. It was purchased by a woman who had a villa on the coast and it remained in the villa when a publisher became the owner. But the carpet became so shabby the publisher finally gave it to a farmer named Vander Stickelen, who carried it in his cart.

The murder case went to the jury on December 22, 1882, at 6:15 P.M. The jury was out only thirty minutes. Armand was found guilty of voluntary murder and Leon guilty of premeditated murder. When the verdict was announced, the audience burst into cheers.

The brothers leaped to their feet. "I am guilty," Leon shouted. "I have been rightly sentenced. But my brother is innocent. His conviction is a judicial crime."

Armand, who had his daughter beside him, pointed his finger at the jury and cried, "May my little girl's curse fall upon the jury." Two days later one of the jurors died and the superstitious attributed his death to the "Peltzer curse."

Many people in Belgium believed Armand and Leon were condemned as much by public opinion as by the evidence, which was largely circumstantial. Their brother, James, spent years trying to prove there really was an American, Henry Murray, that the shooting had been accidental as Leon claimed, and that Armand had no other role than trying to protect his brother. But to most, the weight of the evidence was conclusive. If there had been a Henry Murray, they argued, Leon would have had letters to prove his business relationship or the American would have come forward himself to substantiate Leon's story of the proposed navigation company.

Armand Peltzer died in prison three years after his conviction. The beautiful Julie must have overcome her sex fears because she married again, and then devoted her life to working with the poor people of Antwerp.

Leon Peltzer became a prison hermit at Louvain. He refused to associate with other prisoners and for thirty years never left his cell, where he worked as a translator. He was released on October 11, 1911, on the condition he leave Belgium and never return. He wandered into Germany and then to Ceylon where he worked on a plantation during the years of World War I. He wasn't much help to his employers, they said, because he was "too kind to the natives."

Leon returned to Belgium after the war, using an assumed name. By this time he was seventy-five years old, sick, and feeble. He knew that those who hired him were giving him charity in the form of wages. Despite all that had happened, he still had his pride and life had become too great a struggle. One day he visited his only sister and confided to her that he intended to commit suicide. She tried desperately to dissuade him, but when she saw her arguments were futile, she said, "If you must, you must. I understand. May God forgive you." She wept as she watched him walk from her home.

Leon left his sister and searched out the chaplain of the prison at Louvain where he had spent so many years. He handed the priest his money and the few valuables he had left, without any explanation.

A few hours later, Leon Peltzer stood on the sand dunes looking across the North Sea into the misty distance. He watched a fisherman pass along the beach. And then, alone with the wind and the gulls, he slowly began walking toward the sea.

WEST GERMANY

THE TIME: *1953–1954*

THE PLACE: *West Berlin*

THE CRIME: *Kidnapping—and Perhaps Murder*

The cold war between the Communist bloc and the Western Alliance brought a new and savage kind of crime to Western Europe—political kidnapping and murder by Communist agents.

Men marked for "liquidation" by the Red executioners were found dead on lonely streets and in their rooms. Or else they simply disappeared into an underground which carried them behind the Iron Curtain. Such kidnappings extended even to the United States.

West Berlin became a major center in this silent, deadly struggle because it existed as an island of freedom in the sea of Communist dictatorship. Men and women fled to this haven seeking safety from a system they abhorred—only to be brought back into East Germany, sometimes by trickery but more often by strong-arm goon squads.

West Berlin police say that for several years after World War II, the Reds did not bother to cover up their kidnappings. They simply sent their agents to the home of a victim in West Berlin, dragged him into a car, and then carried him into the Eastern

74

sector. Perhaps his family and friends heard of his fate from whispered messages. But seldom did anyone ever hear of the victim again.

These crude tactics created such an uproar that the Communists changed their methods. They began making painstaking subtle plans to kidnap their victims, arranging things in such fashion that the police themselves were often baffled.

This Red terror, backed by the greatest espionage net the world has ever known, is feared by refugees from communism everywhere. Refugees change their names and take elaborate precautions to hide their old identities, hoping to start a new life free from all Red influences. But after settling in a remote town, the refugee often receives a mysterious telephone call or a message from a Soviet consul—and he knows he has not escaped. Such cases are reported frequently to Allied intelligence sources.

The West Berlin police contend with ordinary criminals as do the police of any great city. But their greatest problems are political crimes.

5. Red Terror in Berlin

It was June, 1953. A squat, gray tank crawled down Stalin Allee in East Berlin, its cannon weaving menacingly from side to side. Inside the red-starred steel hull, Russian tankmen, even above the roar of the engine, could hear the angry cries of German workers whose peaceful parade demanding better working conditions had erupted into violent revolt against Red rule.

The police could not control the rioting. With each passing hour there was growing danger that the challenge to Soviet rule would spread across East Germany. Now the Red Army was moving in to throttle the revolt. A German youth, screaming defiance, picked up a stone and hurled it at the tank commander standing in the turret. Men stood in the path of the tank as though they would pull it apart with bare hands.

Suddenly the tank's machine guns clattered viciously in short, ripping bursts. The bullets cut down the workers like grain felled by the sweep of a scythe. Brutally, efficiently, the Red Army crushed the workers in Berlin just as they would crush the workers in Hungary three years later.

In the city of Bautzen, near Dresden, Robert Bialek heard the news from Berlin—that Russian guns had been turned against German workers. He felt the sick shock of a man who has been slugged low in the belly. He walked home with tired, slow steps. He opened the door to his apartment and sank into a chair. His wife saw the look on his face and cried, "Robert . . . You are so pale! Are you ill?"

Bialek shook his head. "No, Inge," he said. "I'm all right." Then he said dully, "Have you heard the news from Berlin?" When she said no, he told her about the workers' protest parade and how the Soviet guns shot down the people—with not a voice raised in protest among the East German Communist Party leaders. These same leaders were blaming "reactionaries" and "agents of the imperialists" but he knew, in his heart, this was not true.

As he talked with his wife that night, there was a knock at

the door. Bialek saw that his visitors were four men who worked in the same plant where he was employed as a supervisor. He invited them into the parlor.

The oldest of the men said, "Robert, what is the meaning of the news from Berlin? The men at the plant are confused. We must explain this to them."

Bialek said, "You should not have come here to ask me those questions. You know I have been expelled from the Party."

The man nodded. "We know that. But you can tell us what is behind all this."

Bialek said bitterly, "I will tell you. What happened in Berlin is no different than what happened under Hitler. I regret that I have worked more than half my life for a cause that is no better than fascism . . . This is what I thought I was fighting all those years . . ."

When he had finished, the visitors walked out, silent.

And Bialek could look down the years which had become a hideous farce, the now-bitter years in which he had helped to free his people from one tyrant only to bind them with the chains of another tyranny.

It had begun in 1928 when, barely in his teens, he had joined a Communist youth organization in Breslau. Five years later, thoroughly indoctrinated by the Communists, he joined the Red underground and became a leader in the fight against the Hitler government. The Gestapo arrested him and he served five years in prison on a charge of high treason. He was released on his written promise to do nothing more against the government. But almost immediately he began organizing a Communist underground in Breslau.

Bialek remembered his joy when Russian troops arrived in 1945 and Hitler died a madman's death in a bunker in Berlin. Naziism was dead and he would help lead his country into communism. He was named secretary for the Saxon Communist Party. Then he climbed rapidly in the Party and became, for a time, Inspector General of the East German Volkspolizei (People's Police). It was a position of power in which he made certain that the police toed the Party line and that appointments were politically correct. He sat in the councils of the new rulers, with a voice in policy-making.

But then his interpretations of the Marxist line began to dif-
fer from those held by Red Chief Walter Ulbricht and his wife,
Lotte. They began to call him a "revisionist" and an "oppor-
tunist."

He was eased into a lesser position as the "culture director"
at the Bautzen Lowa plant. The downgrading was a blow, but
it did not shake his faith in communism.

Bialek's first real disillusionment came while the Bautzen
plant was building railway express cars ordered by Moscow.
The Russians demanded so many changes in design during construction that the plant's profit of one million marks was wiped
out—a profit already earmarked for workers' bonuses and im-
provements in working conditions at the plant.

The Central Committee in Berlin assured Bautzen plant officials there was no need to worry, that the Soviet government
would make good the loss on the contract. But after a few weeks,
the directors were called into special session and an emissary
from Berlin said: "In recognition of our close bonds with our
Soviet comrades, the decision has been made to strike out the
excessive costs incurred in the construction . . ."

He made it clear the decision meant that the balance sheets
of the plant had to be altered. The workers could not be told
the true reason because it would only cause grumbling and dis-
content and would, in effect, be direct agitation against the Soviet Union. It had been agreed, he said, that Comrade Bialek
would take personal responsibility. He would tell the workers
that, due to his own political mismanagement, there would be
no extra funds as promised. He would confess that the million-
mark loss was due to the fact that he had not been sufficiently
alert in encouraging the workers to greater effort and economies,
and had led them to expect too much.

Everyone in the room turned toward Bialek, waiting for his
acceptance. Bialek arose slowly from his seat. "I refuse," he
said bluntly. "I did not spend six years in a Gestapo prison in
order to tell lies to the workers. The Soviet Union ordered the
construction changes which resulted in this loss—therefore, the
Soviet Union should pay for it. It is a Soviet responsibility and
the workers should know it."

Bialek's comrades pleaded with him to change his mind and

accept the Party decision. The pleading became threats. But he stubbornly insisted he would not be a party to such deception.

Bialek was summoned immediately to Berlin to face the Central Committee. Again he refused to change his stand. The committee expelled him from the Party with veiled threats that if he didn't follow instructions then he obviously was an enemy . . . and enemies were subject to liquidation.

All this Bialek remembered as he sat in his home after telling the workers what he thought about the events in Berlin. He knew, for his own safety and that of his family, he should not have spoken out as he had. But he realized that if he knuckled under now, nothing would have any real meaning in the future.

He was hardly surprised a few days later when a policeman gripped him by the arm and said, "Come with me. You are wanted at headquarters." The policeman led him into a room where he faced men with whom he had worked while helping organize the East German police system. Now his old comrades looked at him with cold hostility. The police chief picked up a paper and began reading. He repeated almost word for word the bitter accusations Bialek had made about the Russians' role in the Berlin uprising.

The chief asked, "Did you make these statements?"

Bialek nodded. "Those are my convictions."

"You must bear the consequences for these statements."

"If you are going to arrest me," Bialek said, "you might as well do it now."

The chief smiled. "Oh, no," he said. "We will not touch you. When we are ready, there are other ways. You may go."

That night Robert Bialek sat in his home alone, thankful that he had sent his wife and son to "visit relatives" in Berlin. Inge had refused at first to leave him, but he had convinced her it was best for them all until he knew what was going to develop. He had received word that she and the boy were safely across the line into the Western sector.

In mid-August, a month after the Berlin uprising, Bialek answered a knock on his door and found that his visitor was an old friend from the secret police. He asked him into the apartment and closed the door.

"So," Bialek said. "You have come for me?"

The visitor shook his head. "No, Robert. I am here as a friend. I came to warn you that you're in great danger."

"What is it?"

"They are going to arrest you in another three weeks. The charge will be that you encouraged the Berlin revolt."

"Why don't they arrest me now?"

His friend said, "They are waiting until Inge returns with the child." The visitor gripped his hand and slipped into the night.

Twelve days later, on August 27, 1953, a tall, dark-haired man walked through the gates of the Marienfels refugee center in West Berlin and stood in the line of men and women shuffling toward the registration desk. Finally, he stood before the clerk, who said, "Name please?" And he answered, "Bialek . . . Robert Bialek."

Thus Bialek joined the stream of thousands upon thousands of men, women and children who were—and still are—slipping into West Berlin seeking freedom from the joys of communism. They came—workers, doctors, lawyers, professors, teachers, schoolboys—asking a haven in the West. A few among them were Communist agents, come to spy on the refugees and to report on their movements and activities to the secret police of East Germany. But the vast majority were those desperately seeking opportunities denied them in the East. Most of the refugees, after establishing their status as political fugitives, were flown from West Berlin to cities throughout Western Germany to be absorbed into the economy.

The news of Bialek's defection spread quickly through Allied intelligence services, which were keenly interested because he was no ordinary refugee—he had an expert's knowledge of the inner workings of the East German Communist hierarchy, of Communist personalities such as Walter Ulbricht, and of the Volkspolizei. If he were truly anti-Communist as he claimed, he could give invaluable information to the West, and help counter the Soviet espionage apparatus operating in West Berlin and West Germany.

An Allied officer called on Bialek and bluntly laid the cards on the table. "We need your help," he said. "But it is only fair to tell you it will be dangerous for you to remain here. We need you—but, of course, you are free to leave Berlin if you wish."

Bialek paced the floor and then reached a decision. "I know the danger perhaps better than you," he said quietly. "I'll stay."

For more than a year, the voice of Robert Bialek was beamed by radio to East Germany, a voice that dissected the theories of Marx, discussed the corruption within the East German Communist Party, and reminded the East Germans they were being used as vassals of Russia. His broadcasts brought cries of protest from the East German press and his old comrades joined in condemning him as a "reactionary," "capitalist puppet," "traitor," and "renegade."

Bialek's broadcasts alone were cause enough for the Communists to rage against him. But then he opened an "office" in West Berlin which became a center of counterespionage. He developed lines of information which led deep into East Germany. Time after time he exposed Red agents who entered West Berlin claiming they were fugitives from the Volkspolizei or had been members of the East German police force.

Bialek—according to West Berlin officials—became one of the most effective counteragents in this city of intrigue, so effective that the Communists decided they no longer could tolerate his activities. He had to be removed, not only to protect the Red espionage net but also to discourage any who might be tempted to follow his path. And so he was marked for death.

As West German police later pieced together the story, two men and a woman were assigned the task of kidnapping Bialek. The Communists had no difficulty finding recruits for their Murder, Inc., operations. The prisons contained many criminals eager to win a suspended sentence, favors for their families, and a fat reward for a job well done in West Berlin.

The plot against Bialek unfolded slowly. It began one September afternoon in 1955 as he strolled down busy Kurfürstendamm, enjoying the bustle of the crowds and the gaily decorated shop windows which were such a glittering contrast to the drabness found in East Berlin. As he passed a sidewalk coffee shop, a man arose from a table and grabbed his arm. "Bialek! I can't believe it."

Bialek turned and saw a former acquaintance, Paul Drzewiecki, a balding, owlish-looking little man whom he had last

seen in East Berlin several years before. He had a vague re-
membrance of having heard that Drzewiecki had been in trouble with the Communist police. He joined Drzewiecki at his
table and ordered coffee.

"What are you doing now?" Bialek asked. Drzewiecki
shrugged. He said he had fled to West Berlin two years earlier
and since then he had managed, doing whatever odd jobs he
could find. It was difficult to find any kind of steady work with
so many refugees coming into the city—but he couldn't com-
plain.

Drzewiecki's story wasn't unusual. In this strange half-a-city,
isolated in a Red sea, men with university educations and distinguished backgrounds often could be found doing menial labor, anything that would keep them alive until their fortunes
changed for the better. Drzewiecki made it clear that he, too,
had become disillusioned with communism and that was why
he had fled. When they parted that afternoon, Drzewiecki had
managed to tie together again the bonds of the old acquaintanceship.

The two men met frequently after that, to sip coffee or to
lunch together, reminiscing about the past and former friends.
At last Bialek confided that he was working in the field of intelligence.

"Perhaps," Drzewiecki said, "I can be of help." He said he
had a friend in East Berlin, Herbert Hellwiig, who worked in
the Rummelsburg prison. Frequently, Hellwiig slipped into
West Berlin to buy things he could not get on the other side. He
always had a great deal of interesting news about what was
going on in police circles. Drzewiecki was certain Bialek would
enjoy meeting Hellwiig—and he might be useful.

A meeting was arranged and Bialek found Hellwiig an interesting man who was surprisingly well informed on what was
taking place in East Berlin, particularly among the police. Soon
he, Drzewiecki and Hellwiig were meeting each fortnight at
Drzewiecki's modest little fourth-floor apartment at Hagow-
strasse 30, to argue, reminisce and exchange information.

One evening in November, Bialek knocked at Drzewiecki's
door and was surprised when the door was opened by a pretty,
dark-haired woman he had never seen before.

"Come in," she said, smiling. "You're Herr Bialek, aren't you? I've heard Uncle Paul speak of you so often."

Drzewiecki appeared behind her. "Robert," he said, "this is my niece, Christina."

"I didn't know you had a niece," Bialek said. "Where have you been hiding her?"

Drzewiecki put his arm about the young woman. "She arrived yesterday—and now she's safe with her old uncle. Already she has changed all the furniture around so I don't know my own home."

Thereafter when Bialek, Drzewiecki and Hellwiig met, Christina was there, pouring beer, preparing sandwiches, and joining in their talk. As the weeks passed, she seemed to grow particularly fond of Bialek, giving him special little attentions she didn't give the others. Sometimes he felt a bit guilty when he left Inge and hurried to meet his friends, knowing Christina would be sitting by his side in that intimate way of hers. But it was nothing more than friendship, and Bialek felt lucky to have such good friends.

Bialek would not have felt so secure and pleased with his friends had he been eavesdropping on a conversation between Christina and Drzewiecki late in January. Christina met "Uncle Paul" in his apartment and announced crisply, "I have found the place. It is perfect. All we must do now is get the fool there. The rest will be easy."

"Where is the place?" Drzewiecki asked.

"In Wilmersdorf—21 Jenaerstrasse," Christina said. She picked up a piece of paper and quickly sketched a floor plan. "It is on the ground floor and has three exits. Here is your room. This exit leads through a plumbing shop facing on Jenaerstrasse. This one goes down the hallway to the main entrance. This one leads through the kitchen into an alley, the entrance the owner wants you to use."

"Who is the owner?"

"Max Schmidt. He's old and hard of hearing. He operates the plumbing shop. He and his wife live in this room, across from the bathroom."

Drzewiecki said, "How much is the rent?"

"Don't worry about money," Christina said. "I have paid the

rent and you will move in on February 1—three days from to-day. I'll arrange to have your things moved from here and I'll buy whatever else we need to furnish the place."

Drzewiecki nodded. "I'm seeing our friend this afternoon."

Drzewiecki was waiting at the Kurfürstendamm coffee house when Bialek arrived. He told him about renting another apartment. "My birthday is on Saturday," Drzewiecki said. "We will have a party and you can see my new place. You will be there?"

"I'll be there," Bialek promised.

On Saturday, Bialek told his wife he was going to help celebrate Drzewiecki's birthday, but that he would be home early.

"Please be careful, Robert," Mrs. Bialek said. "It isn't safe for you to be walking the streets at night."

"Don't worry, Inge. I'll be all right."

It was dark when Bialek walked through the alley to Drzewiecki's place. A few minutes later Hellwiig and Christina arrived, gay and laughing. Soon they were drinking toasts to Drzewiecki, to his new home, to Christina, to life, to love, to freedom . . .

At 9:30, Plumber Schmidt came into the hallway and tried to enter the bathroom but it was occupied. He tried twice more and each time found the door locked. Irritated, he knocked on the door of his new tenant.

Drzewiecki opened the door and Herr Schmidt said, "Three times I have tried to get into the bathroom and each time the door is locked."

"I'm sorry," Drzewiecki said, "something must be wrong with our friend."

He went with Schmidt and tried the door, followed by Hellwiig and Christina. There was no answer to their pounding. Hellwiig and Drzewiecki crashed their shoulders against the door and forced it open. They saw Bialek crumpled on the floor at the end of the tub, lying in his own vomit. His face was a purplish color and his breath came in deep, slobbering gasps.

Herr Schmidt said with disgust, "He is drunk."

But Christina cried, "Oh, no, he's ill. We must get him to a doctor. I'll get a taxi." And without another word she ran through the plumbing shop into the street.

In less than a minute she was back. "I have a taxi," she said.

"The driver will help us." The man who came with her helped Hellwiig lift Bialek from the floor. They carried him out of the front entrance into the street with Drzewiecki following.

Schmidt, watching through a window, saw the two men lift the unconscious man into the back seat of the car and close the door. The woman climbed into the front seat and the automobile drove away, leaving Drzewiecki standing on the sidewalk.

Later, the old man recalled that the car, a black Mercedes-Benz sedan, didn't have the white stripe of a taxi. It seemed strange, too, that the woman could find a taxi so quickly on that quiet street. But at the time, he was too angry over what had happened to give these things any thought. He walked back to confront Drzewiecki. "I gave you permission to have a quiet party," he said, "not a drunken brawl. I will not allow this in my home."

"I'm sorry," Drzewiecki apologized. "I didn't realize my friend was getting drunk . . . Please now, I must get some fresh air. This has been a shock to me, too." And he walked into the night.

Schmidt still was angry on Sunday morning over the party given by his new tenant. Even though only one of them was drunk, that was too much. His wife had had to mop up the bathroom and he would have to repair the damage to the bathroom door. He was muttering to himself when he heard a knock at the front door.

A woman with a pale, worried face stood outside. "I'm Mrs. Bialek," she said. "Where is my husband?"

"I know nothing of your husband," Schmidt said gruffly.

"But you must," she cried. "He told me he was coming here last night to a party. He has not returned home."

"He is not here," Schmidt said.

"He must be here," the woman said desperately.

"Then come see for yourself." He led her to Drzewiecki's room and Mrs. Bialek stepped inside. She looked around the room and then slowly lifted a rumpled jacket from the back of a chair. She buried her face in it and sobbed . . . it was the jacket her husband had worn when he left home.

A rumpled jacket . . . there was nothing else.

West Berlin police patiently pieced together the story, and what they could not document they could easily guess from scattered scraps of information. Of this they were sure: Robert Bialek was drugged, kidnapped and probably murdered. And Drzewiecki, Hellwiig and Christina were well rewarded for the job they performed for the cause of communism.

THE TIME: *1950–1954*

THE PLACE: *West Germany*

THE CRIME: *Counterfeiting*

Crime is not always greed and terror. Sometimes a "criminal" is a quiet, gentle man whose lawbreaking takes on the overtones of comedy. At times even the police smile as they search for a lone little man who has undertaken the task of outwitting the might and majesty of a government.

The U. S. Secret Service had such a case several years ago when crudely forged $1 bank notes began turning up in New York City. They were nothing more than pencil-drawn caricatures of a U. S. Treasury note. But someone managed to pass them day after day, and year after year.

Secret Service agents developed a grudging admiration for their adversary and the pattern of his operations told them a great deal about the man they were seeking. He was obviously a man who lived alone, probably in a shack in some tenement section of the city. His needs were simple because he never passed more than one bogus $1 bill at a time—and then only to buy food and perhaps a bit of clothing. He was a cautious man because he never went back to the same place to pass a second note. And the places he chose to spend his money were dark little shops where the light was bad and no one bothered to look closely at the note being offered.

The trap finally was sprung—as it always is—but not before the counterfeiter had become a legend to the Secret Service.

Karl Peglow, too, became a legendary figure in German counterfeiting. But his ambitions were not modest. He dreamed of world recognition as an artist. And how well he succeeded is our story.

6. *The Gentle Scoundrel*

Karl Peglow was stretched out on his bunk taking an after-lunch nap when a prison guard rattled the iron door of his cell. "On your feet, Peglow," the guard ordered, unlocking the door.

The prisoner came out of the mists of sleep groping for his glasses and his wits, trying to bring his iron-barred world into focus again. "What's wrong?" he exclaimed. And then repeated himself foolishly, "What's wrong?"

The guard said, "Ask the Chief. He wants to see you. Hurry it up."

Peglow scrambled to his feet, a rumpled, formless, middle-aged man with a wispy mustache and vague, near-sighted eyes that were even vaguer once he had his glasses on. He followed the guard down the corridor, trying desperately to think which prison rule he had broken—why he should be summoned before prison authority. Usually it meant trouble and Peglow wanted no trouble. He ran his hand worriedly through his thinning hair.

He was shown into the office of Herr Schmidt, a member of the prison hierarchy. Schmidt sat at his desk, a huge man with huge hands which looked as though they could splinter a desk, or a man's skull, if they pounded it.

Schmidt said in a normal, mild bellow, "Well, Peglow . . ."

The voice made Peglow cringe inside. Loud, rasping voices always did. He stood silent, nervously waiting to see what would come next.

". . . are you a mechanic?"

Peglow was taken by surprise. He stammered, "I am an artist."

Schmidt's laugh boomed out and Peglow flinched again. "Artist?" Schmidt said. "Yes, I know. You are an artist at counterfeiting. That's why you are here. But I hear you can repair radios. Can you?"

Peglow said he knew something about radios, if they weren't too complicated.

"Good," Schmidt said, rising. "Come with me."

They walked through the corridors, through the prison court-

yard and through the prison gate, Peglow half-trotting to keep
abreast of the official. For the first time in more than a year, he
saw the outside of the gray stone walls. He remembered when
the gates had closed behind him in June, 1948, a few hours after
the judge had sentenced him to two years' imprisonment for
counterfeiting ration cards in Hannover. It felt good to be outside again, even for a short time.

As they walked toward Herr Schmidt's home near the prison,
Schmidt explained that he had a good radio but something
had gone wrong with it. This wasn't surprising, he added, because his wife kept the damned thing blaring from morning until night.

"Peglow," Schmidt said, "can you fix it so it won't receive those
bawling singers and their love songs? That's all she ever listens
to." He laughed at his own humor.

Peglow thought it safe to smile. "I'm not that good," he said.

Schmidt led Peglow into the living room of his home and
pointed to the cabinet radio. "There it is," he said. "You will
find any tools you need in the basement." He glanced at his
watch. "It's two o'clock and I'll be back at five. And don't get
any smart ideas like running away." His thick fingers gripped
Peglow's neck briefly, and then Schmidt stomped out.

Peglow inspected the radio. It was a fine one, a Grundig. He
found a small tool kit in the basement and returned to the living
room. Within five minutes he found the trouble, a broken connection which could be repaired in a few minutes. He lifted the
radio from the cabinet onto the floor and was starting to work
when he sensed there was someone else in the room.

Peglow turned and saw a woman standing at the door watching him, her hands nervously smoothing her apron. She was a
small, trim, middle-aged woman with large brown eyes. She had
obviously been a pretty fräulein before life had given her that
frightened look. Peglow realized with surprise that she reminded him of the prisoners with that air about them of suspicion and wariness.

He acknowledged her presence with a nod, acutely conscious
she was the first woman he had seen in many months and that
they were alone. He almost wished she would go away.

"I'm Frau Schmidt," the woman said in a low voice. "Don't

mind me. Go on with your work." She came into the room and
sat in a chair near him, still smoothing her apron over her lap,
looking as though she would take flight if he made any sudden
move.

Peglow fumbled with the radio. His hands were trembling so,
he controlled them only with a great effort. "I am a prisoner,"
he said gruffly. "But you need not be afraid."

"I'm not afraid," she said.

Peglow said, "I'll have the radio fixed soon. Then you can enjoy listening again to the love songs."

"How do you know what I listen to?" she said. "Did my husband tell you?" Peglow nodded. She said in a flat voice, "One
must have companionship—even if it is only the sound of a
radio."

Peglow felt a curious sense of sympathy and understanding.
Her voice was so nice and soft. He wanted her to continue sitting near him and so he carefully inspected each part of the
radio, making no effort to fix the broken connection.

Gradually the feeling of restraint passed and like two people
starved for someone to listen with sympathy—or just to listen—
they were telling each other of their past. Her name was Anna,
and she did not seem to think it shocking that when his dreams
of becoming a famous artist failed him, he used his talent in
counterfeiting. She made it clear to him that she too had ex-
pected more than she had found as the wife of Herr Schmidt,
although his name was never mentioned.

Peglow could never explain how it happened, but before the
afternoon was over the rumpled, vague man in prison garb knew
that he was in love for the first time in his life. He wanted desperately to see this woman again and to talk to her. She made
him feel like a man again—a man whose words were worth listening to.

When Herr Schmidt returned at five o'clock, Peglow had radio parts scattered in one corner of the room where he seemed
to be busily at work. Anna had disappeared when she heard his
heavy steps on the walk outside.

"I found the trouble," Peglow said. "I can have it fixed tomorrow with a little more time."

Schmidt took him back to the prison but next day brought

him to the house again after lunch. The German gods who look down on such affairs must have giggled as Schmidt stalked from the room.

This time when Anna came into the room, there was no shyness between them. And, finally, when Karl Peglow blurted out that he was in love with her, her eyes did not blaze with indignation nor did she laugh at him. She wept.

Peglow stood, blinking helplessly and a little bit awed by what he had done. He patted her shoulder awkwardly and then she was in his arms and they were laughing like two children over an exciting discovery. It was perhaps an unlikely affair, the prisoner clumsily making love to the dowdy wife of a prison official. But to them it was a golden afternoon.

Late in the afternoon, Peglow hurriedly assembled the radio and tested it. The room was filled with the voice of a singer "bawling" a love song. Anna smiled and said, "I really don't need it any more." Before Herr Schmidt returned, Anna whispered to Karl, "I'll be waiting for you."

Karl Peglow served out his prison term and, in 1950, became a free man again. Anna was waiting for him and they slipped away together. Anna left a note for her husband, placed carefully on top of the radio which was blaring a love song when he came home that night. The note ended with the words "goodbye, forever." And Anna meant forever.

Anna Schmidt and Karl Peglow settled in Hameln on the Weser River and when Anna's divorce became final, they were married. Anna adored her husband. Anything he did, in her eyes, was wonderful. To her, he was not a counterfeiter and exconvict. He was an artist and a gentle, kind man.

Anna and Karl were happy together. But even Anna's love was not a complete substitute for the ambition which had become a passion with Peglow—the ambition to be recognized as a great artist. When he found so many doors closed to him because he was an ex-convict, Peglow decided that if he could not achieve recognition legitimately, then he would achieve it as the greatest counterfeiter Germany had ever known. His art might be a "black art"—but it was the kind of art that could not be ignored.

"I'll make them recognize me," he would tell Anna. "I'll make them admit that I am a master." And Anna would adore him with her eyes and say, "Of course, Karl. I'm sure you will."

By day, Peglow worked as a truck driver's helper, delivering furniture to towns and cities throughout West Germany. At night he labored with his cameras, engravings and a small hand press. When neighbors became curious about his night work, Karl would tell them: "I am working on an invention."

Occasionally he turned to poetry to bolster his inner recognition of his own talent. In one of his poems, Peglow wrote:

> *I am a master,*
> *I mix my colors well . . .*
> *I am a master,*
> *And I'll always be*
> *A master in my world.*

When he had finished the poem, he reread it and then signed it with a flourish: "Charles the Great—King in the Realm of the Black Art."

It was the spring of 1951.

In August, 1951, police officials at the Bundeskriminalamt (Criminal Investigation Bureau) in Wiesbaden received several counterfeit bank notes from a regional federal bank which had intercepted them. The notes, all in ten-mark denominations (worth about $2.44 each) had turned up in the Westphalia area. They were remarkably good imitations, so good in fact that they had not been spotted until they reached the banks in the course of normal business operations. Police investigations disclosed the false notes had been passed one by one in cigar shops, beer gardens, small restaurants or grocery shops located in widely separated towns. None of the merchants to whom the bills were traced could say who had passed them or hazard a description of the mystery man, "Herr X." He could have been any one of hundreds of strangers who had made a small purchase.

During the next eight months, the banks intercepted a steady stream of the ten-mark phonies. The police file began to bulge with specimens of Herr X's work. The notes did not resemble the work of any known counterfeiter of German currency. Each

one was uniformly one millimeter shorter than the official bank
notes. The paper didn't have the "crackle" of authentic bills and
a close scrutiny revealed the notes didn't have on them the con-
fetti-like colored dots that appear on all German currency.
There was a slightly fuzzy look about the figures on the bills.

But all these defects were not discernible from a casual look
at the money. They became apparent to the unskilled eye only
upon a close comparison with legitimate bank notes.

Police began the slow task of checking on the activities of ex-
convicts and others known to have counterfeited currency in
the past. This trail even led them into reviewing the names and
checking into the whereabouts of those who had been employed
in the fantastically secret counterfeit operations conducted by
Hitler's government during World War II. Hundreds of millions
of dollars worth of counterfeit British pounds were printed. The
ultimate aim was to flood the world with the phony currency
and wreck the British economy.

In this operation, Heinrich Himmler's lieutenants rounded up
convicted forgers and artisans skilled in printing and engraving
who turned out false pound notes of such excellence that only
the Bank of England was able to detect them. These slave workers had to succeed—for failure meant death. (How near they
came to success is told in a later chapter.) The police could not
assume that Herr X was not one of these.

But weeks of effort by police in this search led only to failure.
The identity of Herr X remained as much a secret as ever. However, the police were certain that Herr X was a lone wolf. There
were no clues that he was using a gang in the distribution of his
notes. It seemed certain he was passing the notes himself, select-
ing only small, busy shops where the cashiers were not likely to
look closely at each bill handed to them.

It was evident that Herr X was someone skilled in photography, engraving and printing. Police experts were certain he
was using the method in which a photograph is taken of a
genuine note and then enlarged some twenty times. The en-
largement is then photographed and reduced to original size on
sensitized plates for engraving. The notes showed Herr X was
working with three color plates in obtaining his remarkable imi-
tations.

Suddenly the passing of the ten-mark notes stopped. For six months there were no new reports of Herr X's operations. Then a new ten-mark counterfeit note turned up, immeasurably better in detail than the first series. Again these notes were precisely one millimeter shorter than the originals and the paper was from the same stock as the first series. The printing was much sharper, indicating Herr X was working from new plates. This time, also, the colored dots were on the paper, expertly placed there by hand-painting.

A few months later, the central bank at Oberhausen, Westphalia, found a counterfeit twenty-mark note which caused a ripple of serious concern among bank officials. This one could not be spotted as a phony by the average person without a magnifying glass to compare its detail with that of a legal note. Except for the "feel" of the paper, it was good enough to have fooled many of the experts—had Herr X not made one mistake. The official bank notes had a picture of allegorical figures standing beside a beehive which denoted the thrift and industry of West Germany. But Herr X had failed to put on his bills the tiny opening used by the busy bees at the base of the hive.

Police sent warning pamphlets to banks, business houses, post offices and merchants pointing out this flaw in the twenty-mark forgeries. But Herr X was obviously a student of all the police literature distributed on the subject of counterfeiting. Soon the twenty-mark falsies appeared with the "hole" in the hive carefully added with pencil.

This new development caused Director Hans Dickhof of the Bundeskriminalamt to step up the efforts to track down Herr X. He organized a special squad whose sole duty it was to find the man. The squad set up headquarters at Hannover and then shifted operations to Düsseldorf. But as 1953 came to an end, there still was no clue as to Herr X's identity. The hunt was all the more difficult because the counterfeiter worked alone and passed only enough of the false notes to meet his needs which obviously were modest. In more than two years, the notes he passed had totaled only $10,497.60 in value.

Director Dickhof called for a special conference at Wiesbaden to discuss the case. "We must broaden our search," he said. "We have checked out the known forgers of bank notes and we've come to a dead end. We are going back into the records for the past thirty years and check on everyone connected with forgery of any kind."

One by one, police went down the list of men who had been convicted of forgeries. Finally they came to the name of Karl Peglow. His record showed he once had been employed as a mechanic in a government printing office. He had been convicted twice of counterfeiting rationing cards. He was an expert photographer and engraver.

About the same time, a woman came to the Hannover police and told them a story of having overheard a woman boasting that she would soon have an unlimited supply of fifty-mark notes which she would sell at a fat discount. In a routine check of what might well have been drunken barroom talk, the police found the boastful woman had once been implicated in the sale of bogus rationing cards. The man who supplied them to her was named Karl Peglow.

Early in the evening of February 19, 1954, two policemen knocked at the Peglow door in Hameln. After a few moments, the door was opened by Peglow, a flannel nightgown flapping about his bare shanks, his vague eyes peering into the night. Behind him stood Anna, her eyes full of fright as she saw the police uniforms.

The police showed Peglow a search warrant. He protested his innocence and raged at this invasion of his privacy—but it was no use. A search disclosed the photographic negatives and, in a hiding place under the eaves of the house, police found a quantity of printing material. They found his workshop, too, in a little used back-alley room. There was a hand press, cameras, photographic equipment, and the plates Peglow had used to turn out his works of art.

They also found that Peglow had completed the plates for quantity production of the fifty-mark notes. This time he had paper with a "crackle" to it and there were no "holes-in-the-beehive" omissions. Bank experts examined one of the notes and shook their heads in amazement. "If this note had appeared," one said, "the Federal government would have been forced to recall all fifty-mark notes in Germany. It's so perfect it would not only have fooled most of the experts—it would have created havoc." The others agreed.

When this opinion was relayed to Karl Peglow in his jail cell, the rumpled prisoner glowed as an artist might who hears a jury of critics acknowledge that his work ranks with the master-pieces.

But Karl Peglow's greatest moment was yet to come. One day as he sat in prison, a police official came to visit him and ask a favor. The official explained that police wanted a documentary film made, showing a counterfeiter at work producing bogus currency, a film that would be an historic record of "the black art." It would be used as a training film by the police.

The official, with a straight face, said, "You will be the film's star, Peglow."

Peglow beamed. "Yes," he said, "I will do it."

Peglow directed the setting up of a counterfeiting shop in prison. All his hand-made equipment was returned to him to-gether with all the supplies he requested. Day after day, he stepped into the glare of floodlights to sit at his work table. When the cameras focused on him he became the star, patiently revealing the amazing skills he used to produce almost-perfect bank notes.

The training film is shown today by the German police to all recruits as a standard part of their training. As the film reaches its conclusion, Karl Peglow looks up from his work and on his face there is a proud smile of triumph. He seems to be saying ". . . I am the master, and I'll stay a master in my world."

Peglow died in prison in July, 1955.

And his wife, Anna? She adored him to the end. After all, he had been recognized by a discriminating jury of critics as a great artist in his field.

THE TIME: *1939–1945*

THE PLACE: *Nazi Germany*

THE CRIME: *Total War*

The world would not at first take seriously the blueprint for world conquest which Adolf Hitler outlined in his Mein Kampf, *because it was madness. It was madness for anyone to dream of a world controlled and directed by a "master race." It was madness for anyone to plan the systematic extermination of all Jews. It was an act of madness to unleash "total war" against defenseless people.*

But this was an era of madness. And one small room in this fantastic madhouse was devoted to perfecting a plot to wreck the currency of Great Britain by counterfeiting on a massive scale—a plot that was hatched before Germany and England were at war.

Government-approved counterfeiting is not unusual in wartime. The manufacture of bogus identity papers, passports, letters, records and passes became a major operation in both the

Allied and the Axis camps. The forgeries were used by secret agents in the elaborate underground and espionage apparatuses that existed around the world.

But Hitler's macabre counterfeit plot was unusual because it had such a startling objective—and it revolved around the skill of one ordinary little criminal.

In corrupting Germany, one of the Nazis' first acts was to corrupt the police and make a mockery of individual rights by creating the Gestapo. A similar corruption had taken place in Japan and in Mussolini's Italy. These police systems, based on terror, were matched only by the secret police of the Communists. Such systems had not been equaled since the days of Napoleon's infamous police.

In this world of madness, Hitler's great counterfeit plot even becomes a reasonable and logical part of "total war."

7. Hitler's Counterfeit Gamble

Hitler's scheme to flood the world with counterfeit Bank of England notes and wreck the value of British currency was by all odds the greatest counterfeiting operation the world has ever known and one of the best-kept secrets of the war.

Hitler forced this task on Jewish slaves, taken from concentration camps and given one choice—succeed or die. The key man in the bizarre drama was a pint-sized criminal named Solomon Smolianoff, who had been in and out of German jails for years for counterfeiting. This was the ironical touch in the grandiose plot—that the Fuehrer, the champion of "the master race," was in the end dependent on the skill of a Jewish criminal, a little rogue who succeeded so well that he saved himself and one hundred and forty slave companions from the gas chambers.

But Winston Churchill and others in the British wartime cabinet were not amused in the midst of the war when Bank of England officials reported the alarming discovery that millions of pounds worth of counterfeit notes were being put into circulation, notes so skillfully manufactured that only the Bank of England itself was able to detect the forgeries.

The story had its beginning in 1939 when Reichsfuehrer SS Himmler and his deputy, Ernst Kaltenbrunner, completed the organization known as the Reichssicherheitshauptamt (the R. S. H. A.), which was a ministry controlling home security and supply. One of the sections within the R. S. H. A., closely controlled by Himmler, was known only to a few trusted Nazis and was officially designated as AMT F6.

Even before the Stukas dive-bombed Warsaw and the gray-clad infantry followed behind the tanks in the invasion of Poland in September, 1939, the chief of AMT F6, Sturmbannfuehrer Naujocks, had assembled equipment and recruited technicians to produce forged documents and identification papers for the German espionage service then spreading throughout the world.

At this early stage, the workers were not Jews and the operation was largely concentrated at Friedenthal near Berlin, where

a research laboratory was set up for the forgery mill. The responsibility for counterfeiting British currency was given to the
Friedenthal group and Sturmbannfuehrer Naujocks summoned
Gerhard Kreische, who had the reputation of being one of Germany's finest engravers. When Kreische stood before him, Naujocks explained the objective and informed the visitor that he
was to engrave the plates for the manufacture of one-pound
and ten-shilling notes. Naujocks shouted, "Herr Kreische, this
is not a request. This is an order. You will produce the plates—
or you will be shot."

But shouts and threats of death could not themselves produce
bank notes of the quality needed to carry out Hitler's plan. The
two keys to success lay in obtaining the finest of engraving for
the printing, and in producing a paper to match the quality of
fine water-marked paper used by the Bank of England.

Day and night the technical laboratory at Friedenthal
worked on the paper problem. Among those impressed into this
work, also under threat of death, were Robert Bartsch, technical
adviser to the Mahnemuhle Mill at Cassell, and five of his old-
time employees, all skilled in analyzing and manufacturing
paper. They struggled with the problem all through the Battle of Britain and while American Army Air Corps planes began
to mount their massive attack on the Reich.

Early in 1942 the breakthrough came on the paper problem.
Bartsch and his men unlocked the secret of producing paper
that only an expert could distinguish from Bank of England
note paper. Almost three years time had been lost in developing
the process. But now Himmler realized the time had come for
the all-out effort. He called a conference of a few trusted SS
lieutenants, among them Sturmbannfuehrer Bernhard Kruger.
Kruger was then thirty-eight years old, a short (five-feet-four),
stocky, aggressive man with a sensual mouth, square chin, and
dark eyes, whose ambition had been noted by Himmler. He had
been an engineer in private life, had joined the Nazi Party in
1929, and then become one of Hitler's SS bullyboys in 1932.

There is no written record of the conference Himmler called,
but from the reports available it is possible to reconstruct the
meeting without any perversion of history.

Himmler and Kaltenbrunner sat in a flag-draped office in Ber-

lin facing their SS lieutenants, close-mouthed men who knew
how to organize a Dachau, a Buchenwald or a mass extermination as well as they knew how to stomp out the brains of an
enemy in a street brawl. They were efficient and trained to carry
out instructions without question. Swiftly, Himmler told them
of the discovery of the new paper-manufacturing process and
the vista it opened in helping Germany to victory. The time had
come to reorganize AMT F6 for a crash program. The plates
made by Gerhard Kreische were good, but not good enough for
what was being planned.

"Kruger will take over direction of AMT F6. You will recruit
the artists and technicians you need from the Jews in the concentration camps." And here, Himmler must have smiled.

"You are surprised at using Jews? It is logical. Many of them
are skilled as artisans and bankers. And if for any reason they
should fail, there will be no trace left of them and no one will
miss a few more Jews. But we must not fail. You understand
that, Kruger?"

Kruger understood. He knew that if he did fail on this mission, his life was worth no more than one of those doomed
creatures staring from behind the barbed wire in the concentration camps, waiting for the day when he would be called to the
gas chamber—or perhaps to the concrete block-houses where
still-living bodies were shoved into fiery furnaces.

Kruger set to work with his usual efficiency. He sent agents to
the concentration camps in search of "volunteer" talent—artists, printers, photoengravers, designers and professional men
accustomed to handling money. None was told why he was
chosen. Each man had to be Jewish or half Jewish.

While the talent search was in progress, a section of the
Sachsenhausen concentration camp was set aside for the project, known in official correspondence as "Operation Bernhard."
The area was isolated from the remainder of the camp by three
rows of electrified fence, and every approach was covered by
machine guns.

The first seven prisoners or *Häftlinge* arrived at Sachsenhausen on August 23, 1942, and before many weeks had passed
another one hundred and thirty-three were housed in the camp
guarded by a special detail of SS troops. The guards were

changed frequently in the interest of security. Regular camp guards were forbidden to enter the compound and the *Häftlinge* were warned that death would be the punishment for any one of them caught trying to communicate with a prisoner outside the compound. Two SS guards, who boasted in drunken barroom talk of the "secret compound" they were guarding, were sentenced to fifteen years in prison.

Among the prisoners who shuffled into the compound was forty-five-year-old Solomon Smolianoff, one of the cleverest counterfeiters and con men in all Europe. He was a skinny moon-faced little man with big ears. He didn't look tough enough to have survived the frightful months he had spent in the terror camp called Mauthausen. But he had, primarily because he had pleased camp officials and guards by doing their portraits. He was not aware of it when he came to Sachsenhausen, but the whole massive project depended upon the skills he had developed as a criminal. In his hands rested the fate of every *Häftling* in the camp.

Smolianoff was born in Poltava, Russia. As a youth he had studied art at the Petrograd Academy of Art under gaunt, bearded Professor Ivan Miassojedoff. This was just prior to the Bolshevik revolution. When Stalin began his pogrom against Jews, the professor and his pupil fled from Russia and, after years of wandering their separate ways, met again in Berlin. When they weren't painting or turning out etchings, they pooled their talents in counterfeiting British and American currency and in forging passports. Both were wanted by the police of half a dozen European countries. The German police first jailed Smolianoff in 1924 and then the professor, who now called himself Professor Eugene Zotow. After Smolianoff's arrest, the London *Daily Express'* correspondent cabled his paper: "So excellent was Smolianoff's work that in the case of 6,000 pounds in English notes which he forged, only the Bank of England itself was able to detect forgery." Professor Zotow at that time was specializing in turning out bogus £100 English notes and $500 American bills. A professional gambler bought the money and, with his glamorous wife, passed it successfully across the gaming tables at Monte Carlo while posing as a member of European society.

After several brushes with the police, Miassojedoff, alias Zotow, slipped out of Germany into hiding in Liechtenstein as the war began. But Smolianoff again was caught counterfeiting British notes in 1940 and was sentenced to five years in prison. Sturmbannfuehrer Kruger found him at Mauthausen as he assembled his strange slave corps for the big secret operation.

When his organization was complete, Kruger called the group to the main building and explained the work they were to do. He said, "I know you are in fear of death. But if you do your work well, I can promise you that nothing will happen to you." And then, insensitive to the implied insult of his words, he said, "You will be given special privileges. Your food will be better than the food of other prisoners. You will be permitted newspapers and cigarettes, and I am having wireless sets installed in the workshops to which you are free to listen. You may organize theatrical performances if you wish, and there will be ping-pong tables in the main room. Best of all, when the war has been won, you shall be rewarded. You and your families—and this promise is made to you by the Fuehrer himself—will live together in a special settlement where you will work for the government. Each of you will have a house and enough land for a garden. But to enjoy this, you must succeed. Any questions?"

One of the bolder of the prisoners asked, "And what happens to us if Germany does not win?"

Kruger flushed and snapped, "You will be eliminated, of course. But Germany will not lose." And he stalked out.

The group was divided into sections and Smolianoff was given the finest tools. His requests for materials received top priority. Day and night, he worked over the plates until his eyes were bloodshot and his lids red and swollen. Always he was urged to speed up his work. In the eyes of all the prisoners was an unvoiced pleading because each realized his life depended on Smolianoff.

One day the little counterfeiter burst out, "I can't do it. My eyes are nothing but blood, and all of you keep staring at me." He buried his face in his trembling hands. The chief photographer gripped his arm and whispered, "You must keep trying, Smolianoff. If you don't succeed, we are finished."

Wearily, Smolianoff went back to his work. And in April, 1943, a great excitement swept through the slave camp. The news spread rapidly that Smolianoff had succeeded. A fifty-pound note had been produced that looked identical to the genuine British note.

Kruger was summoned, but before he arrived Smolianoff spread genuine British notes over a table top and then placed among them one of the counterfeits. Kruger burst into the room and saw the notes spread on the table under a strong light.

"One among them is counterfeit," Smolianoff said. "Can you find it?"

Kruger stood for several minutes looking at the bills, studying each one intently while Smolianoff and others waited with growing tension. Smolianoff knew he could do no better. If Kruger could spot the bogus note, then he had failed and he knew that failure would enrage Himmler to the point that he might well order all of them killed. And so he stared at Kruger in a silence that was almost unbearable.

At last Kruger reached out and put his finger on one of the bills. "This one is the forgery," he said.

Smolianoff was dizzy with relief. He shook his head. "No," he said, "that is a genuine note. Here is the counterfeit."

Kruger was elated. He rushed off to Berlin to show the note to Himmler. Reichsbank officials were called in to study the bill and they agreed it was nearly perfect. There were some flaws in the figure of Britannia, but they were so minute that detection was almost impossible. Kruger was ordered to get into production as quickly as possible.

By this time, the technical laboratory at Friedenthal was turning out thousands of sheets of the bank-note paper which so closely resembled that used by the Bank of England. Two hundred and fifty thousand sheets were delivered to Berlin in June and July. Four bank notes could be printed on each sheet. The production rate was about fifty thousand sheets a month.

Kruger's *Häftlinge* went on a twenty-four-hour schedule with two shifts each working twelve hours a day. Smolianoff also produced copper plates for printing five-, ten-, and twenty-pound notes as excellent as the fifty-pound forgery. As the notes came off the press, they were dried and taken to a sorting workshop where they were packed in cases and pressed. After this, the edges were carefully cut with a file to give them the appearance of hand-made paper. Each bogus note was compared minutely with a genuine note in a search for flaws, and then graded as follows:

Grade 1—notes without an apparent flaw.

Grade 2—good notes with only a single minor fault.

Grade 3—notes of reasonably good quality which had more than one fault, but still were presentable.

Grade 4—fairly good notes, passable if not studied too closely.

Grade 5—the *Ausschuss*, literally junk, which were not usable.

Millions of pounds worth of the best notes were sent secretly to an old mansion at No. 6 Delbruckstrasse in Berlin. The house, in an old residential section, had been converted into a heavily guarded SS headquarters. From this hideout, Himmler's agents handled the distribution of the bogus money.

The best notes were channeled into neutral countries to be used in the purchase of war materials. The second-grade notes were used by the Nazis to pay their own agents abroad, even though detection of the fraudulent currency would expose the agents to arrest and wreck the espionage system. No one yet has explained this curious and foolhardy gamble which threatened the Nazis' supplies of desperately needed war materials as well as their sources of intelligence.

The third-rate notes were used to pay agents and to purchase materials in occupied countries. And the fourth-grade notes, which comprised the greatest number, were set aside for the time when—as Hitler dreamed of it—a fleet of German planes would sweep through the dark skies over England, leaving behind them hundreds of millions of bogus pound notes fluttering to the ground. And next day, every greedy Englishman would pick from the ground, the trees, and the rooftops a fortune in pound notes. Confidence in the value of the pound would be jarred. Normal trade would be disrupted because no one would know whether the money being offered was good or bad. The money channels would be glutted with phony currency and Britain's economy would be shaken for months. So Hitler dreamed.

At No. 6 Delbruckstrasse, bundles of notes were stuffed into big linen envelopes and dispatched by couriers to German commercial attachés stationed in Oslo, Copenhagen, Madrid, Lausanne, Ankara, Lisbon and other cities around the world. Through other channels, bogus bills were sent to secret agents.

But Sturmbannfuehrer Kruger was a prudent man. Not all of the best bills went to No. 6 Delbruckstrasse. Secretly, he arranged to have several million dollars worth of the currency sent to his quarters where he lived with his mistress, pretty Hilde Möller. And while he stoutly proclaimed his faith in a German victory, he ordered his slave workers to provide him with forged passports to ten countries. There is reason to believe that Kruger succeeded in converting his bogus money into foreign currencies which were transferred to a numbered bank account in Switzerland.

"Operation Bernhard" progressed so smoothly with the British currency that Himmler sent orders to Kruger to get into production on phony United States currency. And Smolianoff was put to work to produce plates for a $100 bill. But Allied intelligence agents discovered some evidence after the war indicating that Kruger quietly sabotaged this effort, forcing delay after delay in order to hold onto the tidy little empire he controlled.

Despite the delays, Smolianoff was on the verge of completing these plates when Himmler sent urgent orders for the operation at Sachsenhausen to be moved to the little mountain town of Redl-Zipf in Austria. At this time, the Germans had failed in their desperate gamble called the Battle of the Bulge, and the Russians were advancing steadily on the Eastern front.

A train of twenty trucks, loaded with prisoners, printing presses, printing materials, paper, and tons of bogus currency, left Sachsenhausen in February, 1945, driving to Mauthausen and then to the mountain town of Redl-Zipf where the Germans had hidden a rocket assembly plant in an underground factory. Workers had driven two tunnels into the mountain near the

town and linked them with shafts or *Stollen*. The entrance to
the tunnel was hidden in an old brewery to conceal it from Allied planes.

Sturmbannfuehrer Kruger, accompanied by his mistress,
visited the mountain hideout in early April and ordered the
printing presses set up for operations in one of the *Stollen*. But
Kruger's visit was nothing more than a cover for reaching his
true destination. Even then, he and his mistress were en route to
the Swiss border, deserting the sinking ship. Intelligence agents
are convinced they reached Switzerland and then made their
way to South America.

As the German Army began its death struggle, Himmler's
headquarters sent an urgent message to the SS guards at Redl-
Zipf, ordering them to destroy all traces of the secret counterfeiting operation, and to bring the best of the false notes to the
redoubt area of Berchtesgaden where Hitler had his mountain
retreat. The slave workers in "Operation Bernhard" were ordered taken to Ebensee where the SS commander had instructions to destroy them in a gas chamber. Thus all traces of
the operation would be removed.

On May 2, five days before the formal German surrender at
Reims, SS troops supervised the loading of trucks with boxes of
bogus currency and counterfeiting equipment. Some of the
cases contained a small fortune in gold watches, chains, cigarette cases, jewelry, looted from occupied countries, and gold
fillings pried from the teeth of concentration camp victims.

But American troops were moving swiftly into the area. The
frantic SS men, their escape routes blocked, buried the gold on
a mountainside (it was recovered later). One truck and trailer
arrived at Tauplitzsee and its contents were dumped into the
deepest part of the lake. Cases from another truck were sunk in
the Ebensee, and the guards tossed the wooden cases from another truck into the swift waters of the Enns River near Hieflau.
These cases crashed on the rocks and burst open. Tens of thousands of forged notes floated on the waters. Villagers along the
stream fished fortunes from the water, and these notes were
among those turning up for years throughout Europe.

The SS guards loaded one hundred slave workers onto trucks
and took them to the gas chamber at Ebensee. The officer in

charge of the gas chamber counted the prisoners and demanded, "Where are the other thirty-nine? I have instructions
to dispose of one hundred and thirty-nine prisoners."

One of the guards explained, "We did not have enough trucks
and the others are being marched here."

The officer said, "My orders list one hundred and thirty-nine
men. I'll hold these prisoners until the others arrive. It's simpler
that way."

But the thirty-nine slave workers marching to Ebensee never
arrived. American troops intercepted them along the way and
turned them free. The Americans reached the gas chamber in
time to save all the others—including Solomon Smolianoff.

When Scotland Yard and American intelligence agents, including U. S. Secret Service men, arrived at Redl-Zipf, they
found the furnace in which the SS men had burned many thousands of bogus notes. The ashes had been stirred to a fine dust,
but at the bottom of the furnace were charred bills with the
ashes still intact, plainly showing what it was that had been
burned.

Slowly, the agents pieced together the crazy-quilt story from
scores of interviews with slave workers and others. One of the
most valuable sources of information was Oskar Stein, a Czech
hostage who acted as "office manager" for the compound at
Sachsenhausen. Stein had kept a small diary in which he secretly noted the numbers of bank notes printed and their face
value, along with an amazing amount of information concerning the entire operation.

The Stein records—confirmed by other sources—disclosed
that in a period of about eighteen months, up to December 31,
1944, "Operation Deilhard" had printed almost nine million
English notes with a face value of more than $646,000,000.

No one knows how many millions of dollars worth of the
forgeries were put into circulation. Four years after the war
had ended, approximately $20,000,000 still were not accounted
for. This was a guess based on an assumption that the SS guards
at Redl-Zipf had burned more than $300,000,000 worth of the
notes.

In Berlin, agents found No. 6 Delbruckstrasse a fire-gutted
shell of a building. Germans living in the neighborhood said the

building had caught fire during an Allied bombing raid. But an old caretaker had another story. "I did odd jobs around the place," he said, "and the guards let me sleep in an outbuilding. No one could enter the house without a pass. There was barbed wire out front, and it was guarded by machine guns. In the last days of the war, the bombers came over one night. A bomb did hit nearby—but the bomb didn't start the fire as most people thought. That same night the SS men came with gasoline. They poured gasoline over the roof and splashed gallons of gasoline in every room. Then they set fire to it and ran. The fire was terrible."

The agents sifted through the ashes and found fragments of counterfeit notes, the only physical evidence that No. 6 Delbruckstrasse had been the center of Hitler's scheme to flood the world with bogus English currency.

Little Solomon Smolianoff, after his narrow escape from the gas chamber at Ebensee, wandered into Italy and now is believed to be living somewhere in South America. Somewhere along the way, perhaps he has seen Sturmbannfuehrer Kruger and his pretty mistress, Hilde.

LIECHTENSTEIN

THE TIME: *1947*

THE PLACE: *Vaduz, Liechtenstein*

THE CRIME: *Counterfeiting*

As some men are compulsive gamblers, so there are others who are compulsive counterfeiters. They cannot resist the urge to match their artistic skill against the odds that are against them. And even after they lose, time after time, they convince themselves that next time the wheel of fortune will turn in their favor.

Liechtenstein, hidden in the Alps between Switzerland and Austria, is a strange setting for a man like Professor E. Zotow. The tiny principality is serene and rustic. It was strange that in

114

this environment the old professor should decide to resume counterfeiting to prove a point: that Americans are fools.

Zotow did not prove his point about the Americans. But he did succeed in winning a measure of fame as the only professional criminal in the centuries-old history of Liechtenstein.

And who knows? Someone yet may prove the point he set out to establish.

8. *A Sinner in Shangri-La*

As animals of the forest flee from a fire, so did men scurry across Europe in the 1930's seeking havens beyond the reach of tyranny and, sometimes, justice. In this flight of saints and sinners there was one who stumbled into an unbelievable little valley of peace called Liechtenstein. He was a tall, gaunt, sad-eyed and bearded man, looking as though he might have stalked straight out of one of El Greco's paintings of the Apostles. But, in this resemblance, Fate was merely enjoying a wry little joke because the saintly-looking face belonged to Professor Eugene Zotow, and photographs of it adorned the rogues' galleries of the police in several countries.

The old professor, who had taught the notorious counterfeiter, Solomon Smolianoff, all he knew about art in Petrograd and counterfeiting in Berlin, arrived at the Liechtenstein border in 1939 a few jumps ahead of the German police because of his ventures into forgery. Somehow he wangled permission to enter the little principality tucked into the mountains between Austria and Switzerland. And once across the border of the tiny country, which Europe's wars had by-passed for almost a century, he found himself in a world where the condition of the crops and the milk yield of the cows, grazing in the high mountain pastures, were more important than guns and politics —where the killing and hating and struggles for power had washed against the surrounding mountains for many, many years, but had not spilled over.

Soon after his arrival in the capital town of Vaduz, Zotow was wakened one morning by the sound of gun shots echoing from the mountains. He threw aside the bed covers, hurried from his rooms, and grabbed the arm of a passing townsman. "I heard the shooting . . . where is the fighting?"

The Liechtensteiner looked at the old man in his nightshirt and laughed. "You must be a stranger. The grapes are ripening in the vineyards and a group of men are firing old muzzle-loading rifles to frighten away the birds. You do not want the birds to steal all our wine, do you?" And he walked away chuckling.

The war engulfed other countries, but Liechtenstein was a Shangri-La, magically sheltered from the howling gales of conflict, where life was no more complicated than the rhythm of the seasons. As winter neared, Zotow joined the crowds which climbed up the mountain roads winding above the town of Vaduz, past the ancient castle of Prince Franz Joseph II, to the tunnel which went through the mountain and opened onto the Samina Valley. And soon a great cheer went up, for out of the tunnel came the fawn-colored cows which had spent the summer in the high pastures of the "hinterland" and now were coming back into the valley for winter shelter. The leading cow in each herd wore garlands of wild flowers and was crowned with a milk stool to show she was the champion milk producer for the season and, with her owner, deserving of the people's applause and admiration. He heard, too, the tolling of the church bells signaling the start of the grape harvest. He watched the families picking the luscious fruit which produced a vin rosé of excellent quality. And in the season of the harvest there was much wine drinking, singing, and merriment.

Early one evening when the lowlands and the Alps were covered with February's ice and snow, Zotow saw great bonfires blazing from the mountainsides like giant candles atop a mammoth white-frosted cake. Around each fire danced young boys waving torches in the Liechtensteiners' ancient ceremony dating back to the days when their pagan forebears sought to drive away the winter spirits so that spring would come early. And when spring did arrive, he joined the crowds in their annual Holy Week procession which wound its way through the villages and up to the Castle Vaduz where the elders prayed for a good crop season, and the children munched on the rolls of sugar bread fresh from the bakers' ovens.

Zotow might well have lived out his days in peace among such gentle scenes, forgotten by the police in other countries, had he not yielded to an absurd temptation—the temptation to prove that the American currency was the easiest currency in the world to counterfeit. But we get ahead of our story.

Zotow was a visitor and had no legal right to settle down in permanent quarters, but no one, including the police, could quite bring himself to force the sad-eyed old man into a world in flames. It was easier just to forget the technicalities at a time like this. And so Zotow became a familiar figure in the villages and in the countryside where the hard-working farmers kept their acres as neat as a well-tended park.

Soon the word spread through Vaduz that the bearded visitor was an excellent artist. Somehow Zotow had obtained the necessary materials and was doing delightful etchings of scenes in and around Vaduz. His oil paintings of scenes from Liechtenstein's history had a heroic quality to them.

Among those who admired Zotow's art, particularly his etchings, were the government officials whose job it was to manage the country's profitable production of postage stamps. Liechtenstein stamps, over the years, had become tremendously popular with stamp collectors throughout the world because of their exceptional quality and beauty. Two or three sets were issued each year and their sale brought substantial revenue into the national treasury.

After studying his work, the officials commissioned Zotow to do five stamps for a series that was to memorialize important events in the country's past. When at last they were finished, the jury of judges was delighted because the Zotow stamps were masterpieces in miniature. When placed under a microscope, the amazing detail of his work became apparent. Whether there were two or a dozen figures shown by the artist, the features of each were etched with brilliant skill and sensitivity of expression. The Zotow stamps were applauded by collectors.

This was a proud time for the old counterfeiter. He had longed for recognition as an artist for many years, only to find himself better known in the jails of Europe than in the art salons. But now his work was being admired by experts around the world. Those who examined the stamps carefully would see engraved at the bottom of each the name: Prof. E. Zotow. No longer would anyone have reason to doubt his claim to the title "professor." If necessary, he could produce the stamps bearing his name and show the beautifully engraved scenes depicting St. Lucien, the patron saint of Liechtenstein; the building of Vaduz in 1342; the signing of the first constitution; the 1499 battle of Gutenberg; and the colorful ceremony of 1718 when homage was paid to the Princes of Liechtenstein.

The success with the stamps brought more demand for paintings and etchings. One of Zotow's admirers was Baron Eduard von Falz-Fein, a friendly and energetic young man who, when the war ended, threw himself into the task of making Liechtenstein one of Europe's tourist attractions. Frequently Zotow would stop by the Quick Tourist Center, the Baron's headquarters, to chat with the young man. He particularly enjoyed these visits because the Baron could speak Russian quite fluently.

One day their talk turned to the artistic value of European currencies and Zotow said he thought the most delicate and beautiful color and engraving work were found in the Swiss and French bank notes. "These notes are not merely pieces of currency," he said, "they are works of art."

Casually, the Baron said, "What do you think of the quality of the American money?"

Zotow snorted disdainfully. "The Americans are fools."

Surprised, von Falz-Fein asked what he meant.

"The Americans are fools," Zotow said, "because they make each bank note the same size, regardless of its worth. I don't know of any other major country which makes a small-value note precisely the same size as a note with a large value. They are inviting counterfeiters to prove they are fools."

The old man still was muttering in his beard about the strange ways of the Americans with their money when he walked out of the Baron's office and ambled off toward his workshop, located a few doors from the Vaduz jail. Perhaps it was at that moment that temptation again overwhelmed Zotow—the temptation to prove that the Americans were foolish to make all their paper money of the same size.

At any rate, Zotow set out to prove his point. One day he left Vaduz on a mysterious journey into Switzerland with the announced intention of visiting certain museums. But Zotow was not interested in museums this time. He made his way south to the Swiss frontier where it juts into Italy at Chiasso near Lake Como. And there, on the bank of a small border stream, he sat on a rock and waited.

Soon a man came scrambling toward him, a little man with big ears and a moon-shaped face—the same little man who had almost succeeded in completing the plates for counterfeiting

U. S. bank notes at the Sachsenhausen concentration camp. It was Solomon Smolianoff. He had received a message in Rome asking him to meet his old friend at this time and this place.

For several hours the two men talked across the border. There is no record to prove that anything was passed between them, but soon after returning from the rendezvous with Smolianoff, Zotow had the copper plates he needed for his project. He obtained the necessary paper by bleaching one dollar bills. And he began turning out phony $100 bills which had the appearance as well as the "feel" of genuine notes.

By the time he had printed forty-five of the $100 notes, Zotow seemed well on his way to proving his point. But, alas, there are people in this world who cannot be trusted and just when things were going well there came, as the Americans say, the double cross.

In late July, 1947, two Swiss "businessmen" presented themselves at the American Consulate in Zurich. They were brimming with righteous indignation, they explained, because they had been approached by a low character who made an insulting offer to sell them any amount of American $100 bank notes at a discount. They had followed this man and found, to their horror, that the bank notes he offered them were counterfeit. And so, as good citizens, they had come to warn the Americans of this plot against their currency. Quite naturally, they expected, in return for this information, a token of appreciation—something like a nice fat reward, paid in cash.

This voluntary display of international co-operation was touching to the Americans, but not very. However, it did set off a chain of investigation which prompted American Vice-Consul John A. Lehrs to write the American minister at Bern, "I have the honor to report that the Consulate has received information to the effect that hundred-dollar bills and possibly forged American passports are manufactured by a Russian resident in Vaduz, Liechtenstein . . ."

And so it was that Professor Zotow's bubble collapsed. Liechtenstein police, accompanied by Swiss police and an American Secret Service agent, found the counterfeiting plates and bogus bills in Zotow's apartment. He was sentenced to two years in prison with the added penalty of deportation when he was free.

Shortly before he completed his sentence, the old man sent word to one of his friends in Vaduz, asking him to visit him. "I am sorry I violated the hospitality of your country," he said. "But I ask one more favor. There is in England a famous old firm, Waterloo and Sons, which makes the currency for many countries. It is my dream to work for them. Will you intercede for me?"

As the friend told the story later: "I went to the firm's offices in London and showed them samples of Zotow's work. One of the senior firm members told me, 'There are only four or five men in the world as good as this man, Zotow. But we could not employ a man with a criminal record. We would never know whether he would take his knowledge home with him and begin working for himself again. It is a terrible thing that this man has a criminal record—because so few in the world have his skill. I am sorry . . .' "

Arrangements at last were made in 1953 for Zotow to go to Argentina. Three days after he arrived there he was dead, of cancer.

Liechtensteiners still talk of Zotow with affection. Secretly they are proud of the fact that five of their most beautiful stamps were the work of a counterfeiter, and that his original paintings hang in the stamp museum only one floor removed from the museum displaying the royal family's fabulous collection of masterpieces by Rembrandt, Rubens, Van Dyck, Frans Hals, Botticelli, Dou, and others.

Reminiscing of Zotow, one Liechtensteiner said, with a twinkle in his eye: "With a little more luck, perhaps Zotow would have proved that the Americans are fools to print a one-dollar bill on paper the same size as a hundred-dollar bill. Can you say no?"

AUSTRIA

THE TIME: *1949*

THE PLACE: *Vienna*

THE CRIME: *Murder*

Sometimes a crime—far more than a political event—can illuminate the progress which a country has made from dictatorship to democracy, from suppression of individual rights to the protection of an individual. Such a case was the sensational Mandler murder case in Vienna.

Prior to World War II, Vienna had become the most important police center in Europe because the Vienna Police Department was the unofficial clearing house for information on international criminals who plagued every country on the Continent.

The Vienna police had the most complete files on European criminals then in existence. And largely for this reason, the president of the Vienna police directed the loosely organized international police association in its efforts to combat criminals who skipped nimbly across international borders.

All this was changed abruptly when Hitler's troops marched into Austria in March, 1938, and his puppet chancellor, Arthur

Seyss-Inquart, proclaimed the political and geographic union of Austria and Germany. Then it was that the Vienna police became linked to the Nazis. Important police files were taken to the Nazi central police headquarters in Berlin. And Austria, too, felt the terror of the Gestapo.

Austria was restored as a republic in 1945. Although complete independence from Allied occupation did not come until 1955, the process of rebuilding the police system along democratic lines was started as soon as the war ended.

The Mandler murder case, coming four years after the close of the war, revealed the progress that had been made in a short time. The police made a mistake in this case that almost cost an innocent man his life. But there was no effort to cover up the blunder to save themselves from harsh criticism and embarrassment. The mistake was publicly acknowledged in the interest of seeing justice done to an innocent man.

This was a landmark of progress for Austrian police.

9. *Murder and a Pot of Spinach*

The officer-in-charge at the Vienna Police Station jotted down the date, Tuesday, November 8, 1949. Time: 9:10 P.M. Then he looked up at the visitor standing in front of the desk, a balding, middle-aged man who was shifting nervously on his feet and twisting the brim of his hat in his hands.

"Your name?" the officer asked.

"Richard Kraus," the visitor replied, giving his home address in Vienna.

"What can we do for you?" the officer asked.

"It's about my employer, Mrs. Blanche Mandler. She has been missing since yesterday."

Such reports of missing persons are common in the great city of Vienna as they are in Paris, London, New York and other cities. Most of these reports amounted to nothing more than vague and groundless fears. But each had to be checked by the police as a matter of routine.

The officer obtained the information that Mrs. Mandler owned a textile factory at No. 6 Schmalzhofgasse in the 6th district of Vienna, and Kraus was her factory manager. She lived in an apartment at Trautsohngasse 6–7 in the 8th district.

"Why are you disturbed about Mrs. Mandler?" the officer asked.

Kraus said, "She left the factory at noon yesterday and said she would be back later. But no one has seen her and she doesn't answer at her apartment. This isn't like Mrs. Mandler at all." Then he added with a quick smile, "She didn't return with the keys to lock the cash box."

The officer interrupted Kraus to say: "I note you gave your own address as Trautsohngasse 6–7. That also is Mrs. Mandler's address?"

Kraus nodded and said, "You see, Mrs. Mandler has a large apartment and she rents her spare bedroom to me. I have been renting the room from her for some time."

The officer said, "Now suppose you tell me all that happened yesterday. Sit down, please."

Kraus seated himself and lit a cigarette. He said that when Mrs. Mandler had not returned to the office by 6:30 P.M. on Monday, he went to her apartment to obtain the cash-box keys. When he arrived at the apartment he found the foyer door was closed but not locked, which was unusual. He entered and knocked on Mrs. Mandler's bedroom door—opposite the foyer from his own bedroom. There was no answer.

He stood at the door, listening, but heard nothing. Then he went to his own room, changed clothing, and returned to the sitting room outside Mrs. Mandler's rooms to wait for her return. As he sat in an easy chair smoking a cigarette, he noticed two cigarette butts in the ashtray. He remembered the cigarette butts because Mrs. Mandler was a tidy housekeeper and never left the place without emptying ashtrays and having everything in spotless order.

"Did you enter Mrs. Mandler's rooms?"

"No," Kraus said, "I know where she hides the keys to her bedroom but I made no attempt to enter the room. I did not want her to return and find me in her bedroom."

At this point, the officer said to Kraus: "I believe you had better wait outside in the anteroom, while we check the hospitals. Then we may ask you to accompany our men to Mrs. Mandler's apartment. Perhaps we can find some reason there for her disappearance."

The police made the usual check of hospitals and first-aid centers inquiring about Mrs. Mandler. But when the inquiries brought no results, two officers were dispatched to the Mandler apartment with Kraus. The apartment was on the fourth floor of the apartment building.

The hour was almost midnight when Kraus opened the door and the officers stepped into a small foyer. To the left was a doorway leading to Kraus' room. To the right a doorway led into a sitting room. It was a comfortable room with a large carpet on the floor. Against one wall was an upholstered bench and a bookcase. There were three easy chairs and a large walnut table in the center of the room. The room was in perfect order. The officers noted two cigarette butts in the ashtray on the table. A copy of the newspaper *Neues Osterreich* was on the window sill. The paper was dated November 8, 1949.

Kraus found the hiding place where Mrs. Mandler left the key to her bedroom and he unlocked the door. Nothing appeared out of place in the bedroom. The bed had been made.

Suddenly Kraus said: "I believe I hear water running—there in the bathroom."

The officers had heard nothing but when they walked to the bathroom door, they could hear the flow of water. The bathroom door was locked. They ripped it open and then stood in shocked surprise in the doorway.

The water was running in the bathtub—splashing over the naked corpse of a woman. And the water in the tub was stained red with the blood of Blanche Mandler. Mrs. Mandler's throat had been slashed through to the neckbone. The front part of her right foot had been cut off and there was a deep cut at the joint of the right knee. A blanket had been wrapped around the faucet, apparently to deaden the noise of running water. The bathroom windows were open.

Mrs. Mandler's clothing was lying beside the door. Her coat, hat and dress had been tossed to the floor in a heap and then on top of them a jacket and underwear. The underwear had been ripped from her body. There were blood stains on the upper part of the coat. On a bathroom chair were bloody knife and scissors.

"Oh, my God! Oh, my God!" Kraus repeated over and over again.

One of the policemen called headquarters and asked them to send over a squad from the homicide division and a medical officer. When these trained investigators arrived, they began a methodical search of the apartment. The doctor examined the dead woman's body before it was removed for an autopsy.

In the hallway leading from the sitting room to the kitchen, the officers noted there was blood on the wall reaching to a height of about five feet. There was blood on the floor and, curiously, although the hall rug had no blood on its surface, they found blood stains beneath the carpet.

The kitchen had a scrubbed look of cleanliness. A blood-stained bucket stood in the wash basin. On the kitchen stove was a small pot containing a remnant of spinach. In a closet off the kitchen was a trunk whose contents had been strewn over the floor.

In Mrs. Mandler's bedroom, police found a safe. The key to the safe was on a ring attached to a key in the dresser drawer. They opened the safe and found that it contained more than 100,000 schillings and foreign currency of about the same value. Nothing in the safe seemed to have been disturbed even though the key had hung in plain sight in the lock of the dresser drawer. Robbery did not appear to have been the motive of the brutal murder.

The police theorized that Mrs. Mandler was killed as she had started to leave her apartment, inasmuch as she obviously had been wearing her coat and hat. Apparently she had been attacked first in the hallway and strangled there. The blood on the wall could have come from a severe nosebleed while the killer was throttling her. The killer had then carried the body to the bathroom, torn the clothing from her, and dumped her into the bathtub where she was stabbed and slashed by the knife and scissors.

Two of the most puzzling things to the police were the blood stains beneath the hall rug and the bit of spinach in the unwashed cooking pot. How did the blood get under the carpet when there was no blood on the carpet's surface? And if Mrs. Mandler was as methodical in her housekeeping as Kraus claimed, why had she left an unwashed pot on the stove when the rest of her apartment was in such meticulous order? Neighbors who were questioned said they never knew Mrs. Mandler to leave home in the morning without washing each dish and cooking utensil.

While doctors examined Mrs. Mandler's body, Kraus was taken to the police headquarters for further questioning. "Now tell us all that has happened from the time you last saw Mrs. Mandler," an officer said.

Kraus nervously lit a cigarette and told the police this story:

"Mrs. Mandler came to work as usual Monday morning, carrying her lunch. She seemed to be in good spirits."

An officer interrupted: "Did Mrs. Mandler always bring her lunch to the office?"

"Yes. She is a thrifty woman. She always eats lunch at her desk. I believe on Monday she ate a dish of spinach. After lunch, I guess it was about twelve forty-five, she said she had to return to her apartment. She was meeting someone to discuss a business deal."

"Whom was she meeting?"

Kraus said, "She did not say."

"Continue," the officer said.

"Well, I waited for her in the office until about six thirty. Then I went to her apartment to get the cash-box keys. I found the front door closed, but not locked. I knocked on her bedroom door but there was no answer."

"What did you do then?"

"I sat in an easy chair in the little sitting room that is between the foyer and her bedroom. I lit a cigarette and that's when I noticed there were two cigarette butts in the ashtray. I thought she had stepped out for a few minutes and would be back soon. I sat there for several minutes and then I decided I would spend the night with my parents. So I left."

The following day he was even more disturbed when Mrs. Mandler did not show up at the office. He discussed her strange absence with other employees and told them of his experience the previous night when he had gone to Mrs. Mandler's flat, waited in the living room, and found the two cigarette butts in the ashtray.

He told police that at 10 A.M. on Tuesday he received an anonymous telephone call. A man's voice said: "Your boss is going to the doctor, but she will be back in the afternoon."

"Did you recognize the voice of the anonymous caller?" an officer asked.

"No. It was not a voice that I recall having heard before." Kraus said that at 2 o'clock in the afternoon this same anonymous voice called and told him that Mrs. Mandler had been given an injection and was unable to move. When Kraus asked where Mrs. Mandler could be reached, the voice said "at the Sanatory Union, Lazarettgasse." Kraus said he noticed the caller had difficulty in pronouncing the letter "r" and did not sound like an Austrian.

"Did anyone else in the office hear your conversation?" Kraus was asked.

He shook his head. "No, the calls came in while I was alone but I told the other employees about them. I sent one of our men to the Lazarettgasse to look for the sanatorium but no such place could be found.

"I went to my room about 7:45. A few minutes later Mr. Jezek, who works at the factory, dropped by and we talked about Mrs. Mandler's strange disappearance. We agreed that I should report it to the police. We left the building together and chatted for a few minutes at the entrance. Then I went to the station to make my report."

"What time was it when you left the apartment building after talking to your friend?"

"It was 8:30. I looked at my watch."

The police officer glanced at a note pad in front of him. "Did you come directly to the police station from the apartment building?"

"Yes," Kraus said.

"You didn't stop along the way to talk to anyone?"

"No."

The note pad on the officer's desk showed that Kraus had come to the police station on Tuesday night and the time was listed as 9:10 P.M. If Kraus had not stopped along the way, then he should have arrived at the police station at 8:37—because it was only about a seven-minute walk between the two places.

"Thank you for your information," the officer said, "if we need any other information we'll be in touch with you."

The murder of Mrs. Blanche Mandler was a sensation in Vienna. Newspaper stories disclosed that she had lived in the same apartment at Trautsohngasse 6–7 for about twenty-seven years. She had two sons by a first marriage, one son living in Switzerland and another in France. After the death of her first husband, she had married Rudolph Mandler, the owner of a textile firm. Mandler, a Jew, was arrested by the Nazis in 1938, and he died in a concentration camp in Ysbyca. After his death, Mrs. Mandler took over the direction of the textile firm. She was an industrious woman, and the business flourished under her shrewd management.

Neighbors disclosed to police that Mrs. Mandler was a tight-fisted employer and equally as thrifty in the management of her household. For example, they said, she kept the hallway rug rolled up except when expecting important visitors. She would spread the rug on the floor just before their arrival and in this way she saved wear and tear on the carpet.

In the hours that followed police found these facts. Mrs. Mandler was last seen by a neighbor, en route to her flat at 1:30 P.M. on Monday, November 7. The concierge at the apartment building said he had placed the newspaper *Neues Osterreich* at her entrance door as usual at 8:30 A.M. on Tuesday morning, November 8. At 8 o'clock on Tuesday evening, one of Mrs. Mandler's employees had come to the apartment to meet Kraus and the two had left together at 8:30 as Kraus had reported.

A woman who lived across an alleyway from the Mandler flat said that about 8 o'clock on Tuesday evening, she was in her kitchen when she heard a woman scream two or three times. Police tested this woman's report by shouting in the Mandler apartment. They found that nothing could be heard in the neighboring flat if the windows of the Mandler flat were closed, but when they were opened the calls could be heard distinctly across the way. However, no one had heard the screams who lived on the floor below the Mandler flat. A servant in the flat below said she recalled hearing footsteps between 7:30 and 9:30 on the evening of November 7. She looked from her kitchen window and noticed the glow of a light shining from the bedroom of the Mandler flat. Then she saw the light disappear and she assumed that Mrs. Mandler had switched on her shaded bed light.

Kraus had said after Mrs. Mandler had left the office on November 7, he had remained there until 6:30 P.M., when he had gone to her flat for the cash-box keys. But police were unable to find any employees who could swear that Kraus had been in the office after 4:30 P.M.

They also discovered another interesting fact—that Kraus had had a violent quarrel with Mrs. Mandler. She had promoted him to the position of manager but Kraus complained bitterly that she had failed to give him the authority to carry out his responsibilities. Apparently there had been a crisis in the office for a time. At last Mrs. Mandler had agreed to give Kraus the authority that he demanded. The announcement was to have been made on November 5, but Mrs. Mandler said nothing to the staff, and hedged on her promise.

The autopsy indicated death was caused by strangulation. An examination of the stomach showed that about three hours before her death, Mrs. Mandler had eaten greens, apparently the spinach which had been in the pot found on the stove.

The police reviewed Kraus' movements on the evening of November 8. But they could not account for the time from 8:30 P.M., when he said he left the apartment, until he made his report of Mrs. Mandler's disappearance at 9:10 P.M. This was a vital forty-minute period because the provisional medical examination indicated the body had not been in the bathtub more than three hours before the arrival of the police near midnight. This meant it had been placed there between 8 and 9 P.M.— and Kraus admitted that he had been in the apartment part of this time.

On the basis of the known facts, the police theorized that Mrs. Mandler returned to her apartment and for some unknown reason was delayed in getting back to her place of business. She ate an early supper of spinach from the pot which was found on the stove. About three hours after eating, she put on her hat and coat, preparing to leave the apartment. Kraus arrived. He and Mrs. Mandler resumed their argument over her promise to give him the authority he had asked. There was a violent quarrel that exploded into greater violence. Kraus grabbed the woman by the throat and strangled her to death.

After the murder was done, he met his fellow employee and calmly discussed her disappearance. He pretended he was going directly to the police station, but instead he returned to her apartment to place the body in the bathtub. Then he hurried to the police station to make his report.

Police recalled that it was Kraus who found Mrs. Mandler's keys hidden outside the bedroom door and he who unlocked the bedroom. The police had heard nothing but it was Kraus who heard the water running in the bathroom and led them to the bathroom door. It was even possible that Mrs. Mandler had been killed on November 7 and that the killer had returned on

November 8 to carry her body from the hallway to the bathtub. Kraus could easily have fabricated the tale of the anonymous telephone calls because none of the other employees had heard them.

Acting on this theory, and with approval of the prosecutor's office, police arrested Kraus for the murder of Blanche Mandler. An anonymous letter writer congratulated the police on finding the right man, saying that Kraus' private life, if police investigated, would disclose that he was capable of such a brutal murder.

The police tried to keep Kraus' arrest from the newspapers until their investigation was completed. But the story leaked to the press as such stories always do—and his name was splashed across the pages of Austrian papers, which reprinted details of the bloody crime.

As he studied the police reports, Dr. Franz Heger, Oberpolizeirat (Chief Police Counsellor) in charge of the criminal division dealing with blood crimes, began to entertain a small doubt. The one thing that bothered Dr. Heger most was the pot on the stove which contained a remnant of spinach. The police assumption all along had been that Mrs. Mandler ate a meal of spinach late in the afternoon of Tuesday, November 8, and that she died about three hours after this meal.

Dr. Heger studied a statement made by one of Mrs. Mandler's employees. This witness said he visited Mrs. Mandler on Saturday, November 5. He came to the flat that evening to pick up his tax card and Mrs. Mandler invited him into the kitchen where she was cooking spinach. He recalled her saying that she was expecting a friend from Switzerland in the next few days— but she mentioned no name. Finally Mrs. Mandler invited her guest to supper and she served spinach.

Dr. Heger recalled Kraus' statement that Mrs. Mandler had eaten spinach for lunch in the office on November 7. Supposing, he reasoned, that Kraus was telling the truth. Supposing Mrs. Mandler had left her office and gone home to meet someone in her apartment—a "someone" who killed her that same afternoon. Then it would follow that Mrs. Mandler already was dead when Kraus went to the apartment later that day for the cashbox keys.

Continuing on this line, Dr. Heger noted that Mrs. Mandler was a thrifty woman who had no maid. She took care of her own apartment and cooked her own meals. He speculated that a woman of her habits, living alone, would cook enough food on Saturday to last her over the week end. Very likely she bought about one kilo (a little more than two pounds) of the greens, from which she could have obtained no more than five servings. On Saturday, November 5, she had served her visitor one dish of spinach and had eaten one dish herself. If she had eaten spinach for lunch on Sunday and another dish for supper that evening, then on Monday she had one serving of spinach left in the pot. And Kraus swore that Mrs. Mandler had eaten spinach for lunch on Monday, November 7.

If the noon meal on Monday was her last meal, then Mrs. Mandler had been killed probably about 3:30 P.M. on November 7 and not the following evening. If she died during the afternoon of November 7, Kraus was innocent because he could account for his whereabouts until the hour of 4:30 P.M.

Who was the mystery visitor Mrs. Mandler had been expecting? There were statements from more than one person that Mrs. Mandler had said she was expecting an unnamed visitor at her flat. Police had found among her papers a telegram dated November 7, 1949—the day of her disappearance—which had been sent from the Vienna Post Office #101 at 8:15 A.M. The telegram said "Prevented from coming. Will come to see you on Friday evening. Signed, Dr. Bossard."

While the circumstantial evidence still pointed to Kraus as the probable killer, Dr. Heger pushed forward with the investigation and a search began for the Dr. Bossard who sent the telegram to Mrs. Mandler. In questioning Mrs. Mandler's employees, one of them said that his father-in-law, Mr. Rudolf Lutz, had recently been in Switzerland where he had met a Dr. Bossard, who was a friend of Mrs. Mandler. The doctor had sent greetings to Mrs. Mandler from her son living in Switzerland. The employee recalled Mrs. Mandler saying that Dr. Bossard was supposed to come to Austria on business and also to visit the fair in Graz.

Police inquiries disclosed that a Dr. Bossard had entered Austria from Switzerland, driving a Packard automobile with a

Zurich license plate. He had driven to Graz and registered at the Hotel Union. The hotel records indicated he had checked out of the hotel on the morning of November 7, giving Zurich as his destination.

At this point Dr. Heger uncovered a staggering fact. One of the most damning points against Kraus had been his story of leaving the apartment building at 8:30 P.M. and going directly to the police station to report Mrs. Mandler's disappearance. It was a seven-minute walk to the station—and yet his appearance there was timed at 9:10 P.M. The police had found no one to account for the thirty-three minutes missing in the chain of Kraus' movements that night.

But Dr. Heger discovered that Kraus actually had gone from the apartment building straight to the police station. He had spent those thirty-three missing minutes sitting in the waiting room, nervously twisting his hands while waiting his turn to make a report. Witnesses were found who remembered him sitting there, smoking cigarette after cigarette.

It was appallingly evident to Dr. Heger that false assumptions had led police astray from the beginning of the investigation. The preliminary medical report, which indicated the body had been in the bathtub only about three hours before police arrived on the scene, had been the false clue. Accepting that report as accurate, police had come to the conclusion that Kraus was the killer—and the conclusion had seemed entirely logical.

But now Kraus could account for the time that it had taken him to go from the apartment to the police station to make his report of the disappearance. And the police knew his whereabouts until 4:30 of the previous afternoon. He could not possibly be the killer.

Police centered their attention on the movements of Dr. Bossard. Had he actually gone to Switzerland when he left the hotel at Graz, or had he instead come to Vienna to meet Mrs. Mandler in her apartment as the telegram indicated that he planned to do? The telegram had been sent from a Vienna post office.

This line of inquiry was barely under way when the Ministry of Foreign Affairs reported that Dr. Bossard had been issued a visa on November 5. He had come to Graz on that date. But the report also said that Dr. Bossard had crossed the Austrian border into Switzerland on November 7. He could not have been in Vienna on either November 7 or 8. And so Dr. Bossard was ruled out as a suspect.

The investigation was at a dead end when the police made a routine check on Rudolf Lutz, who one witness said had talked with Dr. Bossard and had brought greetings to Mrs. Mandler from her son in Switzerland. Checking through their criminal files, police found that a Rudolf Lutz was at that moment in jail on suspicion of burglary in connection with the theft of typewriters stolen from various offices and sold for approximately 135,000 schillings. Lutz had confessed to the burglary. Lutz's file showed that he came from a well-to-do Austrian family. For many years his parents had operated a stove factory in Vorarlberg and Lutz had worked in the factory. But in 1923 he had been arrested and convicted of fraud. In 1930 he was convicted of burglarizing a post office delivery wagon of 38,000 schillings. And he was convicted of fraud in later years.

Police questioned Lutz. He denied knowing anything of Mrs. Mandler's murder. He said that on November 7 he left Vienna and went to Tyrol where he spent the nights of November 7 and 8. But in checking Vienna hotel registers police found that Lutz actually had spent those nights in a Vienna hotel.

The telegram allegedly signed by Dr. Bossard—found in Mrs. Mandler's flat—was taken to the Vienna Post Office #101 where it was checked against the original copy. Handwriting experts returned the report that the handwriting of the original message was identical with the handwriting of Lutz.

Police went to the little town of Tyrol and searched Lutz's living quarters. They found a bank book showing a credit for 35,000 schillings deposited in a Tyrol bank. Their inquiries disclosed that Lutz had gone on a spending spree in Tyrol after November 7.

Lutz maintained at first that the money in his bank account and the money he had spent in Tyrol after November 7 had come from black-market operations—but he refused to say with whom he had made the deals.

The police confronted Lutz with the evidence that he had spent the nights of November 7 and 8 in Vienna and not in Tyrol as he claimed. They laid before him the telegram in his own handwriting. Bit by bit, they broke down his claims as to his whereabouts during those two days.

Finally Lutz confessed. He admitted he had known Mrs. Mandler for several years, and they had made some deals together in foreign currencies. He had cautioned her never to mention his name to any of her friends. A month before the murder, he convinced her the two of them could turn a tidy profit in another foreign currency deal.

"I visited her several times in her flat to discuss the deal. She was to invest fifty-six thousand schillings," he said.

An officer asked, "What about the telegram signed with Dr. Bossard's name?"

Lutz shrugged. He admitted the telegram was part of his murder plan, to throw suspicion on Dr. Bossard and confuse the police.

"I went to her apartment about 2 P.M. on Monday. She had left the door unlocked. I sat in the living room and smoked a couple of cigarettes while I waited for her. She came in and we talked over the deal.

"Finally she went into the kitchen. When she came out she had on her coat and hat and was carrying a brief case. I knew she had the money in the case. I grabbed her by the throat."

When he saw she was dead, Lutz said, he carried her body to the bathroom and slashed it to leave the appearance that the murder was a crime of passion. He wrapped a towel around the faucet and turned on the water. Then he washed his bloody hands in a bucket in the kitchen sink. As he left, he noticed the hallway carpet was rolled up. He carefully rolled it into place, covering the blood on the floor.

Lutz was sentenced on December 5, 1950, by a Vienna court to life imprisonment. And the judge decreed that on each November 7, for the remainder of his life, he must spend the day in solitary confinement in a darkened prison cell to ponder his sin against society.

HUNGARY

THE TIME: *1945–1960*

THE PLACE: *Hungary*

THE CRIME: *Patriotism*

There can be no true account of crime and police operations around the world without a reference to "political crimes," the police system of Soviet Russia and her satellites, and those who are the victims of this system.

Within the Communist bloc, the major crimes are "crimes committed against the State." The criminals in this weird system of justice are those who are opposed to communism or whose acts are judged to be detrimental to the welfare of the State. In short, the political criminal can be anyone who does not agree with the existing Red regime and is not sympathetic to its policies.

The police of the satellite states are organized along the same lines as the police in Soviet Russia. Every change in the organization of the Soviet police is promptly aped throughout the satellites. In addition to the ordinary police force which handles the usual police duties, each country has its net of secret police who are aided by informers planted in every factory, office, shop, farm group, and association.

In West Berlin and in Austria, refugees from communism will tell you of this police terror. There is a gray, terrible sameness to their stories—the pounding on the door in the dead of night . . . the arrests without explanation . . . the days, weeks, and months in a cell without a hearing . . . the endless questioning and beatings . . . and then a farcical trial.

The refugees also tell bitter little jokes about the Red police. An example: Mrs. Tildy was terrified when awakened by a pounding on her door. Only the police pounded on doors at midnight. And so, shaking with fright, she crept downstairs, wondering what crime she had committed. She opened the door and a policeman stepped in. "Don't be afraid," he said. "There's nothing to worry about. It's only your house on fire."

10. *"The Police Are the Criminals . . ."*

Arpad Taby is a rough-hewn, sixty-four-year-old rock of a man whose craggy brows overhang eyes as blue as bright Hungarian skies. His shoulders are broad and slightly stooped and thick with the muscles of an outdoor man accustomed to hard toil. His face is leathery and seamed from years in the sun and rain and winter winds . . . and from suffering of a kind known to few men in the free Western world. But it is the eyes you remember about Arpad Taby . . . eyes that are clear and steady and unafraid despite thirteen years of mental and physical torture at the hands of Communist police.

In the files of the AVH, the secret police of Hungary, he is listed as a criminal and a fugitive from justice—a dangerous man to be loose. But you shall judge how dangerous he is, how just was the "justice" from which he fled, and who, in fact, should be classed as the criminal in this case.

When the Soviet Army rolled through Hungary in World War II, the Communist political cadres marched behind them, to seize political control in each village and city and to prepare the country for a Communist-run government. The authority of the politicians was backed by the guns of the Red Army and the secret police of the AVH, which is the Hungarian counterpart of Russia's dread MVD. Their first job was to seek out the "enemies of the State"—meaning those who were anti-Communist or who had had any connection with the former anti-Communist government.

Among the hundreds swept into the police net was Arpad Taby, an enemy of communism for almost forty years. In 1919, when Hungary had its first Communist government, young Lieutenant Taby, a highly decorated war hero, was a fiery rebel who damned the Marxist doctrine and passionately opposed Communist control of his homeland. An Austrian military science publication says of Lieutenant Taby: "After World War I, during the period of Soviet government in Hungary, he organized an anti-Communist movement in the area of Eger, the former garrison of his regiment. He had to flee, however, when the undertaking failed to succeed . . ."

Later, Taby joined the Hungarian gendarmerie and rose to the rank of major. In 1939, he was elected to the Parliament on a platform of land reform to aid the peasants. But when the Red Army approached the borders of Hungary, Major Taby reported again for military duty to fight the invader.

This record placed Taby high on the Reds' list of those marked for arrest. He was "held for investigation" in the prison on Andrassi Street in Budapest while police began looking for witnesses to testify against him. Then he was taken to the prison in Gyongyos, the main town of the district which he had represented in Parliament. The Gyongyos newspaper carried an announcement: "All those who have any complaints against Arpad Taby, former member of Parliament, please report them to the police."

The police waited for Taby's enemies to appear and give evidence against him. But no one came. The time for Taby's trial was nearing, so police agents went into the countryside seeking witnesses. At the last minute, one enterprising secret policeman reported he had obtained a statement against Taby, signed by a farmer living near Gyongyos, which would be used at his trial. The Communists were determined to expose Taby as an enemy of the people, and to use his trial as a showcase of Communist justice, displaying for all to see how the new government would protect the people against their enemies.

Taby was led from his cell to the largest meeting hall in town where six judges waited to hear his case. The judges formed the "people's court" and each represented, at least in name, one of the country's political parties, with the Communists in firm control.

As he looked around the crowded room, Taby saw many familiar faces. He knew most of the spectators by their first names. He had sat in their homes and listened to them talk of their hopes and fears. He had always believed he was close to these people. But now they looked at him without recognition, their faces like masks carved from wood. And Taby's heart was heavy.

At last the prosecution brought forward the farmer whose statement was a key point in the state's case. He was a stringy-tough old man who kept his head cocked to one side like a giant bird. He was a bit hard of hearing.

The presiding judge quickly disposed of the preliminaries and then turned to the witness. "Now, tell the court what you have to say against this former member of Parliament."

"How's that?" the old man said, leaning forward.

"Tell the court," the judge repeated, "what it is you accuse this man of."

The old man shook his head. "I don't accuse him."

There was a stunned silence. The witness said, "Taby's a very good man and always helped us. We liked him very much."

"What are you talking about?" the judge demanded angrily. "The written statement I have from you tells quite a different story."

The farmer said, "I gave a written statement?"

Someone in the courtroom smothered a laugh. And then laughter swept the room. The judge pounded for order and threatened to expel everyone from the room unless they were silent. Taby could have wept from joy because he knew now these people were on his side.

The judge said, "I'll read the statement myself which you signed." He read a charge that Taby had persecuted the people and worked against them in Parliament. It was a bitter denunciation.

The old man sat listening with his hand cupped to his ear, and when the statement was finished, he looked over the courtroom and said, "Why, I can't even write. Show me the man who said I signed that statement and I'll spit in his eye. If it's signed, it was signed by that policeman who talked to me. I didn't sign it."

The audience by this time was convulsed with laughter and the old man, still mumbling with anger, was led from the room. The Communist court learned in that embarrassing moment that no witness should be asked to testify until the presiding judge was certain he would say what the police claimed he would say.

When Taby was led from the courtroom to be taken to his cell, men and women lined the market place to shake his hand.

Taby said to the police lieutenant guarding him, "I wish I had been this popular during the elections."

Next day, the police tried to lead Taby around the market place to avoid the crowds. But people saw them coming through the narrow streets and soon the passage was blocked. A woman cried, "Let the man free. He was the only one who spoke up for us!" The crowd became menacing in its demands and Taby pulled the police lieutenant to his side. "The trial will have to go on," he told the crowd. "You have made me very happy— but don't try to prevent the court action. It would only make things more difficult for me and for you."

On the fifth day, the trial was abruptly ended when the Communist judge withdrew from the case without explanation. But before the court adjourned, Taby asked to make a statement. "The people have acquitted me," he said, "therefore, I cannot understand why the court cannot pronounce a clear-cut acquittal. This is a 'people's court,' isn't it?"

But no one bothered to answer. He was taken from Gyongyos to the prison in Eger where he remained until November when he was taken back to Gyongyos for retrial. This time there was no public announcement. The judges met in a small room and the only spectators were those who could produce tickets issued by the police. The trial lasted fifteen minutes and Taby was sentenced to eight years at forced labor.

Taby appealed his conviction to the court of appeals, the so-called NOT, which convened in the House of Parliament in Budapest. Taby and his prison mates learned that the appeal would be heard by a Communist judge named Bojtha. "You are doomed, Taby," a friend said. "That man will let you hang. He has sentenced everyone to death so far who had any prominence in the old government."

But Bojtha was no fool. He wanted Taby on the side of communism. If he could be persuaded to join the Party, it would help influence many of the small landholders. And so he announced that Taby's sentence would be reduced to six months.

"You are guilty because you did not stand on our side," Bojtha said. "Do you plead guilty?"

"No," Taby said. "It would not be just if I am punished."

"You had better talk to your lawyer," Bojtha said dryly.

Taby's attorney took him into a conference room. "Listen, Taby," he said. "Six months from that judge amounts to something like an honorary degree. For God's sake, take the plea. He can hang you if he likes. Don't challenge him."

When Taby returned to the courtroom, Bojtha said, "Have you talked to your lawyer?"

"Yes," Taby said.

"Do you agree to plead guilty?"

"Yes."

Bojtha smiled. "I am sending a letter to Eger to set you free."

Taby was released from prison, but the freedom he found was constant surveillance by police, constant pressure to join the "Peasant Party" and to bring others into the Red orbit. Taby's doorbell rang two, three and sometimes four times each night. He answered the bell always to find an AVH man waiting to make a search of the house or to repeat the question—"Have you changed your mind about joining the Party?"

Each day someone followed him. He could not leave the village without a special permit. All he had left from his small estate were two horses and a wagon. He tried to make a living with these—but few people dared do business with someone always followed by the police. Even old friends began to avoid him. Taby understood, because he knew the danger that anyone risked who associated with him.

He managed to support himself for a time by hauling coal. One day he asked a friend to use the horses and wagon to fetch coal from the mine. But the mine owner said, "I'm sorry, but the wagon and horses of Taby will get no more coal from me."

For seven years, the Communists permitted Taby to exist in this nightmare world, giving the village a lesson in what happens to those who oppose the will of the Party. And then in October, 1954, he was arrested again. By this time, Taby was ill and weak from malnutrition. His big body had shrunk and his clothes hung on his gaunt frame, but his eyes had not lost their hard brilliance and he had not joined the Party.

This time he was not permitted to have a lawyer. The trial was quick. Taby said later, "I don't even remember the charges, but

it would have made no difference. All I can remember was that
I was sentenced to hard labor for fifteen years. But you must
understand that the fifteen-year sentence made me feel good.
At last I knew that it was not to be death."

They sent Taby to the big fortified prison at Vac, located on
a bend of the Danube near Budapest. This was the prison
where the Communists kept murderers, former army officers,
priests, Jehovah's Witnesses, degenerate criminals and those
considered dangerous politically.

Taby was hardly a threat to anyone, politically or otherwise.
He was too ill, and too weak from the years of struggle merely to
stay alive. He was placed in a hospital ward with others who
had little hope that they would ever be free again. They feared
the doctor who visited them because they never knew when he
gave them an injection whether it was for their good—or
whether he was conducting one of his private experiments, using them as guinea pigs.

Some of Taby's companions had been sentenced to death.
But the Communists let them live month after month with no
hint of when the day of execution would come. Each day these
doomed men awakened with the knowledge that it might be the
last. No one was surprised when some men's minds broke and
they had to be carried away.

One day in late November, 1956, Taby and the other prisoners sensed a tightening of security around the prison. Work
stopped in the button factory. No one was permitted to talk in
the prison yard. From a window in the hospital wing, Taby and
the other patients looked down the Danube to a bend in the
river and saw men cutting the big Soviet star from the top of a
monument. The monument had been a reminder to Hungarian
boatmen for years that the Red star of Soviet Russia hung over
Hungary.

"Now they're going to put up a bigger star, as if that one
wasn't big enough," one prisoner said.

That night Taby awoke and listened to the stillness around
him, the stillness filled with the small, familiar noises of the
prison. And then he heard faraway voices singing an old and
beloved song. The melody was faint but unmistakable. It was

the Hungarian national anthem . . . the forbidden anthem.

He sat up in bed. The melody was still out there in the darkness.

"Wake up! Wake up!" Taby shook the bed next to his.

"What is it?"

"Listen . . . it's the national anthem."

The other said, "Go back to sleep, old man. You are dreaming."

Taby said, "I'm not dreaming. I've got good ears and I know it is the anthem."

The others in the hospital were wakening. They listened, too, and then they heard the singing and wondered who dared to raise their voices outside the prison walls. All through the night they sat and talked. Taby told them, "I have a feeling we will not be prisoners long. Something is happening out there."

When daybreak came, they saw the guards on the watch tower, peering down the Danube through binoculars. Then came a rifle shot. One of the guards turned toward the prisoners crowding the windows. He saluted them, threw away his red-starred cap and hurried down the tower ladder. Then came the clear, sharp sound of a machine gun.

Throughout the prison, three thousand prisoners set up a chant: "We want freedom . . . We want freedom . . ." A convict broke through the barred hospital door with an iron bar and shouted, "You are all free!"

The prison of Vac became a battleground. Prisoners somehow obtained rifles and pistols, many of them from the guards themselves. One AVH guard came to the hospital ward and said, "Gentlemen, you know I have never done anything to you . . . I want to join you." And they welcomed their first recruit.

All day the prisoners battled the AVH guards who had climbed to the hospital roof and refused to surrender. Taby shouted to the AVH men, "Give up and we will not kill you. We are not hangmen." When they refused, Taby shrugged and said, "Those who die now fall in battle—and not from our vengeance." The fight went on until the last AVH resistance was crushed.

The doors of the prison were battered open. The prisoners

streamed out to be welcomed by the villagers. Taby was given medical care by friendly physicians. When his strength returned, he took over direction of guerrilla fighting against the Russians, using his old skills as a soldier to harass the enemy's supply lines and to direct sudden raids against reinforcements moving on Budapest.

But the odds were too great. Russian tanks and infantry smashed the Freedom Fighters on orders from Moscow. The bright flame of freedom that blazed through Hungary and stirred the world slowly dimmed. The AVH returned to avenge the deaths of the secret police killed by the people in their fury. And the world watched in horror as the Red Army strangled Hungary again.

Taby was preparing to join the guerrillas in the woods and hold out as long as possible. But he knew he was too old to survive such a life. Youth and endurance were needed for the rugged existence of a guerrilla fighter. And then his friends sent word from Budapest that the Communists were seeking him and he was certain to be condemned to death for his part in the revolution. They sent him money and urged him to flee to Austria.

And so Arpad Taby slipped across the border into Austria, a fugitive from Communist "justice."

This was the story Arpad Taby told me as we talked in Vienna. Today the old soldier gathers used clothing to send back to his people in Hungary. He lives in a barracks with other refugees and receives a few schillings a month from refugee relief agencies.

"It is the young people of my country I think about," He said. "They need counsel. We are old, but only we can teach them the traditions and the greatness of Hungary. Without us, they will forget . . . and we must not let them forget."

Vienna is a refuge for thousands like Taby. Not far from the Opera House live Mrs. Anna Molnar and her husband. They, too, are "fugitives from justice." Their home is a big, drafty room on the third floor of an old building full of dust and shadows and echoes of the past.

Mrs. Molnar is a small, middle-aged, dark-haired woman with a sweet, gentle face. Her husband towers over her, a gray-haired distinguished man who once was one of Hungary's well-known engineers. There is, in their voices and in the glances they give each other, a communion so electric that they might be young lovers.

In one corner of the big room is a bed, made from packing cases, and when the Molnars lie down together at night, they can shut out the meanness of the room by drawing together drapes made from old sheets. In another corner is a crude table where Mr. Molnar still works on his drawings while his wife paints at a nearby easel. Their coffee table, made of packing cases also, is covered by a fine white linen. And when Mrs. Molnar pours coffee into the chipped cups there is an illusion that she is still presiding at a table set with flawless crystal, fragile china and gleaming silver.

After the coffee, Mrs. Molnar begins to talk in a voice so soft and controlled that the listener does not sense at first the strength and passion hidden beneath the surface. It was a trick she learned in prison as a protective shield, the only shield she had against the fists of the AVH guards. . . .

We lived in Budapest (Mrs. Molnar began). Several years ago some friends who were in trouble with the Communists came to us and asked our help. We could not refuse them although we knew it was dangerous if the secret police learned about it.

I was very foolish to tell anyone what we had done. But one day I confided in a friend, a woman doctor we saw quite often and who led us to believe she felt about the Communists as we did. I told her my only fear was that if I were arrested, the AVH would torture me into betraying others.

She said, "I can give you some poison. Put it in some plastic material and hide it between your toes. That is the only place which the AVH doesn't check."

I began to wonder then how she knew so much about the ways of the AVH. But I didn't learn until later that she was working for the AVH, and getting a reward each time she gave them information.

A few days after this conversation, the police rang our door-

bell. It was about ten thirty P.M. My husband went to the door
and four men shoved him aside and walked in. The oldest of
the men said, "We are from the secret police."

"Where is your identification?" my husband asked.

They stood and laughed as though my husband had made
a big joke. One of them waved a card under his nose and said,
"This is our identification. Both of you are under arrest."

I was wearing high-heeled shoes but they refused to let me
change to walking shoes or take anything with me except my
hat and coat. They pulled me out the door and I looked back
before the door closed to see my husband putting on his coat.
In that moment he looked so defeated, so helpless. We had not
even kissed each other good-bye. And I thought: "Oh, my darling. What have I done to you? I have killed you . . ."

For five months I didn't know whether he was dead or alive.
They took me to a room in the prison where a man sat at a
bare table. A light shone in my eyes. He was writing something
—but I could never see what he was writing. I was terrified, of
course. Always I had been afraid of being beaten—of physical
violence. I wondered whether I could stand the pain.

They didn't let me sit down. At times I heard a door opening
behind me but I was afraid to look around. I answered the questions as best I could. But if the man at the desk didn't like my
answer, he would lift his pencil and the man behind me would
hit me with a whip or with his fist. I tried not to break into
panic. I forced myself to answer the questions in the same quiet
voice no matter what happened. I knew somehow that if I
showed anger or panic, they would hit me again.

I learned quickly that if I hoped to survive, I had to control
the awful panic that was at the edge of reason. I had to keep
thinking and observing what was happening. I had to remember
the answers I gave to the questions or I was lost.

The whole purpose of the AVH questioning is to keep the
prisoner in a state of constant emotional strain, a sort of dy-
namic excitement that no one can endure forever. I remember
once I was badly beaten by three AVH men. All of them jumped
on me at once and hit me when I didn't give the right answer.
But later I realized they really had been staging a scene. Any
one of them could have killed me with one blow if he had

wished. But that wasn't their purpose. They wanted to break my spirit. Even when I knew their purpose, I couldn't keep from screaming before they hit me.

But when they did hit me, something happened inside me. Call it anger, stubbornness, spirit or what you will. I felt a hardening against them. Gradually I knew that the more they beat me, the harder this inner resistance would grow. And it made me feel somehow happy and more secure.

The worst experience I had actually made me stronger. Once I was put into solitary, a filthy hole crawling with bugs. Finally a guard came and told me to stand facing the wall. He blindfolded me and forced me to stand there. I thought he was getting ready to shoot me and I shook with fear. It was an agonizing experience. But then he took off the blindfold and laughed. He was just having his little joke . . . but after that, when they tortured me, I always thought: This can't be any worse than that moment when I was blindfolded—and I didn't die then. I can stand this, too.

They questioned me for eight hours every day except Sunday, asking me again and again to recall everything I had done from the time I was a child. There was one period of a month when they questioned me for only two or three hours a day. Perhaps the regular interrogators were on vacation or had more urgent work to do. The men who substituted were less intelligent than the others and I realized their main job was to keep us in a state of fear until the other AVH men were available.

During the first five months, I was questioned by nine different men. Two of them were not only brutal, they were intelligent and well educated. I began to have a certain admiration for them. No matter how horrible the system was, it was efficient. And with one part of your mind, you had to admire their efficiency even though you hated it.

It was strange, too, that in this conflict the captors and captives almost unconsciously protected each other at times. Sometimes my interrogators would become so exhausted they would fall asleep. It was wonderful for me when this happened because I could relax and get a few minutes of blessed relief from the pressure. But when I heard footsteps outside I would cough and waken the sleeping man who was my enemy. My impulse to

warn him was instinctive. But when I analyzed it, I saw there
was a selfish motive. Because if an inspector caught the AVH
man asleep, he would be punished—and in turn, he would take
it out on me. So we became dependent on each other even
though we were enemies, and there was a bond between us.

Often the questioning developed into a kind of psychological
showdown which was as bad as the beatings. One man—the
worst of the lot—looked like a Gypsy and maybe he was. He
would put a watch on the table before him and then repeat
eight questions over and over until you wanted to scream, trying to remember the exact answers you had given before. He
would repeat his questions and I would repeat my answers in a
mechanical way—like a broken phonograph record repeating
the same phrase again and again until I felt I couldn't bear it.
But I did. I had to.

Through it all, I feared these men. But I didn't hate them. I
began to feel they were prisoners as much as I . . . prisoners of
a system from which they could not escape. At times I felt a
great pity for them because they were the ones who were weak.

And then the time came for the trial. The AVH took several
of us women from our cells to the courthouse and we stood outside the courtroom waiting to be called. A group of men was led
into the waiting room with us and I saw my husband among
them. He was standing six feet from me. We stood and looked
at each other. I can't tell you what was in my heart. I could have
cried with joy. I wanted to rush into his arms. But a guard
gripped my arm and said, "Don't you dare speak to that man!"

My husband was led with the others toward the courtroom.
As he passed me I could not help myself. I whispered, "Darling
. . . do you still love me?" He did not speak, but he blinked his
eyes and I knew he was saying . . . yes. That was what I
wanted to hear.

After the trial—I was sentenced to five years—I was taken to
the Szombathely prison and put to work sewing underwear for
the military. I wasn't skilled in sewing and so I never was able
to achieve more than thirty-five percent of the quota. But after
a time they moved me to the Kalocsa prison south of Budapest.
There were twelve women in my cell, a filthy hole with no
toilet, a single slop jar, a table, a bench, one water bucket and

three wash basins. Most of the women were common criminals and they hated the political prisoners. When I entered the cell, one of them said, "Well, look who's here. Another one of the 'ladies.'" And she spat on the floor.

The women in my cell insisted on keeping the windows closed at night. The stench was terrible because none of them bothered to wash. They were afraid they would get "typhus of the head." It was a disease that existed only in their minds but it was real to them.

The cell was cold and the water was icy, but it wasn't long before I had all of them washing themselves from head to toe every day and keeping the place clean. I was the weakest of the lot physically—but I had a powerful weapon: I told them stories each night.

I told them fairy tales or the plot of a book I had read. I told them the story of George Orwell's *Animal Farm*, *The Magic Flute* by Mozart, *The Idiot* by Dostoevski and dozens of others. I went through the plays of Shakespeare and every opera I knew and what I couldn't remember, I made up. It didn't matter. At that hour the room became quiet and those women would lie in their beds and listen to every word. It was a magical hour for them, perhaps the only release from reality they had ever known. All of them, somehow, became different beings. Perhaps they got a glimpse of beauty they had never known. I don't know. But I did know this hour was my weapon. I could make them agree to anything I really wanted. I would say: "Tonight there will be no story. Unless all of us are clean—we may get the plague. And unless all of you co-operate, I will tell no story." I didn't have to say more. After that the newcomer who had washed only her hands and face that day was certain to be scrubbed the next day.

Then the prison officials learned that I had done some amateur painting. They put me to work painting dolls' eyes. My production record jumped to two hundred percent of the quota. I could paint two thousand dolls' eyes a day, imagine it, and none of the others could come close. Even now, sometimes, I wake up in the middle of the night and realize I've been painting dolls' eyes in my sleep.

Because of my production record, I won a year's reprieve from my sentence and my husband was released about the same time. It took us quite a while to recover, physically and mentally, from our experience. We had to be on guard every waking hour because we knew the AVH never forget former prisoners.

And then came the revolt. Our arrest was inevitable so we decided to escape. At the border we almost ran into Russian troops. We hid and saw them arrest one refugee. At last we decided to make a try. We were caught but, thank God, they were Hungarian guardsmen. We told them frankly we were trying to escape into Austria. They looked at us for a moment and then the leader said, "We are just as good Hungarians as you. Now hurry . . . and don't stop."

Mrs. Molnar sat silent for a time and then she said, "Too many people don't understand the difference between the police systems of these two worlds. In most of the Western world, the purpose of the police is to protect the people from criminals. But over there, the police are the State . . . and *they* are the criminals."

She poured the last of the coffee from the pot into our cups. But now the coffee was cold and bitter and it was time to leave these people to their memories.

Outside the old building the dark streets were wet with rain, and the cobblestones glistened briefly under the headlights of an occasional automobile. You wondered how many Molnars and Tabys were sitting behind the shuttered windows, waiting in shabby surroundings for someone to seek their talents and make them feel useful again . . . make them feel that their fight was worth all the agony of spirit and pain of body they had endured.

And suddenly you remembered a day in Italy during World War II, a bitterly cold, bleak day when the mountain hid its peak in the low, gray clouds and the sounds of the cannon were muffled. Down the mountain trail came the casualties, limping slowly through the mud or lying silent on the stretchers to which they were strapped. Some had their limbs in splints. Some had their arms in slings, and some had their faces swathed in bloody bandages. Some of them, lashed to the backs of mules, would never fight again. They had met the enemy face to face and they were the casualties. But who would dare say their fight had been useless even though it won only a few yards of barren earth? None but a cynic or a fool.

In your heart, you gave a salute to those men on the mountainside in Italy. And so it was in Vienna you saluted the casualties of the cold war.

ITALY

THE TIME: *1958*

THE PLACE: *Milan*

THE CRIME: *Robbery*

The American influence in crime is felt more strongly in Italy than in any other country on the Continent because of the close ties that have existed for many years between the American and Italian underworlds.

Italian hoodlums see evidence every day that crime in America does pay. They see big-time criminals Lucky Luciano and Joe Adonis, among others deported from the United States, living in luxury in Rome and Naples on the profits from a lifetime of crime. If these men can make crime pay in America, they reason, why can't the same thing be done in Italy?

American-style gangster methods have been tried in Italy, particularly in the great industrial city of Milan, which is the center of the country's criminal activity, rather than Rome or Naples. The most carefully and skillfully planned robbery ever executed in Italy was the Via Osoppo robbery. For a time this case created such a political uproar that it threatened to cause a reshuffling throughout the entire Italian police force.

One reason the Italian gangsters have never quite succeeded in gaining more power than they have has been the modernization of the Italian police techniques and equipment since World War II. Another has been the deliberate government effort to regain public confidence in the police, which was destroyed during the days of Mussolini.

Once a country's police system has been perverted to an instrument of oppression, it becomes the enemy of the people and not their protector. Such an image is difficult to erase. But Italy has been making this effort with remarkable success under a democratic government. The police are aided in their rebuilding program to recruit and train able young men by one of the finest crime laboratories in all Europe.

And sometimes, aid comes from unexpected sources as you shall see.

11. St. Rita and the Robbers

In a little church in the city of Milan, there is a shrine where the candlelight flickering in the shadows creates the illusion at times that the image of the gentle St. Rita is smiling, as though sharing a special secret with those who bring their troubles to her. Many come from the streets with problems which seem insoluble, to kneel in this little pool of peace. And when they leave they feel they have found an ally.

Among those who come to the shrine are members of Milan's Squadra Mobile, the special police unit charged with handling the city's major crimes. They have a special feeling about St. Rita, because the solutions to the most baffling cases have come after these visits to the church. And that is why they mention her name when they talk of how they solved Milan's great bank robbery of 1958—the Brink's case of Italian crime which became known throughout Italy as the Case of the Blue Overalls.

The Milan police tell this story of underworld intrigue and violence: In February, 1958, six men came secretively to a midnight rendezvous at No. 24 Via Chinotto in answer to a summons from bull-necked Enrico Cesaroni, a kingpin in Milan's underworld. It was as select a gathering of thugs as ever assembled in Milan; those present were Cesaroni, Arnaldo Bolognini, Eros Castiglioni, and Ugo Ciappina, all expert gunmen; and Luciano DeMaria, Arnaldo Gesmundo and Ferdinando Russo, a trio as skilled at stealing automobiles as they were at driving them on their forays into crime.

During 1956 and 1957, this gang, with other recruits drifting in and out, had netted more than 47,000,000 lire ($78,000) in raids executed with military precision on two banks, a jewelry shop, and a post office. Not once did they leave behind them a clue from which police could build a solution. This was largely due to Cesaroni's skill as a planner. And now he had another plan.

Cesaroni explained to the group that he had found another target worth their attention. For five months he and Ciappina had studied the Popular Bank of Milan's method of transferring money from the main office to branch banks throughout the city.

The transfers were made with a small panel-type delivery truck, manned only by a driver, a bank clerk and one armed guard. Usually there were eight to ten suitcases in the truck, stuffed with millions of lire. And the truck's pattern of travel from bank to bank never varied. Its arrival time at any given point on the route could be timed almost to the minute.

Cesaroni spread a map of Milan on a table and, like a general briefing his captains before a battle, explained what each would do at H-hour on February 27, the date chosen for the robbery.

"The bank truck will enter Via Osoppo from the Piazza Brescia about nine thirty A.M.," he said. "DeMaria will be waiting in a parked truck at this corner where Via Osoppo intersects with Via Caccialebroi. Russo will follow in a car behind the bank truck when it comes out of Piazza Brescia. The rest of us will be waiting in two cars parked here on Via Caccialebroi.

"When the bank truck approaches Via Caccialebroi, DeMaria will drive into the intersection and crash into the bank truck. Russo will turn his car broadside in the street behind it to block the approach from Piazza Brescia. At this moment, all of us will put on the masks and rush the truck. Russo will take care of the guard who sits just behind the bank clerk. The operation should take no more than sixty seconds if all goes well. Then we will put the money into the waiting cars and get out fast."

He followed this briefing with detailed instructions on abandoning the stolen cars and then meeting later at 24 Via Chinotto to divide the loot.

On the evening before the robbery, Ciappina met Cesaroni at their favorite bar on the Piazza Napoli to report that everything was in readiness. A truck and three cars had been stolen in and near Milan during the past few days and were parked in convenient places. DeMaria had obtained seven pairs of blue overalls to be used as part of the disguises and he would bring them to Cesaroni later that night.

While most of Milan slept, Cesaroni was busy with last-minute details. A late caller knocked at his door and he opened it to admit an old man carrying a heavy canvas sack across his shoulder. "Come inside, old man," Cesaroni said.

The visitor was seventy-year-old Ermenegildo Rosi who had traveled across town from his home in a quiet, respectable neighborhood. No one suspected that his house was the armory for Cesaroni's gang. Rosi's name had never been linked with crime and that was one reason why Cesaroni had paid him 1,000,000 lire ($1,666) to be keeper of the weapons.

Rosi laid the sack on the floor. "Everything is here as you ordered," he said, and then slipped back into the night.

Cesaroni opened the sack and lifted out three machine guns, four pistols and several hand grenades. The grenades were to be used if anyone attempted to give chase from the scene of the robbery. Around each of the guns, together with a knitted hood, Cesaroni wrapped a pair of the blue overalls which De-Maria had delivered earlier. When he was finished, he placed the bundles in his car and drove to the Piazza Napoli where he parked on a side street. One by one, members of the gang drifted from dark doorways and received one of the bundles. With this task completed, Cesaroni returned to his hideout.

At 9:29 next morning, Via Osoppo looked as peaceful as any other residential street in Milan. A few pedestrians walked the street with their coat collars raised against a chill wind. A small delivery truck came out of Piazza Brescia, followed closely by a Fiat sedan. The bank clerk in the front seat of the truck was mentally ticking off the number of blocks to the next stop at Agency No. 28 on Via Rubens. He had made this journey hundreds of times until he knew every tree and apartment house and store window along the route. There had been a time when he had wondered what he would do if anyone ever tried to rob the truck. But he soon grew tired of such make-believe and rarely thought about it any more since the daily trips had become monotonous routine.

He saw the intersection of Via Caccialebroi ahead, empty of traffic. But suddenly a big truck wheeled from the side street straight into the path of the bank truck. "Watch out . . .!" the clerk cried. There was a crashing jolt, the grinding of metal against metal, and the sound of shattering glass.

The shaken clerk exclaimed, "The damned fool . . ." But then he swallowed his words and stared in disbelief as the truck was surrounded by hooded men wearing blue overalls. One of them smashed the rear window with a hammer and knocked the guard unconscious before he could draw his pistol. Another bandit poked a machine gun through the glass beside the clerk and commanded: "Don't move!"

The bandits signaled to each other with peculiar howling noises that sounded like barking dogs. They yanked the cases of money from the truck and tossed them into a Fiat sedan that pulled alongside. The hooded men then scrambled into the Fiat and a waiting Alfa Romeo sedan, and the cars raced from the scene without a shot being fired.

The robbery was executed so swiftly that the robbers had vanished before most passers-by knew what was taking place. The robbers had made only one mistake in carrying out the operation. Ferdinando Russo, driving the Fiat which followed the truck, swung his car across the road behind the truck to cut off any traffic from the direction of Piazza Brescia. He leaped out of the car and donned his mask, but failed to set the car's brakes. The Fiat careened across Via Osoppo and crashed into the front of an apartment house. But the mistake actually turned out to be a well-timed diversion. Some passers-by saw only the runaway car and they ran to it to see if anyone were injured. By the time they realized the car was empty, the robbery across the street had been completed.

Police cars, with sirens wailing, reached the scene a few minutes after the robbery. The police found utter confusion when they sought to get a description of the robber gang from the excited crowd.

"They howled like dogs . . ."

"They sounded like Frenchmen to me . . ."

"No, no! They had the accents of Corsicans . . ."

"I counted four robbers . . ."

About the only agreement among the eyewitnesses was that the bandits wore hoods and blue overalls. The police later discovered that the truck and automobiles used in the robbery had all been stolen during the four days preceding the holdup.

The robbery on Via Osoppo became a newspaper sensation when the bank disclosed that the bandits had escaped with 114,000,000 lire ($182,400) in cash plus 476,000,000 lire ($771,-600) in securities and money orders, most of them negotiable. This was the biggest bank robbery in Italy's history, executed with American-style gang methods. The police could not dis-

count the possibility that the mastermind behind the crime
might be one of the hoodlums deported to Italy from the United
States.

At the police headquarters on Via Fatebenefratelli, Dr. Paolo
Zamparelli, chief of the Squadra Mobile, studied the reports of
the robbery with his lieutenants, Ricardo Pennetta and Mario
Iovine. The reports provided no clue to the bandits' descriptions. The only revealing part of the reports was that the bandits'
modus operandi was strikingly similar to the methods used by a
mystery gang in the major unsolved robberies of the preceding
year.

In each of these cases, the robbers' faces were masked with
hoods. The swiftness with which they struck indicated careful
advance preparations and disciplined leadership. They always
used stolen cars, which were abandoned near the scene of the
crime.

Zamparelli reviewed these crimes and said to his aides, "I believe there is only one man in Milan capable of organizing such
disciplined operations. He is Enrico Cesaroni."

But while the police suspected Cesaroni, they had no proof
against him. He was questioned, but the police reluctantly
had to release him.

The first break in the case came six days after the robbery,
quite by accident. For several years, citizens had complained
that the old Olona canal near Via Washington was a mosquito-
breeding health hazard. City authorities at last agreed to have
it drained, and when the stagnant water was drawn off, a workman was startled to see two Beretta automatic pistols lying in
the muddy bed of the canal. Nearby was a hammer, several
pairs of mud-soaked, oversized overalls and a knitted hood.
The workman reported his discovery to the police.

Zamparelli and his men examined the pistols and clothing
for any identifying marks, convinced they were used in the Via
Osoppo robbery. "If we can trace these overalls," Zamparelli
said, "we'll find the gang."

By means of a trademark label, the overalls were found to be
the product of a small garment factory in Milan. The manager
examined the overalls and told the police, "These are our overalls. Perhaps our sales record will show who bought them."

He sent for the records and studied them. "Yes, here it is. We

made only ten pairs of these large-size overalls and sold them
to a small store in Piacenza. It was a special order."

In Piacenza, some seventy kilometers from Milan, the police
found the merchant who had made the purchase. He, too, remembered the overalls and recalled selling them to a peddler
who carried his stock of merchandise in his automobile, visiting
the Saturday market places in the villages around Milan.

The search for the peddler began. The police found him but
the peddler was no help. "Yes, I bought the overalls," he said,
"but then some son-of-a-dog steals my car and everything in it,
including the overalls."

Police reports showed the peddler's story was true. The car
theft had been reported four days before the Via Osoppo robbery. And the police could find no one who had seen the thief
make off with the peddler's car. Again the police were at a
dead end.

By this time, almost a month had passed. The clamor for
the capture of the gang was becoming a serious political issue
in the national election campaign. The government's opposition was asking embarrassing questions. The Communist press
flatly stated: "The police are interested only in politics and
efforts directed against the workers, not against the criminals
. . . They are not interested in solving the case . . . There
are not enough police to protect the people's money, but there
are more than enough police available when the workers
strike . . ."

The pressure on the police became so great that Zamparelli
moved from his Squadra Mobile headquarters and set up a special office in the police barracks where he could concentrate
on the case without interruptions. He and his men often worked
around the clock. They knew their careers were at stake in the
political heat being generated—and that nothing less than a solution of the robbery would halt the attacks. The press hinted
that high police officials in Rome and in Milan might find themselves transferred to the hinterlands of Sardinia unless the case
were solved.

Dozens of known criminals were questioned but no trace was
found of the thief who had stolen the peddler's car. If only this
man could be found . . .

One blustery morning in late March, Zamparelli and his top

lieutenants, haggard of face and bone-weary from a fruitless all-night session of checking the stories of suspects, watched the dawn brighten the windows of their office. They listened to the sounds of the awakening city as they sipped cups of strong coffee.

"Well, what now?" someone asked.

Zamparelli said suddenly, "Let's go for a drive."

They walked outside and climbed into two waiting cars. Zamparelli gave the drivers instructions and the cars moved into the flow of traffic. After a few minutes the cars pulled up before the Church of St. Rita, and the small group walked into the quiet shadows where the candles glowed with tiny flames of eternal hope. And again they saw on the face of St. Rita the secret smile reserved for those who are troubled.

When the familiar service was ended, they left the church to return to the task of trying to find the missing clue in the puzzling Case of the Blue Overalls. And suddenly, the pieces of the puzzle began to fall into place. An aide burst into Zamparelli's office and said, "We've found a man who saw the theft of the peddler's car."

The witness, discovered that morning by a persistent detective, said he saw a stranger drive away with the peddler's car, but he had thought nothing of it at the time. He looked at photographs of criminals brought from the police files and at last he pointed to one and said, "This looks like the man."

The face on the photograph was that of Giorgio Puccia, well known to police for past robberies. A squad of police went to Puccia's apartment but he saw them coming and barricaded himself in his rooms. Police battered down the door and arrested him. Taken to headquarters, Puccia confessed he had stolen the peddler's car.

"What happened to the overalls that were in the car?" he was asked.

"I sold them to Luciano DeMaria," he said sullenly.

Squads of detectives fanned out into the city and, in sudden raids, picked up DeMaria, Russo, Gesmundo, Bolognini and Ciappina and others they suspected might have been linked to the robbery. Hour after hour the suspects were questioned and their stories crosschecked one against the other. The stories grew more confused. And at last one of the gang (the police never have disclosed who it was) broke and told the whole story. Other confessions followed.

After the robbery, they told police, the gang abandoned the stolen cars and switched to their own automobiles. That night the disguises were tossed into the canal and they met Cesaroni at 24 Via Chinotto to divide the loot. Each received 14,000,000 lire ($23,000) but Cesaroni had taken an additional 6,000,000 lire ($10,000) to cover the cost of buying the hideout on Via Chinotto. He took another 3,000,000 lire ($5,000) which he claimed he had paid to Rosi as keeper of the weapons, when in fact he had paid the old man only 1,000,000 lire ($1,666).

The Squadra Mobile raided Rosi's home and found an arsenal of eight machine guns, six pistols and four hand grenades. In Bolognini's home they found two plastic buckets stuffed with a fortune in lire, hidden in a secret compartment beneath the kitchen sink. One of the buckets of currency belonged to Ciappina. Another cache was found under a grating where it had been hidden by Gesmundo. One member of the gang had wrapped his money in a package and left it in the care of his unsuspecting parents. Bundles of lire were recovered from other hiding places, along with money orders and securities. Most of the loot was recovered.

But while police were rounding up DeMaria and the others, Cesaroni slipped from the city along with Castiglioni. (Cesaroni fled to Venezuela where he finally was located and arrested in the summer of 1958. He was returned to Italy under heavy guard in the fall of 1959. Cesaroni was sentenced to eighteen years and four months in prison and fined 439,000 lire. Eros Castiglioni was sentenced in absentia to eleven years and ten months' imprisonment and fined 192,000 lire. The others were sentenced to prison terms ranging from nine to twenty years.)

When Zamparelli made his final report on the solution of the robbery, it ended the pre-election clamor and shattered the Communists' campaign issue.

And then once more the chief of the Squadra Mobile and his lieutenants went to the Church of St. Rita where the candles flicker in the shadows, and they said prayers of thanksgiving as is their custom when a major crime is solved.

INTERPOL
(International Criminal Police Organization)

THE TIME: *1954*

THE PLACE: *Two Continents*

THE CRIME: *Narcotics Smuggling*

Around the world today there exists a shadowy criminal combine, loosely connected from country to country, which does a multibillion-dollar traffic in narcotics, smuggling of aliens, precious stones, counterfeit currency, forgery, and other profitable lines.

It is not new, this sprawling syndicate which operates around the world. International crime has always existed. But since World War II it has increased tremendously because of faster and easier communication between continents and countries. No country is entirely free from it. The combine shifts its operations from place to place, and from product to product, as the promise of profits dictates.

There is no czar or board of directors sitting in obscurity and running the affairs of the combine. The personnel is constantly shifting. There are many men pulling the strings from many cities, with no traceable connection between them.

A tin of opium smuggled through the mountains of northern Thailand and slipped aboard a motorized junk south of Bang-kok would seem to have no connection with a man found murdered on a dark street in Vancouver, B. C. But there was a connection.

Such world-wide crime operations have forced greater and greater co-operation between countries. The need for co-opera-tion brought into being the agency known as Interpol—the In-ternational Criminal Police Organization—with headquarters in Paris. It is now the focal point of police co-operation between many countries.

12. Co-operation vs. Crime

In January, 1954, an American narcotics agent in Rome, Italy, dropped a letter into a mailbox and triggered a crime hunt that was to spread across two continents in a dramatic cat-and-mouse game of modern police co-operation.

The letter was flown to London, England, and delivered to the Royal Canadian Mounted Police officer who maintained close liaison with Scotland Yard. This officer opened the letter and read ". . . I have information that a Canadian citizen named Lippe, often flies from Canada to Brussels to pick up kilogram packets of pure heroin. The drug is brought to Brussels from Paris by French traffickers in narcotics. I am told Lippe has a blond woman accomplice who helps him smuggle the drug into Canada. We are vitally interested in this man and his operations because we believe the drugs smuggled into Canada are delivered to a New York syndicate. Lippe is reported to receive from $6,000 to $7,000 for each kilogram packet of heroin."

The information given by the American agent was relayed from London to Toronto, and Canadian police began searching for the mysterious Lippe and his blond friend. The hunt went on for months without any luck. But eight months after the letter was posted in Rome, a pasty-faced little man was murdered in Vancouver, B. C. Police found the bullet-punctured body of a man they identified as Daniel Trent, a known peddler of narcotics. In a search of his home, they found twenty-three ounces of heroin.

One by one, Trent's companions were questioned. The police were as interested in the source of the heroin as they were in Trent's killer. And finally an underworld informer admitted he knew who sold Trent the drug.

Sullenly, he said, "He got it from the Nipper."

"Who is the Nipper?" an officer asked. "What is his real name?"

"Lipa, or something like that. That's all I know."

Police carried on their investigation in Montreal, Toronto, and Quebec looking for the man known in the underworld as the "Nipper." They picked up traces of his movements in one city, only to lose them and then find them in another. But gradually the identity of the hunted man became clear until the police were certain that he was Jake Rosen.* Rosen's Canadian citizenship records showed that he was born October 28, 1903, in Warsaw, Poland.

Jake Rosen didn't know it, but during the latter part of 1954 and the early months of 1955 he was shadowed by detectives wherever he went. The police wanted to know the source of his heroin supply and who his confederates were before they made an arrest. They were in no hurry.

Early in May, 1955, Rosen entered the Montreal ticket office of Air France. The man who stood beside him at the ticket counter, leafing through a timetable, was a detective.

A ticket clerk said to Rosen, "Can I help you, sir?"

"I would like a seat on your May 18 flight to Paris," he said.

The clerk checked the reservations list. "We can give you a seat on that date," he said.

Rosen obtained the ticket and went directly from the Air France office to a steamship line's office nearby. There he reserved a cabin on the *Arosa Star*, which was leaving Quebec on May 22 for Germany.

"What name shall I put the cabin under, sir?" the ticket agent asked.

"Miss Hannah Blum," Rosen said.

When Rosen left the steamship office, a young man standing nearby watched him leave and then followed at a discreet distance.

The police learned that Hannah Blum was indeed going to Germany—according to the papers she signed when applying for a visa. This information was passed on to the Canadian Embassy in Paris, suggesting that European police be asked to watch the movements of the pair from the time of their arrival in France and Germany.

A representative from the Canadian Embassy carried this request to the International Criminal Police Organization at 37 Rue Paul-Valéry near the Arc de Triomphe. Interpol is used

---

* At the request of Interpol, the real names of the criminals involved have been changed. But all other information is factual.

by sixty-four nations as a clearing house and co-ordinating agency for the detection and suppression of international crime. Through its secretary-general, Marcel Sicot, Interpol arranged for police surveillance of Rosen and Hannah Blum.

Rosen stepped from the Air France plane at the Orly airfield on May 19. A detective from the Sûreté Nationale stood watching as Rosen passed through the customs and immigration routine and hailed a taxi. An unmarked police car followed the taxi which deposited its passenger at a hotel in the Place de la République. Rosen entered the hotel, registered, and was shown to his room by a bellboy.

When the detectives checked the hotel registration papers, they found that Rosen had registered under the name of "Alick Angel." He identified himself as a British subject born in London, in 1909. He had a British passport issued in London in May, 1947.

Through its international radio net, Interpol asked Scotland Yard to check the validity of the passport issued to one Alick Angel. Within a short time the reply came back that a British passport had in fact been issued to an Alick Angel, allegedly born January 1, 1909, in London. But when Scotland Yard forwarded to Interpol the photograph which "Alick Angel" had used in obtaining his passport, the photo showed the face of Jake Rosen. Obviously he had used false papers to obtain his British passport.

Rosen remained in Paris for several days, and detectives found that his favorite hangout was a restaurant in the neighborhood of a Jewish temple. He met old friends there but police made no attempt to identify his companions. They did not wish to arouse Rosen's suspicions.

Rosen left Paris for Hamburg on May 26. When he boarded the train, the Interpol radio was asking police in Brussels and Wiesbaden, Germany, to continue the surveillance when he crossed the borders. Rosen went from Paris to Hamburg where he checked into a hotel under the name Angel. He left the hotel with his luggage the following day, and for a time the police lost track of him. But they picked up his trail a few days later in Bremen where again he was using the name of Angel.

During Rosen's stay in Bremen, police discovered that he

secretly was meeting Hannah Blum, who had arrived on the *Arosa Star*. The couple remained in Bremen for several days. Then on July 22 Hannah boarded the *Kolumbia* which was sailing to Canada by way of Southampton and Cherbourg.

The day after the woman left Bremen, Jake Rosen left the city. He returned to Paris where French detectives—alerted through Interpol by the German police—picked up the surveillance. They were still following him on the evening of July 28 when he entered the air terminal at the Invalides. At midnight he boarded a plane at Orly for Montreal.

Interpol passed on this information to the Canadians. And the Royal Canadian Police were waiting when Rosen arrived at Montreal. They were also watching when Hannah Blum arrived in Montreal on August 27 and joined Rosen.

For three days Canadian police watched the movements of Rosen and his blond companion and then they decided to take action. The couple was arrested in Toronto with an accomplice. Police seized nearly two kilograms of heroin and a half kilogram of opium. This was more than enough to convict them of trafficking in drugs.

When the Canadians sent Rosen's fingerprints to Interpol headquarters in Paris, a comparison of prints showed that his real name was Lipa Stultz, born October 1903 in Warsaw and a known international criminal. He had been sentenced in Germany previously for theft and impersonation and also as a pickpocket.

And thus it was that Interpol acted as the clearing house for the police in breaking up one of Canada's drug rings.

Since World War II, Interpol has become a key center in a widespread battle against international crime and international criminals. It employs no detectives. It has no police force of its own. It is solely the co-ordinating agency for police in Europe, the Middle East, North Africa, and Brazil. Its identification files contain information and descriptions on a gallery of cutthroats, thieves, forgers, confidence men, drug traffickers, murderers, and pickpockets.

The idea of an international co-operative organization for criminal police was first conceived in 1914. At that time the heads of several police organizations met in what they called the First International Congress of Criminal Police. This congress made tentative moves toward forming an international organization but World War I interrupted the effort. Then in 1923 the president of the Vienna police, Johann Schober (who later was to become Austrian Chancellor) invited the police of European countries to a second congress of criminal police.

Even though the Austro-Hungarian Empire had ceased to exist at the close of World War I, Vienna had the most complete file on international crime of any country in Europe. The city had become, in fact, a sort of headquarters for an international police bureau. But there was no system for co-operation between countries in suppressing crime. As a result, criminals who committed a crime in one country were comparatively safe as soon as they crossed the border into another country.

Schober's invitation brought 138 delegates from twenty countries to the Vienna meeting. Article I of the statutes adopted defined the purpose of International Criminal Police Commission—ICPC—in these terms: "To insure and officially promote the growth of the greatest possible mutual assistance between all criminal police authorities, within the limits of the laws of their countries; and to establish and develop all institutions likely to contribute to the efficient suppression of ordinary law crime . . ." This remains the aim of the modern agency.

An international working arrangement among the police of Europe was being developed when World War II shattered it again. In this case, Hitler's lieutenants moved into the picture, took over the police files in Vienna and peremptorily removed the operation to Berlin with all the files and correspondence accumulated over the years. The entire file was lost during the fall of Berlin a few years later.

But the pressing need for international co-operation in suppressing crime was even greater after World War II than it had been before. The idea of an international organization was revived by the inspector general of the Belgian police, Mr. F. E. Louwage, who called a conference of police heads to meet in Brussels in June of 1946. This meeting was attended by representatives from nineteen countries and once again the ICPC came into being. This time Paris was chosen for the organization's headquarters and it was decided that rather than have only a president to direct the organization—as had been true prior to the war—the president would be assisted by an executive committee which would be a true international council.

Within ten years the organization had grown from nineteen members to fifty-five members and then to sixty-four members. The name was changed from the International Criminal Police Commission to the International Criminal Police Organization, or Interpol.

Interpol now is a going organization whose operations spread around the world. It has a central radio station in the Parisian suburb of Lagny–Pomponne which is in direct communication with nineteen police radio stations throughout Europe, the Middle East, and North Africa. Through this network flows an average of more than 125 messages a day as central police bureaus in the member companies pass information back and forth and request co-operation in tracking down international crime operations. Hundreds of other messages and inquiries are exchanged by telegram and mail.

In its files are 286,000 individual cards dealing with the criminal histories of about 100,000 persons. There are more than 21,000 fingerprint cards, either complete or single prints. There are 605 identification description cards and more than 3,000 photographic index cards. This gallery of the world's known international criminals is grouped into three classifications. The first grouping covers murder, burglary, assault, theft, pocket picking, the money-change swindler, car thefts, stolen articles, and missing persons. The second grouping covers substitution theft, breach of trust, fraud, worthless checks, banking infractions, smuggling, and document forgery. The third grouping includes drugs, currency counterfeiting, immorality, and trafficking in women.

Because of this co-operative effort between police, the international criminal and confidence man is finding it more and more difficult to operate. The borders between countries no longer are the protective barrier they once were.

GREECE

THE TIME: *1945–1951*

THE PLACE: *Athens*

THE CRIME: *Espionage*

The war in Europe was nearing a close. General Dwight D. Eisenhower's armies were smashing toward the Rhine River after defeating Hitler's last desperate gamble for victory in the Battle of the Bulge. The Russian armies were battering back the German defenders on the Eastern front. And at Yalta, Joseph Stalin, Winston Churchill and Franklin D. Roosevelt were holding their historic conference, agreeing among other things on a principle of self-determination for nations freed from Nazi occupation.

But as the last of the German occupation forces pulled out of Greece to defend the homeland, the Communists made a farce of the Yalta agreement. They opened a bold campaign of guerrilla warfare and subversion to draw Greece within the sphere of Communist domination. Civil war wracked the country and Greece was not to live in peace for many months.

The Communist espionage and subversion apparatus established in Greece was one of the first to emerge after World War II. Here was the real beginning of the cold war. And slowly the West realized that Stalin's words promising self-determination for liberated peoples were one of history's great deceptions. The realization of the danger to Greece shocked Washington into action, and Congress into approving military and economic aid for the Greek government.

This was the backdrop against which our story of treason was played to its bitter end in Athens.

13. Death of a Traitor

The soft gray gauze of dusk was dropping over the ancient city of Athens and yellow clusters of lights were winking on in homes across the Athenian plain. The waters of the Mediterranean already had changed swiftly from azure to deep blue-black, and small boats trailing streamers of foam were scurrying back to the shelter of Piraeus harbor. Above the darkening valley and the sea, the Parthenon's classic white columns were etched in cold silvery beauty against sky, ageless sentinels looking over the city that was settling itself for the night.

This was Athens on the night of November 13, 1951, giving the illusion of a city at peace with itself. But beneath the surface serenity, men were moving secretively in the final act of a tragedy of treason, violence and death that would shake all Greece.

One of these men was thin, hawk-faced Nicholas Vavoudis, Moscow-trained leader of a Communist espionage ring which had operated successfully for five years. As darkness came, Vavoudis walked along Lykurgus Street in suburban Kallithea. His pace slowed when he approached the small villa marked No. 39. Then he saw that the window shades were only half-drawn, which meant that his confederate, Nicolas Kaloumenos, had seen nothing suspicious in the neighborhood and it was safe to enter. Had the shades been fully drawn, Vavoudis would have continued past the house and gone into hiding until he received an all-clear signal.

Vavoudis knocked at No. 39 and the door was opened by Kaloumenos, clad in a nightshirt. "You are early," Kaloumenos said, locking the door behind his visitor.

"There's work to be done," Vavoudis said brusquely. "Go on to bed."

"Would you like something to eat? I'll call Maria."

"I've already eaten."

Kaloumenos shrugged. "As you wish," he said. He went into the bedroom and closed the door.

Vavoudis walked through the kitchen into a lean-to laundry

room at the rear of the house. He passed through the laundry room and stepped down three concrete steps onto a patio. He stood listening to the sounds of the night, peering into the shadows to be certain no one was watching.

Satisfied that he was alone, he knelt quickly and tugged at one of the laundry-room steps. It swung aside, disclosing a passageway. He slid into the opening and pulled the step back into place. He drew an iron bar through steel rings anchored in the concrete, locking the step so that it could be moved only from the inside.

Vavoudis switched on a light, which revealed that he was standing in a crypt that had been dug beneath the laundry room. It was a crude room, but high enough for a man to stand and move about freely. Air was supplied through an eighteen-inch pipe running up the wall alongside the washroom chimney and opening onto the low roof. The room contained a bed covered with rumpled, dirty covers, a couple of chairs and a table. On the table was a radio transmitter.

Vavoudis seated himself at the table and pulled a code book from a hiding place. He took a sheaf of papers from his pocket and was quickly absorbed in preparing messages in code. The code was in numbers and the key to it was known only to Vavoudis and those on the receiving end of his transmissions.

Soon the radio in the crypt came to life. A Communist receiving station in Rumania picked up the signals and recorded them on tape. For five years Vavoudis had been transmitting military, political and economic information to his Red confederates—information to be relayed to Moscow.

The espionage operation had been so successful that the Party had smuggled tens of thousands of dollars into Greece to keep the apparatus functioning. But the clandestine station in Rumania was not the only radio station listening to the mysterious broadcasts emanating from Kallithea. As the messages flowed from the crypt that night, its signals also were picked up by special task forces of government radio technicians with monitoring equipment. Reports that the mystery station was in operation were relayed to a central control point manned by government security officers and police.

The security group pored over a map of the city. And at last an officer gave a pre-arranged signal over the telephone. Army and Navy helicopters, carrying special radio monitoring equipment, whirled upward into the night and moved over the city in a pattern to pinpoint the location of the hidden radio.

For months, the security forces had been intercepting and recording messages from two illegal radios hidden somewhere in Athens. No move had been made to locate them because officials wanted first to discover all those involved in the underground operation before closing in.

Now the time had come to act. Gradually the pins on the map moved nearer to the Kallithea area. Then they came closer and closer to Lykurgus Street. In the darkness, city police cars carrying squads of security officers slowly began to converge on the house at No. 39.

It was almost daybreak when Kaloumenos, rubbing the sleep from his eyes, climbed from his bed and walked to the front of the house. He peered from the window and saw a policeman. And then came a pounding on the door. Kaloumenos opened the door and police shouldered by him into the house to make a search.

Kaloumenos followed the officers about the house protesting the "invasion" and shouting that innocent, law-abiding citizens should not be treated like criminals. When the police entered the laundry room, Kaloumenos stamped on the floor as though in a fit of anger.

In the crypt below, Vavoudis heard the warning signal. He switched off the radio and leaped to his feet. He picked up the revolver from the table and stood listening . . . waiting . . . waiting . . .

Nicholas Vavoudis was trapped like an animal in his dank hiding place. He had reached the end of a long trail of treason. This trail had led through the dark sewers of Communist intrigue to the most sensational spy plot of modern-day Greece— a plot that almost succeeded in dragging Greece behind the Iron Curtain.

It began in February, 1945, at the same time that Franklin D. Roosevelt, Winston Churchill and Joseph Stalin were meeting at Yalta and agreeing on concessions that would bring Russia into the war against Japan. The wartime leaders also agreed that in the postwar world they would support stability and free elections in the countries freed from the Nazis.

But while Stalin was agreeing in Yalta to the principle of self-determination for the liberated countries, Greek Communist leaders were meeting with Soviet strategists to plot the overthrow of the Greek government. The top-ranking Greek Communist at this conference was Nicholas Zachariades, who was head of the Greek Communist Central Committee and a trusted agent of Moscow. The conference agreed the time had come for the Party to make an all-out drive to overthrow the Greek government by guerrilla warfare and subversion. Zachariades was chosen to co-ordinate the training and activity of guerrillas with the work of the Greek Communist underground, including its espionage unit. The underground operation was entrusted to Nicolas Ploumbidis and Vavoudis was named to direct the espionage operation and its radio transmissions.

Vavoudis had been a Party member for many years. He was born in Odessa, Russia, in 1903. His mother and father brought him to Greece after the Russian Revolution. He joined the Communist Party as a young man and became one of its most active and devoted members. He rose to the rank of instructor for the Aegean area, and then was arrested in 1932 for his illegal Communist activities. He was sentenced to four years in prison. But, acting on instructions from Zachariades, he escaped from the Aegina prison two years later by tunneling beneath the prison wall. Communist friends were waiting to spirit him into hiding.

Vavoudis slipped out of Greece into Russia and was assigned to a responsible post in the technical branch of the Cominform, then the agency of International Communism. He proved to be so able he was given many confidential assignments. Acting on orders from the Cominform, he returned secretly to Greece to take over the espionage assignment.

The Communists could not have chosen a better time for their effort. Greece was in turmoil. Civil war had broken out soon after the Nazis withdrew their troops from Greek soil in late 1944. The underground resistance forces in Greece—a great many of them Communists—had fought the Germans throughout the occupation. But when the end of the war came, the Communists refused to lay down their arms. Brother fought brother. Father fought son in a tragic, bitter conflict that ravaged the country.

Vavoudis managed to get into Athens and immediately went to work setting up the espionage apparatus under the direction of Zachariades who selected his helpers carefully from the ranks of trusted Party members. One of the first men chosen by Zachariades was his old and trusted friend, Nicolas Kaloumenos, with whom he had worked in the underground before and during the war. Zachariades sent for Kaloumenos and asked him if he had enough room in his home to house another person.

Kaloumenos shook his head. "I'm sorry," he said. "But I'm living with my two daughters in a bomb-damaged house and there is no room for another."

Zachariades handed him twenty gold pieces and said, "Well, find a place where there is enough room."

Kaloumenos rented the modest house at No. 39 Lykurgus Street in Kallithea and moved in with his two handsome daughters. A short time later, Vavoudis arrived at the house carrying a suitcase in which was concealed a radio transmitter.

For a while Vavoudis operated the radio from a bedroom. But when city authorities issued an order for all home owners to list the names of persons living in each dwelling, he decided it was too risky to continue the radio operation so openly.

Vavoudis discussed the problem with Kaloumenos and they decided to build a crypt beneath the laundry room. At night, Kaloumenos carried dirt from the excavation and scattered it carefully over the garden at the rear of the house. The neighbors noticed nothing unusual.

When the crypt was completed, Vavoudis moved into the hiding place. He also used the room when necessary as his living quarters and his presence in the house went unreported to the police. He taught Kaloumenos' daughter, Maria, how to operate the radio and after a while he began to combine business with pleasure. He became Maria's lover.

Zachariades was too cautious to depend on a single radio. He decided to have a second transmitter in case one should be discovered by the police. He called in Elias Argyriadis, a clerk in

the Communist office on Piraeus Street and one of his trusted
friends. Zachariades arranged for Argyriadis to move into Villa
Avra at No. 23 Artemdos Street in suburban Glyfada, with his
mistress, Catherine.

Argyriadis posed as a chicken raiser. He quit his old haunts
and publicly played the role of a right-wing sympathizer, even
subscribing to anti-Communist newspapers and frequenting
cafés and clubs preferred by conservative Athenians. Not even
his closest neighbors suspected his double life.

After he was settled at Villa Avra, Zachariades came to the
house with a man he introduced as "Mr. Costas" and Argyriadis
was told he would take his orders henceforth from the visitor.

Costas returned soon with a radio transmitter concealed in a
suitcase and Argyriadis learned that his new boss's name was
really Vavoudis. They built a crypt beneath the house similar
to the one at No. 39 Lykurgus Street. The entrance was concealed by a concrete block which fitted into the basement wall
so perfectly that when the block was in place, the wall looked
solid and smooth.

Sometimes the radio transmissions were made from the house
in Glyfada and then they were shifted to the hideout in Kallithea. While the underground was establishing itself, the Communists were pushing forward with their program of training
"recruits" in the neighboring satellite countries.

In December, 1946, these guerrillas began to pour across the
border from Albania into the rugged mountains of northern
Greece. The Communists were making their great drive to conquer Greece by force. No longer was the Red strategy concealed. Greece was a target for conquest.

The British, who were helping the Greek government organize its postwar army, found the nationalist forces were not strong
enough to control the mountainous terrain. The guerrillas, moving in great numbers, seized towns, mined the highways, terrorized the people, and disrupted the economic and political
life of the entire country. Because of serious financial circumstances at home, the British were unable to carry the burden of
giving Greece protection against this armed aggression.

At this critical time in history, President Harry Truman came
forward with his Greek-Turkish aid program—the program that

became known as the Truman Doctrine. Congress quickly approved the program, and on May 22, 1947, President Truman signed the measure. Now the lines were drawn for the West to resist the raw aggression supported from Soviet-controlled soil. The United States was determined that Greece and Turkey would not be hauled behind the Iron Curtain.

Shortly after the measure was approved, General James Van Fleet was dispatched to Greece with a military mission to see that the Greek government got what it needed to throw back the Red threat. Gradually the Greek Nationalist armed forces were strengthened to the point where they were able to defeat the guerrillas in battle after battle and to drive them back across the border.

The Greek government had an early warning of the Communist plans for subversion and espionage. Two young Greek guerrillas smuggled into Greece by the Red underground surrendered to police. Tired of the bloodshed and disillusioned, they disclosed that the Cominform had set up espionage schools which were training Greeks for underground work.

This was the story, in part, told by one of the defectors, J. Logothetis: "I was with the guerrilla forces fighting in Greece. I was injured and was taken into Albania. Before I recovered fully, I was sent with a group to Budapest aboard a Russian plane.

"In Budapest, Ioannidis, a member of the Central Committee, told us we were going to attend a school. He gave us no more information and no one asked any questions. Anyhow, nobody was in a position to object because it was either follow orders or be sent to a concentration camp.

"I was taken to a school and trained in espionage activities—that is, the use of radio, code procedures, disguise and forgeries. The technical instructors and civilian personnel of the school were all Hungarians. But the teaching of economics, the history of the Communist Party and the theory of materialism was done by a Greek Party member.

"Eventually, they told us our job would be to return to Greece and work for the liberation of the country and that we would have support from all the other Republics."

After six months of training, Logothetis and several of his school comrades were sent to Bulgaria. There he was given a portable radio set, sixty gold pieces of French currency, and twenty million Greek drachma. Then he was taken across the border into Greece by a Greek named Vasvakas.

"Vasvakas organized our departure to Greece," he continued. "He gave us clothing, liquid for the batteries, envelopes containing instructions and crypto codes. He told us, 'You are going there to build up a solid secret net for the Party which you must keep active until other members arrive.'

"We were ordered to collect political, military and economic information. We slipped across the border at night and hid. Eight or ten days later we got instructions from the Central Committee of the Greek Communist Party. We were told to learn everything possible about the defensive works at Porto-Lago . . . and the intelligence we collected was to be given to our superior in the locality who would be responsible for its transmission."

The other defector, named Masmanidis, told authorities: "After the defeat of the People's Army in Vitsi in 1949, the guerrillas withdrew into Albania and Bulgaria and many of them also went into Yugoslavia. I went to the last country. In September we left for Czechoslovakia, where they had established a political-technical school. Our lessons included radio operations, photography, producing forged documents and sabotage.

"At the end of six months, we were given a rest while our passports were being prepared. In Sofia, we met Vasvakas, who said we had to go to Greece to build up a secret organization, and that someone in Greece would assign us specific tasks."

Alarmed by this and other information, Greek security officials began a drive to uncover the underground and its members. To their amazement they found journalists, doctors, lawyers, and even the son of a famous Greek admiral were involved in the Red underground.

The admiral's son, Dimitrios Batsis, had no criminal record and no known link with the Communist Party. Yet he was a key figure in the underground's financial operations. Couriers com-

ing from France, Switzerland, and many other foreign countries
smuggled funds to him to be passed on to Zachariades, Ploumbidis and other Party chiefs.

A seaman was arrested who told police of smuggling money
to Batsis and others by way of Marseilles and Beirut. "Eventually," he said, "I was trusted with 1,625 gold pounds. When I
got to Piraeus the police found the money on me. The money
was seized because it was illegal at that time to bring foreign
currency into the country. But when the trial was over, the
money was returned to me and I deposited it in the Ionian Bank.
Then I got in touch with Batsis and gave him a check. He
protested that I was supposed to give him cash—not a check.
But he took it."

Batsis was arrested and confessed his role. Too late, he
turned against his confederates. "These people," he said bitterly, "pretended that everything they did was being done
merely to bring peace to Greece. I really swallowed it because I
trusted them and their arguments . . . If the court wants me to
be punished for what I did, I can say that I am not afraid of
death. I'm only thinking of my old father, of the dishonor of
sitting here as a spy."

The news of the arrest of Batsis and others spread quickly
through the underground. Zachariades and Ploumbidis saved
themselves by fleeing across the border, leaving the others to
shift for themselves as best they could.

Throughout this crisis, Vavoudis continued his radio transmissions, seemingly unaware that the police net was closing
on him also. And so he sat at his transmitter on the night of
November 13, 1951, as the security forces closed in.

One of the security officers recalled: "The raid began at three
A.M. We were certain one of the radios was in or near the Villa
Avra where Argyriadis lived with his mistress. We searched the
house for an hour and found nothing. We knocked on the walls
and went over the floors inch by inch.

"There was a laundry room in the basement which had walls
made of big concrete blocks. We knocked on the walls, but they
seemed absolutely solid. The search was beginning to look hopeless when I noticed that between two shelves on the wall there
was one concrete block with a small crack around it. I shoved

heavily against it and it moved. The block was set on ball-bearing rollers on a track that was slightly inclined, so that when pressure against the block eased, it slid back into place of its own weight. Behind the block was the crypt and the radio transmitter.

"When Argyriadis saw me shove the block from the wall, he shrugged and said, 'All right, you've found it.'"

With the discovery of the Glyfada crypt, the search shifted to Kallithea. Police closed in on No. 39 Lykurgus Street. Vavoudis heard the warning signal from Kaloumenos stamping on the floor, and he waited in silence. He must have heard the shouts of police through the ventilator and the scrape of shovels digging in the backyard. But hour after hour passed and the crypt still was undiscovered.

Kaloumenos continued to protest he knew nothing of a secret radio. But then a policeman saw him edge his way slowly to the side of the laundry room where he reached up quickly and dropped a chunk of bread and a piece of cheese into a pipe.

Caught in this act, Kaloumenos sullenly admitted that the pipe led to a crypt below. The officers urged him to appeal to the man to surrender because he had no chance to escape. But Kaloumenos said, "The man down there will never come out alive. He'll kill himself first."

A police official shouted down the ventilator to Vavoudis promising him safe conduct and a fair trial if he would surrender. There was a moment of silence and Vavoudis cried, "Give me ten minutes to think it over."

But then smoke began curling from the ventilator as Vavoudis frantically tried to burn the messages and code book. And from the ventilator also came the muffled sound of two pistol shots. At last the concrete step was torn aside. Two policemen entered the crypt to find Vavoudis lying on the floor with a pistol in his hand. He had shot himself twice in the head. He was still breathing as he was lifted from the crypt and rushed to a nearby hospital, but he lived only a few minutes.

The traitor Vavoudis succeeded in destroying some of his messages—but the code book was virtually intact. Greek authorities were able to decode more than three hundred messages containing a shocking amount of political and secret military information, in addition to the names of key members of the underground. The code book revealed that the number "60" was used to refer to money, "15" to Batsis, and "38" to Ploumbidis. For example, there were exchanges of messages between Vavoudis and the Rumanian station such as these: "Do not forget to take from 15 (Batsis) 60 (the money) received from 43 (Paris)." And the reply: "15 (Batsis) gave a total of 7,000. 38 (Ploumbidis) took 1,000. Once again we have nothing in our pockets." And then: "20,000 are at your disposal. It will be sent to you in one and a half months."

When the swift roundup of the underground was completed, the Communist radio screamed that Vavoudis had been "murdered" by the government, and added, "You will be drowned in the blood you yourselves spilled! Murderers!"

Zachariades, from his asylum behind the Iron Curtain, violently attacked the Greek government and declared Vavoudis' death was not suicide, but a murder supervised by the government. The radio also said, "Greece is living under such terrorism that working people are killed even in the streets like dogs, as Vavoudis was killed."

For twenty days the Communist radios paid tribute to Vavoudis as a martyr who died for the Party's cause. But then, abruptly, the Party line switched. Vavoudis, instead of being a hero, became overnight a "traitor and tool" who had been used by the Americans.

The Red radio beamed on Greece said: "When the war between Greeks ended, Vavoudis was used for organizing a great case of high treason against the Greek Communist Party. He set up a fake espionage and radio network. The stories of his suicide, as well as the messages and codes, are just a big fake. Vavoudis is alive and the Americans have taken him to America where he collects ransom for his treason."

Thus was Vavoudis—who gave his life for the Party—"honored" by his comrades because he was fool enough to be caught in a plot which damaged the prestige of the Party.

The courts gave death sentences to Batsis, Argyriadis, Kaloumenos, and Nikolaos Beloyannis and long prison terms to sixteen others swept up in the police net.

And so ended this phase of the great Communist plot to destroy freedom in Greece.

TURKEY

THE TIME: *1958*

THE PLACE: *Istanbul*

THE CRIME: *Murder*

The twentieth century has come to Istanbul. Bulldozers smash their way through buildings, carving out paths for broad, new boulevards above the Bosporus. Huge planes, en route to the Far East or heading for Europe, disgorge passengers by the thousands at the modern airport. The restless, well-to-do passengers can find shelter at the brassy Istanbul Hilton Hotel which provides American-style plumbing conveniences and a kidney-shaped swimming pool.

The Hilton guests can stand on the hotel balcony and look across the Bosporus at ancient mosques whose minarets rise above a city from which Sultans once ruled a mighty empire.

Istanbul is a crossroads between Europe and Asia. The old

city, once known as Constantinople, sprawls across the Bosporus with one half in Europe and the other half in Asia. Through it passes a strange assortment of humanity. And sometimes one among them is a murderer

This city seems an improbable place in which to find the police using modern, Western-style methods of crime detection and prevention. But the pull of the West has been stronger than the tug of the East on all of Turkey. And the police have had their training in the United States and in Scotland Yard's police schools.

Perhaps the murderer who came to Istanbul in 1958 didn't know this.

14. *Murder by Chance*

The murderer was in India and his victim was in Germany when each began the journey that would lead one of them to his death, the other to prison. They did not know each other. They were wanderers whose paths came together by chance.

The murderer, Johann Golkowski, pretended to be a physician. At times he called himself Raschad Hussein Golkowski or Johann Leonhard when a confidence game required an alias. He had a wife and child in Germany waiting for him to return to them—and sometimes, when in deep trouble, he thought of them—Lilo and the boy. But more often his thoughts were occupied by the lady with whom he happened to be sleeping at the time.

The victim was Gerhard Moritz, who had found it profitable to drive automobiles from Germany into Syria, where they could be sold for as much as $12,000 on the black market. This was Moritz' aim when he left Germany early in 1958 in a Mercedes-Benz sedan, heading once more for Syria.

But his final destination was a rendezvous with death on a dusty road outside Istanbul, Turkey.

A diary kept by Johann Golkowski tells much of the weird story. On the flyleaf was written:

Name: Dr. Golkowski
Address: Every place in the world or homeless.

On the next page the story began:
January 1—Madras, India
A new year came. What will it bring new to me or to us? Today Angela is in much better condition than she has been for some days. For this year, I wish that she will not become an addict.

From using narcotics during these last two years, she has arteriosclerosis. This evening she demanded a narcotics injection. There was only one way to bring her away from this—I had to beat her with the belt. Afterward she was all right.

January 2

Angela slept two nights without waking up. Today she is not so thoughtless as she was a few days ago when it was very terrible. I was ashamed even to go out with her. I am so glad that my treatment shows such quick effect. This is the first day, she told me, that she has felt like she was newly born. For an undisturbed night I treated her with 1.5 cc of Coramine and 3 grains of phenobarbital orally. It works pretty well. The reaction of her pupils is not so irregular as it has been.

Angela seems to be very happy today. And that is the way she must be for my own happiness.

January 3

It seems to me that since Angela has been without pethidine injections, she cannot give me the same love that she does during the time she is taking narcotics. But it should not worry me if she is becoming all right again. I bought for 12 rupees medicine for her treatment. For my own handbag I bought 24 tablets for the hypodermic. Every day I must explain to her the use of Coramine or she forgets it. I get very angry about this. So much so that I have advised her to go away because she often says such thoughtless things I get nervous and forget myself. In the evening we went to the picture, *The Burglar.*

January 4

Angela's treatment and condition are still the same.

What is it about my life in India since I have had to treat Angela? My hands are tight and I can't do what I want with them. The way I must treat her keeps me always busy. Sometimes I think about leaving her, but my conscience won't allow me to do so. I have to care very much and stay with her, but who knows where our ways are going? I don't believe that life is fate. I will say it is directed by our conscience.

January 5

Sunday is no different from all the other days, and I will say it is tedious. In the evening I wrote a letter to Angela's father about her condition, treatment and expenses for the medicine. I will be very glad when Angela can care a little more for herself and can stand the pain without so many injections. I don't know about her blood condition and so every injection hurts my conscience because I don't know what will happen to the blood.

January 6

During the morning I had terrible rheumatism pains in the muscles and joints of my legs and I went out to buy some medicine. The pain got so bad in the afternoon that I couldn't stand it any more. In the night for the first time in my life I gave myself an injection. It was Impletol to take care of the pain but it didn't help so much. This night is the first night I stopped the injection for Angela. She got only 4.5 grains, and she slept.

January 7

During the day I took my second Impletol injection but my terrible pain doesn't go. I thought about taking a pethidine injection but I fight against it until my thoughts are lost. In the evening I had to beat Angela again because she demanded an injection I couldn't give.

January 8

Before I went to sleep last night I took my first pethidine injection but only 1 cc. I had a nice feeling for some hours but I can't say that I slept well.

For what reason did I get Angela out of this only to get myself in? To treat her has made me nervous and sick. This evening again she made me so angry that I couldn't go to sleep without the injection.

January 9

This morning I went to the general hospital to see the surgeon. I asked him for help but he was unable to do it. After lunch I took Angela for a medical check-up. In the evening Angela was becoming jealous because I spent a few hours with some friends. She went away with the remark "The police will find me on the beach." She meant, of course, she wanted to commit suicide. But after two hours she came back and said, "I couldn't do it."

January 10

I am so fed up with Madras that I often feel like vomiting. Today I took pethidine again.

January 14

Four times today I took injections and now I am sure that I will be an addict. Angela and I are feeling very sad about it. Also my sex feeling has gone because of the injections. When we went out for lunch in the Pals restaurant, Mr. Bath came to see us. I was angry because I didn't invite him to our table.

January 15

When I woke up this morning I felt very well but when I returned from the Spencers' I was very nervous. My hands were trembling so much that I couldn't even sterilize my syringe. From this time until evening, I took 4 injections. Very bad. Feel sick about it. For the night I will take one tablet and hope to sleep well and then start a new day without an injection.

January 16

Today I had a breakdown. I don't know whether it is the result of narcotics or from too much phenobarbital. Had a terrible headache and was very dizzy. Couldn't leave my bed. Angela and I talked about committing suicide because if something should happen not even our best friend will help us now. We were expecting Angela's mother and only she can help us now. But she did not come today so we lost all hope for her visit. How can a mother not be interested in the life of her own daughter? I did such a lot for her, sold all my things for her treatment, and now my hands are tied so I can't do any more for her. Now I don't even have the money for medicine to treat myself. I have a fever and need antibiotics.

January 17

I am still sick with a horrible headache and fever. It is very bad to be sick in a foreign country and without money. We are getting more and more into debt. The hotel account today is 181 rupees. I am in debt also to two shops. The account in the Pals restaurant must be about 200 rupees. When I think about my debt I get even more sick.

Angela is sweet and trying to help herself up. She only had two injections today. Angela feels very happy because I told her she must be pregnant.

January 19

I feel a little better and can hope to be all right tomorrow. I had a conversation with Mr. Khan. He offered me every help I need and then he pushed some rupees into my hand. I was very thankful. It is funny because always when my money comes to an end, I find somebody who likes to help.

January 21

Tried to get Angela a passport but couldn't. Nothing is to be done. Can I leave her alone without any difficulty? I will try from another country to get her out of India. We are so right together, but it is so difficult for each of us to stay alone. We will find a way.

January 22

I approached an engineer about getting a guarantee for Angela's passport. He said he could do it for ten thousand rupees. I was shocked at such a fantastic sum. Our feeling now is funny and we are laughing and crying. We feel now the time is running against us, that the day we have to say good-bye comes so near.

January 25

Mr. Khan brought the 1000 rupees.

January 26

We feel our parting is coming in a great hurry. Our feeling is really sad and our hearts are breaking.

I bought the tickets for my departure on January 28.

January 27

In the afternoon we spoiled two hours with packing. Angela cried so much and I could not keep from crying myself. In the evening we went with Hilal to buy whiskey. We took a little for us. Angela got tipsy. Angela affects me always when she cries and she wanted to be all night in my arms. I was bad and wouldn't accept it because we cried so much about our parting today. I feel sorry for Angela because she is so lonely. I love her and feel lonely myself. I left for Delhi.

February 23

Arrived Teheran by bus and train. Went to Shimrah Road to see Mr. A.R.D., the Ford agent. He gave me 100 toman. In the afternoon I saw a picture and went back to my hotel. I don't want to go out in the crowds and I also don't like to see people. I feel like killing them.

(Golkowski's notes indicated that he left Teheran and went to Tabriz where he arrived broke and sick. He apparently got a room at the Metropole Hotel and noted "This was the first time I have been able to go to sleep without a pethidine. Pawned watch for 1,000 rials. Got 2,000 rials also for personal belongings.")

February 28
Sometimes I am afraid of what is happening to my character.
When I am without the hypodermic I am thinking about mur-
der. I can't help it.

March 1
Went to a drug store to buy dolantin. An elderly gentleman
asked me to have a look at his wife. She doesn't feel well. I examined her but nothing serious. I was invited to have lunch
there and after this her daughter, twenty years old, showed me
the family album. She is very well built and gave me a lot of sex
feeling. I had to hold on to myself. Her father gave me 200
rials for examining his wife.

March 2
I returned to see the woman who is my patient. They told me
after I gave her the injection she felt like dying, but I told them
there was nothing to worry about.

March 3
I saw the lady again. She looks much better today. Her room
was full of visitors and I was the only man. I didn't feel very
comfortable.

Sold my pistol for 7,000 rials.

March 4
6½ hours by bus to Khoy. We arrived there at 11 A.M. The
lady of the house is very pretty and has sex appeal. I like her
very much. In the afternoon I drove her car to the village.

March 5
We arrived at the Turkish border. On the Turkish side, I saw a
Mr. Moritz. It seems he has done something bad and cannot get
into Syria because he doesn't have a visa for Iran. I advised him
to go to Ankara and apply for the visas. He has a Mercedes 220
but no money for benzine. I agreed to buy the benzine for the
trip.

(Golkowski arrived at the Turkish border with his papers in
order and was permitted to enter Turkey. While he was clearing
his papers with border officials there was a violent argument
going on nearby between border officials and a German who
was driving a Mercedes-Benz sedan. The German, Gerhard
Moritz, did not speak Turkish. One of the police officials asked
Golkowski to act as interpreter. Golkowski was told that Moritz
could not enter Iran because he had no visa and also because

Turkish police had been advised that Moritz on previous occasions had entered Syria with automobiles and had sold them
illegally on the black market. Golkowski who was on his way to
Istanbul had no difficulty in convincing Moritz that they should
team up and perhaps in Ankara they could obtain the visa which
was necessary for Moritz' entry into Iran. They left the border
station together.)

March 6

Moritz and I arrived in Erzurum at 10 P.M. The roads were
very dangerous, full of snow and ice. Today at 12 A.M. we
started for Ankara. In the evening we were in Gumushane and
slept there. In return for driving his car, I am paying for all the
benzine, his boarding, and the food. I have the feeling Moritz
is not very satisfied but I can't help it.

March 7

We drove through the snow and mountains to Trabzon. The
Iranian counsel refused to give Moritz a visa because last year
it seems he had done something illegal in Teheran. During the
night we arrived in Samsun (a port on the Black Sea) very
tired. In the morning we left Samsun for Ankara and arrived
there at 8 P.M.

March 10

In the afternoon I saw Fitnat. We had lunch together in Zeki's
house. Fitnat loves me very much. As soon as I am free I will
marry her.

At 4 P.M. Moritz and I left for Istanbul.

Here ended the diary of Dr. Johann Golkowski, alias Johann
Leonhard, alias Raschad Hussein Golkowski. But the story was
continued in the files of the Turkish police like something from
the irrational dreamworld of an opium smoker.

As they left Ankara, Moritz was gloomy. "Why do you think
we can get help in Istanbul?" he growled.

Golkowski laughed. "I have important friends there. They
will help you. Now stop worrying."

At one time, Golkowski did have influential friends in Istanbul. He had come to the city posing as a professor and had
given lectures to classes at the university. He had been wined
and dined by university faculty members and the city's intellec-

tuals who had been duped by his clever masquerade—until Golkowski's checks began to bounce.

Golkowski perhaps was thinking of all this as he threaded the Mercedes through the ancient streets of the city once known as Constantinople, from which Turkish emperors had ruled an empire that threatened even to engulf Western Europe. The afternoon sun was gleaming on the domes and minarets of the city's mosques when he found a garage near the Golden Horn of the Bosporus. The two men walked past the great cathedral of San Sophia to a small hotel, the Yayla Palas, where they registered and obtained rooms. It was Tuesday, March 10, 1958.

Who can say, except the murderer, when the first thought of a murder is born? But somewhere between the Turkish border and Istanbul the idea of murder came to Golkowski. On Friday afternoon, Golkowski strolled through the teeming cavern of the great covered bazaar until he came to the shop of a pawnbroker. He stepped inside and stood looking into the display cases until a customer left the shop. Then he said to the shopkeeper: "I wish to buy a pistol."

"I have no guns," the shopkeeper said. "It's illegal for me to sell them."

Golkowski laughed. "Don't worry. I'm leaving town and the police will never know."

The shopkeeper hesitated and then drew Golkowski into a back room. He took several pistols from a hiding place and placed them on a table. Golkowski finally selected an Italian-made Beretti automatic.

"You like it?" the shopkeeper said.

"It's not for me," his visitor said. "I have a friend who is driving an automobile to Germany. He needs a gun for protection. It's a long journey." He examined the mechanism of the pistol carefully and then said, "I don't know whether my friend will like this one or not. How much is it?"

"It is in excellent condition—750 lire."

"I'll take it," Golkowski said, "but only on condition I can return it if my friend doesn't like it."

The shopkeeper nodded. "If your friend doesn't like it, you bring it back and I'll return your money."

Golkowski paid for the pistol, stuck it in his pocket and walked into the bazaar. That evening the desk clerk at the hotel saw Golkowski and Moritz leave the hotel together, but he did not notice when either returned.

The following morning, Golkowski came downstairs carrying his battered suitcase and black medical kit. He asked for his bill.

"Where is your friend?" the clerk asked amiably.

For a moment Golkowski looked at him coldly, and then he smiled and winked. "He spent the night with his girl friend. He'll be in later."

From the hotel, Golkowski went to the bazaar to the shop of the pawnbroker. He pulled the Beretti pistol from his pocket and said, "I'm sorry, but my friend didn't like the gun." Then he chuckled and said, "He didn't like it at all."

The shopkeeper returned the 750-lire payment. Golkowski walked swiftly to the garage. He stowed his luggage in the back seat of the Mercedes, slid behind the wheel, and headed the car into the Saturday morning traffic.

Occasionally, drops of liquid oozed from beneath the luggage compartment of the car and dripped to the roadway. They were drops of blood.

At 4:30 P.M., a Turkish laborer was walking along a lonely stretch of road outside the village of Gebze, about two hours by automobile from Istanbul, when he glanced over an embankment and saw a body lying in the weeds. The man was dead. His clothing was soaked with blood and his face and head were badly battered.

The worker hurried to a nearby police station and reported what he had seen. The Istanbul central police station dispatched a doctor and two policemen to the scene.

The doctor examined the dead man and found a gunshot wound in his head and knife wounds on the body. The face was torn and bruised, obviously in a desperate struggle. There was nothing in the pockets to identify the victim—his pockets had been rifled.

"I believe he has been dead about eighteen hours," the doctor said.

The policemen examined the road but found no signs of a struggle and no bloodstains even though the victim had bled profusely.

"This man wasn't killed here," the doctor said. "His body was brought here and dumped over the bank."

Carefully searching the area, police found a lone clue—a small key that looked to them like an automobile key. On it were the initials "G. M." A locksmith examined the key and said, "This key wasn't made in Turkey. It is German-made."

With this slender lead, police began checking hotel registers throughout the city, looking for someone with the initials G. M., and perhaps having a German name.

At last a policeman arrived at the Yayla Palas hotel. He checked through the names on the register and found the name Gerhard Moritz.

The clerk said, "He spoke with a German accent and was driving a grey Mercedes sedan. Here is the license number that was on his papers."

"Was anyone with him?"

The clerk nodded. "He had a friend with him." He pointed to the name, Dr. Johann Golkowski. "Golkowski checked out early this morning. When I asked about his friend, he laughed. He said Moritz had spent the night with a girl friend and would return later. But he hasn't returned."

"I don't think your guest will be back," the policeman said. Within minutes, Istanbul police had broadcast an alarm throughout Turkey, asking for the arrest of Dr. Johann Golkowski. His description was given, along with the license number of the Mercedes, B U K 6. Border control stations were notified to be on the alert and warned to be extremely cautious in making an arrest because the wanted man was perhaps armed and desperate.

Police could not find a murder weapon at the scene of the crime so they began a methodical check of pawn shops throughout the city. At the shop in the bazaar, the shopkeeper admitted he had sold a pistol to a man answering Golkowski's description —but that it had been returned to him. He turned the pistol over to the police.

Ballistics experts fired several shots from the Beretti and found that the barrel markings on the bullets were identical with the marks on the bullet which had been fired into the head of Moritz. There was no doubt that the Beretti was the murder weapon.

A man cannot lose himself so easily in Turkey as in the United States. Within six hours after the police broadcast the alarm, a telephone call came into the central police station at Istanbul. A Mercedes sedan answering the police description had been found abandoned in a garage at Mersin, a town on the Mediterranean sea in southern Turkey. There was blood smeared on the floor of the car's trunk. Three hours later, a message came from Adana, about an hour's drive from Mersin. A man answering Golkowski's description had been seen at the railway station. He had asked the ticket agent about train schedules to Halap, Syria. By this time, all the morning newspapers of Turkey were carrying stories of the brutal slaying along with a picture of Golkowski found in police files. Slowly the net closed on the hunted man.

Golkowski saw the newspapers at the railway station at Adana. And he realized it was hopeless to try to cross the border into Syria. In desperation, he decided to double back to Istanbul by train and then seek another escape route. Perhaps the police wouldn't expect him to come back to the scene of the crime.

Golkowski arrived in Istanbul, unrecognized, in the early morning hours of March 18. He took the ferry across the Bosporus and went to the Cordon Hotel, about a four-minute walk from the ferry station. But when he asked for a room, the clerk told him nothing was available unless he shared a room with another guest.

"I must have a room alone," Golkowski pleaded.

And then the clerk recognized Golkowski from the description carried in the newspapers. He said, "Well, I do have one single room that is reserved—but I'll let you have it." He called a porter to show Golkowski to his room.

When Golkowski left the lobby, the clerk called the police and five minutes later Golkowski was taken into custody, protesting that he had done nothing. He was taken to the central police station for questioning.

"I came from the Iranian border alone," he insisted. "I don't know anyone named Moritz. I don't know anything about a murder."

But then police told him they had found Moritz' car in a

garage at Mersin. They told him he had been recognized near Mersin and had been seen in the railway station where he asked about the train schedule to Syria. They told him they had found the murder weapon in the pawnshop. As they questioned him, the door opened and the clerk from the Yayla Palas hotel entered.

The clerk looked at Golkowski and said, "He was Moritz' friend."

Golkowski broke down. He admitted that he had killed Moritz, shoved his body into the trunk of the car, and then thrown it over the bank near Gebze.

"We left the hotel to go to a restaurant for dinner," he said. "But before we got there I got the shakes. I told Moritz I had to return to the hotel for an injection. He refused and attacked me. I had to kill him in self-defense."

But Golkowski's story of self-defense hardly tallied with the fact that he obtained the murder weapon in what seemed to police a clear case of premeditated murder. The police theorized that Golkowski—desperate for narcotics—lured his countryman to the lonely road, knocked him unconscious and, in a murderous frenzy, shot him and stabbed him until he was certain he was dead. Then he had robbed Moritz and taken the car in the hope of selling it himself for a fat black-market price.

Golkowski was charged with murder and held in the Istanbul jail for months. His case dragged slowly through the court, but in October, 1959, the court found Golkowski guilty as charged. He was sentenced to twenty-four years in prison.

As he sat in his cell, Golkowski's letters were not to Angela in Madras or to Fitnat in Ankara. They were addressed to "Dear Lilo," the forgotten wife in Germany.

But neither "Dear Lilo" nor anyone else could help Golkowski, the man whose address was "Every place in the world or homeless."

HONG KONG

THE TIME: *1947–1960*

THE PLACE: *Hong Kong*

THE CRIME: *Piracy*

The visitor strolling along a street in Hong Kong heard the thin, high skirling of bagpipes and the throb of the drums which could have come straight out of Scotland. He sought the source of the music and turned into a parade ground alongside the police barracks.

The kilted pipers and drummers marched toward him in military formation, the leader's baton flashing in the sun. And then he saw that not one among them was a Scot. Every man jack of them was Chinese, and a member of the Hong Kong police force.

Hong Kong is full of such surprises for the stranger, a city of startling contrasts. On the island of Hong Kong, the wealthy live in mansions on the hills high above the harbor. Across the way in Kowloon, a part of greater Hong Kong, refugees from Red China huddle by the hundreds of thousands in poverty. One street has the solid, stolid look of a financial street in London. Another nearby could have been lifted out of the slums of Shanghai.

There is an electric awareness everywhere that the city lives under the dark shadow of Communist China. Everyone knows the Red Chinese could seize this great port in one quick grasp if they wished to take the risks involved. And yet millions of dollars are being invested in new hotels, apartment houses, homes, and business places in cheerful disregard of any danger from the north.

Beneath the surface ferment of Hong Kong, there is always a conflict between the police and criminals who are members of the strangest crime syndicates in the world—the Chinese secret societies. Normally, the police function as any ordinary police force. But in times of emergency, such as a riot, the police force becomes a military organization and every able-bodied Englishman in the city is duty bound to answer a call to arms.

Red China is the threat to Hong Kong from without. But within the city, the danger lies in the Chinese secret societies.

15. The Secret Underworld of the Orient

On December 12, 1947, the sturdy, 4,551-ton motor ship, *Van Heutsz*, glided slowly into Hong Kong harbor. Her Dutch flag snapped in a stiff breeze and almost all of her 1,672 passengers seemed to be crowded at the rails for a look at the Crown Colony which the Japanese had controlled such a short time before.

Captain Klaas Alberter Vliek stood on the ship's bridge viewing the panorama with the fascination he always felt when he brought his ship into this exciting Asian port. Each arrival carried with it a new sense of adventure.

On this day gray clouds drifted low across the mountains towering above the harbor, hiding the peaks in a misty veil. Occasionally the clouds parted to give a glimpse of white mansions clinging to the peaks. Then the clouds closed in again, leaving the illusion that the mansions really didn't exist. They were like people trying to isolate themselves from the struggle that went on below among Hong Kong's swarms of Chinese.

The captain looked down at the Chinese motorized junks moving swiftly through the water and the gangs of coolies heaving freight from junks anchored beside towering freighters and passenger vessels which came from all parts of the world to pause here briefly. The ferries shuttled back and forth busily between Kowloon and Hong Kong Island, carrying their odd mixture of humanity. Through the streets moved limousines alongside rickshaws drawn by spindle-legged coolies whose endurance was unbelievable.

Captain Vliek was cheerful because this night he would dine in the quiet elegance of the Peninsula Hotel or beneath sparkling chandeliers in one of those mansions in the clouds. He would have almost two full days in which to visit with old friends and catch up on the gossip from Amsterdam, Rotterdam and The Hague. Hong Kong always provided a pleasant break in the monotony of the run from Belawan in Sumatra to Penang, Singapore, Swatow and Amoy.

There was nothing to cause Captain Vliek any alarm and he would have laughed outright had anyone suggested that within forty-eight hours he and his ship would be the prisoners of a murderous pirate gang. Piracy seemed so improbable that the *Van Heutsz* did not even carry an antipiracy guard as some smaller vessels did while plying the waters from Hong Kong to Swatow and Amoy. Pirates had seized some small vessels in these waters but none had ever dared attack a ship the size of the *Van Heutsz*. The only piracy precaution taken by Captain Vliek was to issue arms to his European officers once his ship was outside Hong Kong harbor heading for Swatow.

Captain Vliek watched over the docking of the vessel and the disembarkation of the passengers. On this voyage his ship carried seventy-six first-class passengers and 1,596 deck passengers, most of them en route to the China ports. Virtually all the travelers were Chinese returning to their homeland after years of enforced absence caused by World War II. Many of them did not know whether their families had survived. Among the first-class cabin passengers were businessmen carrying merchandise, and cash, with plans to reopen markets which had been closed to the millions of Chinese scattered throughout Southeast Asia.

When the last of the passengers had crossed the gangplank, Captain Vliek turned over the vessel to his chief officer and made his way ashore. A few hours later while the captain was enjoying the long-anticipated meeting with friends, a nondescript Chinese named Sam Piu walked the streets of Kowloon seeking out brokers who dealt in black-market ship passages. Sam was searching for tickets which would permit him and twelve confederates to board the *Van Heutsz* before it sailed for Swatow. Because of the postwar shortage of transportation, many Chinese en route to Hong Kong purchased tickets good for passage to points beyond. The unused portions of the tickets always could be sold in Hong Kong at a fat profit.

Sam, however, was not greatly concerned over the availability of the tickets. If necessary, he knew he could bribe Chinese crew members to smuggle him and his men aboard the *Van Heutsz*. He also knew that once his gang was aboard, it would be easy to become lost among the hundreds of deck passengers. The ship's officers could not possibly check out the credentials of so many passengers. They had to be satisfied if the boarding count tallied with the official passenger list.

The ship's casual security precautions had been of special interest to Chan Kwok Ching, a guerrilla general who controlled a small empire in southern China. Chan's gang, between periods of fighting the Japanese and the Chinese Nationalist forces who encroached on their territory, had found it profitable to smuggle wolfram ore and salt from China into Hong Kong. But with the political turmoil increasing in China, and the currency deteriorating because of corruption and Communist successes, Chan had found smuggling unprofitable. He decided to turn to his old profession of piracy.

While the *Van Heutsz* was in Belawan, Chan called members of his gang to a meeting in the town of Lin Shan in the Wai Yeung district on China's east coast not far from Hong Kong. It was decided that eleven gang members would slip into Hong Kong and board the *Van Heutsz* with the aid of two confederates who lived in Kowloon—one of them Sam Piu, who had traveled aboard the ship and knew its general layout as well as the ship routine.

Chan knew the ship carried no anti-piracy guards, and also that, after leaving Hong Kong, the captain would distribute weapons to his sixteen European officers. The pirate chief wasn't worried about the ship's 158 Chinese crew members because they could easily be cowed by armed men.

Chan told the gang, "We know that four hours after the *Van Heutsz* leaves Hong Kong, the captain will issue arms to the officers. This is the critical period. You must get control of the ship before the arms are distributed. When you seize the ship, you will force the captain to sail into Bias Bay. We will be waiting for you at Reef Island."

The gang members, each armed with a revolver, slipped into Hong Kong and dispersed. They found lodging at small Chinese boarding houses where they waited for Sam to arrange their passage.

At midday on December 14, Captain Vliek was back on the bridge of his ship, watching the last of the passengers hurry aboard with their bundles and packages. Then the gangway was lifted, and the *Van Heutsz* moved into the main channel and headed for sea.

At 4 P.M. the ship was nearing Bias Bay. All seemed well. Only eight new passengers had boarded the ship at Hong Kong, according to the ship's passenger list. The deck passengers were settled amid the usual shrill babble of many voices. The sea was glassy smooth, for which the captain was grateful because rough seas created havoc on board, especially among the deck passengers who were continually frightened and seasick.

Captain Vliek was in his cabin having a cup of hot tea when there was a knock at the door and the third officer and two crew members entered. "I have come for the weapons, sir," he said.

"Very well," the captain said.

Captain Vliek selected a key from his key chain and opened a large steel case. He gave the third officer and the crew members seven revolvers, six automatic pistols, five rifles, two machine guns and ammunition. They stepped from the cabin and the captain started to pour another cup of tea when he happened to glance up. Through a porthole he saw the third officer with his hands above his head.

"What in hell . . ." he exclaimed and started for the door to investigate when five armed Chinese burst into the cabin.

The leader was a fat, squat man wearing a cheap Western-style business suit. He waved a revolver and said, "Sit down, Captain. We are taking over your ship."

Captain Vliek, his face red with anger, took a step toward the pirate, but one of the gang shoved a pistol into his stomach and pushed him back. As he watched in outraged disbelief, the fat man sat himself in the captain's favorite chair and then laughed insolently. He selected a cigarette from a box and poured himself a cup of tea. He said, "Will you join me?" The gang members laughed uproariously at this jest.

When Captain Vliek did not answer, the leader shrugged his shoulders and issued rapid orders in Chinese. Members of his gang began ransacking the cabin. They forced the captain to open the ship's safe, where he kept emergency cash for paying crew members and for buying ship's stores and where many of the first-class passengers had deposited cash, jewelry and other valuables.

Elsewhere on the ship, the pirates went into action swiftly and efficiently. Chief Engineer G. Van Kleeveren heard a bab-

ble of voices outside his cabin. When he stepped outside a gun
was shoved into his side. Chief Officer A. Matterkoorn was coming up a companionway when he looked up and found himself
staring into the muzzle of a pistol.

Quickly the gang rounded up all the European officers, who
were caught totally off guard. They were forced onto the
bridge and guarded by a Chinese armed with one of the ship's
own machine guns.

In less than ten minutes, the pirate gang had gained control
of the *Van Heutsz* without firing a shot. Then they calmly went
about looting the vessel and its passengers. Terrified passengers were stripped of money, jewelry, and even clothing and
shoes—everything of value that could be sold in China. Many
of the deck passengers were robbed of their life's savings.

While the looting was under way, the fat little leader was
smoking opium in the captain's cabin.

Throughout the night, the *Van Heutsz* ran through the China
Sea without lights, a ghostly shadow moving toward Bias Bay
for a rendezvous with the main pirate gang. Captain Vliek was
forced to stand behind the helmsman to guide the ship through
the treacherous waters where it had never sailed before. He
had no choice, since there was a gun at his back.

The Chinese quartermaster steered the ship into Bias Bay and
slowly she made her way toward Reef Island, where anchor was
dropped. As dawn came there was a babble of consternation
from the pirate gang. They anxiously watched the shore. And
at last it became obvious to Captain Vliek that something had
gone wrong. He gathered that the gang had been thrown into
confusion because their confederates who were to meet them
and unload the booty onto junks were nowhere to be seen.

Finally, the leader ordered Captain Vliek to maneuver the
ship to cut off a passing junk. Shots were fired across the junk's
bow and it was forced to pull alongside. The pirates swarmed
onto the junk and the booty was transferred from the *Van
Heutsz*. Along with the loot, the gang took with them six
wealthy Chinese to hold for ransom.

When the last of the loot was transferred to the junk, Captain
Vliek, the chief officer and six seamen were ordered into a small
ship's boat which was lowered and secured to the junk by a tow

line. The junk headed for Tai Sami inlet. About halfway ashore, the pirates cut the tow line, leaving the little boat bobbing in the wake of the junk.

The fat leader waved. "You are free, Captain."

Captain Vliek watched the junk pull away. It seemed like a terrible dream. This gang of thirteen ruffians had seized the largest ship ever pirated in these waters, looted it of a fortune and escaped with hostages whose ransom would bring them perhaps another $500,000. And they did it without a drop of blood being spilled. The episode was a disaster—but the captain realized that he and his officers were lucky that the pirates had left without slitting their throats.

The seamen rowed the small boat back to the *Van Heutsz* and Captain Vliek immediately radioed details of the piracy to Hong Kong authorities. Then he turned his ship back to sea.

Four months after the piracy, Hong Kong police arrested Sam Piu on a tip that came from the underworld. They found over $50,000 in cash and jewelry in his room. Sam told police he made the money dealing in wolfram ore, but none of the wolfram dealers in the city had ever heard of Sam. Letters in his room indicated the wily Sam had pulled a gigantic double cross on his mainland pals. In one of these letters, Piu explained that the loot had been seized by Chinese customs officers and for this reason there was nothing to split with members of the gang. The kidnapped Chinese merchants were returned safely to Hong Kong—but police never were able to learn how much ransom they paid for their freedom.

The case of the piracy of the *Van Heutsz* was never satisfactorily closed by the police because the Nationalist authorities had so many problems of their own they couldn't bother with helping the British run down the pirate gang. One man was sentenced to six years in prison for his role in aiding the pirates and Sam Piu was tucked away behind bars, too—but is now free and living well for a man with no known source of income.

From the Hong Kong underworld came rumors that the pirates were linked to a Chinese secret society whose power extended from the mainland to Hong Kong. The police were not surprised at such reports. Almost every major crime committed in Hong Kong for years has had some connection with the secret societies, known to the British as Triads, because their basic insignia is the triangle, symbolizing heaven, earth and man. They form the most sinister underworld in all the Far East, controlling prostitution, gambling, extortion and all other forms of crime including organized murder.

In the United States, such groups would be known as crime syndicates. But the Triads have a more exotic background than the ordinary American criminal gang. The Triads are the Mafia of the Far East and they present a much greater threat to the security of Hong Kong than a mere crime syndicate because they are a potentially dangerous political force.

The British police fear the time may come when the Triads will be maneuvered by the Communists of Red China to create incidents of a political nature. These societies, many of them headed by men who present a respectable front in the city's business community, owe their allegiance only to their own success. And while the Hong Kong police have cracked down hard on them, they have been unable to wipe them out. Tens of thousands of Chinese in Hong Kong are more fearful of the power of the secret societies than they are of punishment from the police.

These societies had their beginnings in the seventeenth century during the early part of the Ch'ing dynasty. Originally they were branches of a patriotic organization dedicated to the overthrow of the Ch'ing emperors. The Ch'ing rulers had come out of Manchuria to overthrow the Ming dynasty; the southern Chinese regarded the Ch'ings as foreign invaders. Some of the loyal Ming followers—so the legend goes—took refuge in the Siu Lam monastery in the Fukien Province. The Siu Lam monks were perhaps as devout in their religious beliefs and practices as other Buddhist priests but with a difference. These monks specialized in the study of military strategy and the use of arms. They had been strong Ming supporters. The monastery became a center of revolutionary plotting against the Ch'ing rulers, who decided to rid themselves of the threat by blowing up the monastery with gunpowder.

A disgruntled ex-monk named Mah Leng Yee smuggled a group of saboteurs into the monastery. They succeeded in caching several tons of gunpowder in the fortress-like retreat without arousing suspicion. Ch'ing soldiers surrounded the monastery; and at a given signal, the gunpowder was ignited and a violent explosion shook the monastery, which was soon enveloped in flames.

Under cover of a dense fog, eighteen of those in the monastery escaped and made their way through the lines of the Ch'ing soldiers. One of those who escaped managed to take with him a pair of straw sandals that had belonged to the founder of the monastery. The fugitives made their way to a place called Ting Shan, where thirteen of them died from severe powder burns and starvation. The remaining five, known in the Chinese secret societies as "the First Five Ancestors," pushed on to the Yangtze River with Ch'ing soldiers in pursuit. They found the only bridge across the river guarded by Ch'ing soldiers. When capture seemed inevitable, so the story goes, three stepping stones miraculously appeared in the river and the escapees crossed over them to safety. At a second river crossing, one of the straw sandals salvaged from the monastery was transformed into a boat which carried them across the river.

Another version of the escape has it that the fog which shrouded the fugitives in their escape from the Siu Lam monastery was composed of two clouds, one yellow and one black. When the group was trapped at the Yangtze, the two clouds formed themselves into a bridge of brass and iron over which they walked to safety.

The fugitives made their way to the city of Muk Yeung in the Fukien Province where they joined forces with five other devout Ming supporters known in society history as "the Second Five Ancestors." This group made Muk Yeung a rallying center for Ming sympathizers—but the Ch'ing army defeated them in battle and the survivors scattered to all parts of the country where they set up branch societies. As the years passed, these groups gradually lost their original patriotic purpose but continued to be powerful pressure groups used by their leaders for political and even criminal purposes.

The British in Hong Kong took note of the secret societies, or Triads, and their menacing character in 1845 with the passage of Ordinance No. 1—an ordinance for suppression of the Triads and other secret groups. At that time, the penalty for membership was three years in prison, branding by a red-hot iron on the left cheek, or deportation from the colony. When Lord Derby, who was then Secretary of State for the Colonies, objected to the cheek branding, Hong Kong officials placed the brand under the left arm. But even this harsh treatment failed to stamp out the organizations.

After World War II, as the Communists pushed down from the north to threaten the Chiang Kai-shek government, Chiang's military men sought to use the Triads to rally public support against the Reds. This effort, according to British records, was handled largely by General Tai Lee, chief of the Nationalist intelligence bureau. The general exhorted the societies to fight "foreign domination" and to combat Communist infiltration into the army and the government. General Tai's deputy for organizing and expanding this move was General Kot Siu Wong, who was himself a long-time Triad member.

Kot Siu did succeed in bringing virtually all the branch societies under his control. Thousands of Nationalist soldiers were conscripted into the societies and required to take the oath of allegiance, pledging loyalty to the Nationalist cause and "death before defection." Ordinary citizens by the thousands joined these secret societies, because if they did not join, the implication was that they were pro-Communist. But this sort of rattle-brained mobilization was useless. It merely underlined the desperation of the Chiang government as it groped for any kind of support it could find to fight the Communists.

As the Communists pushed southward, tens of thousands of Chinese fled to Hong Kong. Most of them maintained their secret-society membership. Out of this turmoil, the Triad known as 14K emerged as the most powerful in Hong Kong, but only after a series of bloody street battles between members of the 14K Society and the Yuet Tung Society over protection rights in Kowloon's Shek Kip Mei village. The protection rights included control over brothels, opium divans, prostitution, pimping, drug peddling, street hawkers, waterfront workers, dance-hall girls and small businessmen, who were forced to pay some form of tribute to the society.

A Hong Kong police report sums up the menace of the 14K in these words: ". . . The 14K is an extremely powerful force for evil, which wields tremendous influence over the lower-class people in the Colony . . . The problem is a grave one and there appears to be no practical solution to it as long as the public, through ignorance or fear, continues to regard these societies as more powerful than the organized forces of law and order."

SINGAPORE

THE TIME: *1956*

THE PLACE: *Singapore*

THE CRIME: *Kidnapping*

The name Singapore, for the romantic-minded, conjures up visions of water-front brawls between drunken sailors . . . a man found knifed to death on a dark street . . . beautiful Eurasian women available for a price . . . the monsoons, when the steaming rains come in drumming downpours . . . and Old Bill Bailey sitting behind his bar strumming a guitar and cackling a bawdy song beneath the coconut-shell masks leering from the walls.

Singapore is also sleek men and women in limousines . . .

214

the Orient with a British accent . . . beautiful homes hidden in luxuriant tropical gardens . . . a mingling of brown and yellow and white skins . . . the cool bite of a Singapore Sling . . . and the old-fashioned elegance of the Raffles Hotel.

Singapore is all of this. There is the civilized surface. And there is the underworld of crime and violence—controlled and directed largely by the secret societies whose influence has degenerated into organized terror.

16. Number 7 Is Death

The hour was midnight. One by one, six Chinese men slipped through the shadows of a side street on the outskirts of Singapore and knocked softly on the door of a dingy house. When the door was opened slightly each of the visitors whispered a password; then they were led into a small room lighted only by the guttering flames of oil lamps set behind an improvised altar. They squatted on their haunches and nervously watched a little man who sat cross-legged on a low platform in front of the altar. He wore a black robe similar to the robes worn by Buddhist priests. It was belted at the waist with a white sash. About his neck was a string of beads and on his head was a red turban, symbolic of his position as the Heung Chiu, or area leader, of a secret society.

By day, the little man on the platform—whose real name was Ah Chai—shuffled through the streets of Singapore wearing the ragged, dirty clothes of a man on the edge of poverty. He blended into the background of Singapore so well that few people ever gave him a second glance. Only a few Chinese knew that he was one of the most powerful and dangerous criminals in the city's strange underworld. Not even the British police had found reason to pay any attention to Ah Chai.

On this night in March, 1956, Ah Chai had called before him the recruits who were to be initiated into the secret society, one of the powerful "18 Group" which controlled the underworld of Singapore and had connections with similar Chinese secret societies in Hong Kong. Each recruit, as his name was called, stepped forward and repeated solemnly the thirty-six oaths of loyalty required of ordinary members. This series of oaths was known as "Sze Kau" or "49" (4 × 9 equals 36).

When these ceremonies ended, Ah Chai reached into a box and pulled out a squawking white rooster which struggled futilely in his hand. Ah Chai held the rooster above his head and said, "You will swear by the blood of the white cock that you will never disclose any of our secrets. If you do, you will be branded as Ah Chiit (traitor)."

Those who heard Ah Chai knew the meaning. A society member who betrayed his comrades was certain to have the number 7 marked beside his name on the society's rolls. And the number 7 meant that he was marked for execution. There was no appeal. The initiates watched in the dim light as Ah Chai drew a knife and with one swift movement cut off the head of the rooster. The neophytes stepped forward and spat on the bloody head and then Ah Chai opened the door and threw the fowl's head into the darkness—an act symbolizing what would happen to those who violated the oaths which they had taken.

Two days after this weird ritual, a wealthy Chinese rubber broker, Tam Puay Choo, left his office on Chulia Street, just off Raffles Place in the heart of downtown Singapore. He stepped into a waiting trishaw—the bicycle-propelled version of a rickshaw—and the coolie driver headed for the rubber market where the midday trading session was about to begin. Tam had amassed his fortune by shrewd trading on the volatile Malayan rubber exchange, where prices soared or dipped with nervous twitching over every rumor of war or peace from Washington and Moscow.

It was only a half mile from Tam's office to the market place. And while many of his colleagues drove to the mart in their chauffeured limousines, Tam was content to ride in the trishaw. It was cheaper. The trishaw had traveled only a few blocks when a small black Morris sedan suddenly swung over and forced the trishaw to the curb. Before the coolie could shout an insult at the car's driver, two men stepped to the side of the trishaw with pistols in their hands and ordered Tam into the car. "The boss wants to see you," one of them said.

"No," Tam said. "I won't . . ."

One of the men shoved the muzzle of the gun into Tam's ribs and said, "Get out—or we'll blow you out of there." They forced the broker into the car which swerved into traffic. One of the abductors pushed Tam to the car floor while the other bandaged his eyes and tied his hands and feet.

It all happened so quickly that passers-by did not realize they had seen a kidnapping until the trishaw driver began shouting. The driver ran into a nearby shop and called the police emergency number, 999. Rapidly he told them what had happened and gave a description of the automobile and the license number.

Central police headquarters immediately radioed an alarm to squad cars throughout the city. A cruising police car spotted the Morris racing along Bukit Timah (Tin Hill) Road, which leads toward Johore, and gave chase with its siren screaming. The police car pulled even with the Morris and a policeman shouted, "Pull over."

One of the kidnappers cried, "Keep driving—and shoot!" The burst of gunfire from the little car forced the police to drop back. Afraid of hitting the kidnap victim, the police aimed their fire at the tires of the speeding car—without luck.

Police at headquarters followed the running gun battle by radio. A riot squad of specially trained police was ordered to move onto Bukit Timah Road ahead of the fleeing car and to block the road. When this big police car swung from a side road into the path of the Morris, the kidnappers' driver slammed on his brakes and the Morris skidded to the side of the road.

The driver and his two companions leaped out and darted into the jungle-like undergrowth, leaving Tam knocked unconscious on the floor of the car. When the police plunged into the undergrowth, the gangsters opened fire with their pistols. But the police were armed with riot guns and powerful rifles. In a short skirmish, two of the kidnappers were killed. The third man, Teo Eng Bee, escaped. But police found him three days later, hiding in the Indian section of the city.

Bee was a young tough known to police because he had been involved in several vicious street brawls between rival gangs. Obviously he had graduated from the ranks of the strong-arm boys to faster and more dangerous company. Bee was sentenced to death for his role in the kidnapping, but not once did the name of Ah Chai escape from his lips. To him this death was infinitely better than a traitor's death and having his memory symbolically spat upon and tossed into the darkness like the ceremonial bloody cock's head.

At police headquarters, Inspector B. W. F. Goodrich of the Criminal Investigation Department put together bits and pieces of information which seemed to confirm his suspicion that the kidnapping of Tam was not an isolated case. He heard whispers from the underworld that a powerful "Mr. Big"—

somewhere in the city—had engineered a series of abductions and pay-offs which had been hidden from the police for more than two years.

Goodrich's informers gave him the names of several alleged victims, all men of wealth in the Chinese business community. When police questioned the businessmen about the rumors, they refused to talk. It was obvious that they wouldn't talk because they were afraid of something or someone they believed to be more powerful than the police.

Goodrich was convinced that this fear which caused men to tremble in silence was linked to the Chinese secret societies, which were as powerful in Singapore as they were in Hong Kong. But it wasn't until October, 1957, that the police got their first big break in the long investigation. It came with the kidnapping of sixty-year-old Ng Sen Choy, who owned a prosperous tailoring establishment and had important interests in other Singapore businesses.

Choy was well known to the British because he had worked with them in underground operations against the Japanese during World War II, risking his own life and that of his family. His wife came from a wealthy family and his big home on Wing Loong Road, twelve miles out of Singapore, was a beautifully landscaped show place. The house sat in luxuriant tropical growth near the beach, looking out toward the Singapore harbor.

Perhaps it was the remoteness of the home which caused Ah Chai to select Ng Sen Choy as his next victim. For weeks, his agents watched the merchant's movements, noting the time he left home each day and the pattern of his travel which varied little from day to day.

One day Choy left home in his chauffeur-driven limousine, accompanied by his wife and a grandson. As the big car turned out of the driveway and headed toward Singapore, it was blocked by a black Hillman Minx and forced to the side of the road. Two gunmen jumped from the small car and climbed into the limousine. They knocked the chauffeur unconscious, grabbed Choy and hauled him, struggling, into the Hillman. Mrs. Choy saw them pull a sack over her husband's head as the small car raced away. Their parting words were: "You will hear from us soon."

The gangsters gambled that Mrs. Choy, the child and the
chauffeur would be so hysterical with fear they would do nothing until contact had been made by an intermediary. But Ah
Chai and his men made one fatal mistake. They underrated the
courage of Mrs. Choy. As the kidnap car disappeared, Mrs.
Choy saw a truck approaching. She hailed the driver and persuaded him to drive her and her grandson home where she
called police. She told them what had happened and described
the abductors and their car.

Minutes later, a police cruiser spotted the Hillman and gave
chase. The kidnap car skidded to the roadside and the bandits
opened fire. In the exchange of gunfire, one of the gangsters
was wounded and captured. The other two escaped. The
wounded man talked enough to cause Inspector Goodrich to
suspect that the leader of the gang was operating from a downtown headquarters. A careful check of small business houses led
detectives to a small import-export firm near Raffles Place. The
office was similar to dozens of other small business places in
Singapore. The front room contained several display cases and
a desk. Behind the front office were two other small rooms.

Three men worked in the office, one of them a ragged-looking
fellow named Ah Chai. All of them came to work on bicycles or
in trishaws and none of them was ever seen in a limousine,
which was the trademark of most wealthy Chinese. They
seemed to live frugally.

But Inspector Goodrich made an interesting discovery. While
Ah Chai by day gave the appearance of being one jump ahead
of starvation, at night he could be found in a gambling house,
playing for big stakes.

The police also learned that one of Ah Chai's colleagues in the
little office was a drug addict who had once been fined $1,000
for illegal possession of opium—and was known to be a Triad
member.

Gambling on a hunch, Goodrich ordered the office raided.
Police found some morphine and a syringe in a desk—enough
evidence to justify the arrest of the drug addict, who was
placed in a closely guarded cell and denied any drugs.

As the hours passed, the man's craving for morphine became
unbearable. Perspiration poured from his body. He shook in an
agony of pain and then he began to babble. His babbling re-

vealed that Ah Chai, perhaps the most unlikely candidate in all Singapore, was the brains behind the chain of kidnappings.

With this information, police rapidly pieced together the story of perhaps the most daring kidnap gang that ever operated in Southeast Asia. One by one, Ah Chai's victims began to talk when they began to suspect that perhaps, after all, the police had more power than Ah Chai.

Inspector Goodrich was amazed to learn that over a three-year period, Ah Chai had engineered the abduction of eleven wealthy Chinese merchants, using Triad members as his finger-men and abductors. Once a likely candidate was chosen, the victim's every move was watched for days. Then he was kid-napped and taken outside Singapore where he was thrown into a pig pen or chicken pen—to live in the filth of the animals and in his own filth.

When the victim was almost crazed by fear and revulsion, he was forced to write a note pleading with the family to meet the ransom demands. Ah Chai's intermediary would contact the family and arrange for the pay-off. The pay-offs averaged more than $200,000 each, and Ah Chai collected a total of $3,740,000, which he invested in apartment houses, small businesses, and parcels of valuable land.

Ah Chai surrendered meekly to police. An officer asked him, "Why did you keep on with this business when you already had piled up a fortune—more than you would ever need in a life-time?"

Ah Chai shrugged. "I had to keep on," he said, "to pay off the blackmail by gamblers." He said after he had won huge sums at the gambling tables, the gamblers came to him and threatened to disclose his kidnap operations to police if he refused to meet their demands. And so the kidnapper was blackmailed.

In a small notebook kept by Ah Chai, police found the tele-phone numbers of his victims, telephone numbers and ad-dresses of prospective victims, and the names of gang mem-bers. In his office they also found the Triad ceremonial robes which Ah Chai wore when initiating recruits into his Triad.

Ah Chai paid with his life for his crimes. Somewhere in Singapore, another Heung Chiu—chosen by the Triad—has picked up the underworld reins dropped by the wizened little criminal. The police battle against the secret societies goes on.

SOUTH VIETNAM

THE TIME: *1945–1956*

THE PLACE: *South Vietnam*

THE CRIME: *Treason and Murder*

Crime is unusually ugly and violent in many Southeast Asian countries, where the struggle for life itself is violent and primitive. The major crimes always reveal something of the history of the country itself and its people. Too often the full story of these crimes are exposés of official corruption.

Our story that follows is set against the background of the struggle for independence that swept Southeast Asia after the surrender of Japan in 1945, the Communist move to conquer all of Vietnam, and the emergence of South Vietnam as a free country.

In their desperation to hold onto Vietnam as part of their colonial empire, the French colonials made the cynical move of turning over police powers in Saigon to a native society that was nothing more than a crime syndicate with its own private army. The society collected its own tax on gambling, prostitution, smuggling, and even on the trade and commerce of Saigon.

The French thus bought the fire power of the society to help control a restless people, but they could not buy the allegiance of the people with government-by-criminals.

In this turmoil, there emerged men such as Ba Cut, the cunning cutthroat who terrorized the villages and established himself as a war lord by leaving a trail of dead men behind him in the jungles and rice fields. But Ba Cut at last collided with a man with whom he could not make a deal.

17. The Jungle Killer

On a stormy night in 1929, as legend has it, a twenty-year-old Vietnamese youth named Hunyh Phu So awoke from a deep hypnotic sleep in the village of Hoa Hao in west Vietnam and startled his parents and neighbors by advocating a religious philosophy which was to influence tens of thousands of his countrymen.

Phu So's suddenly acquired intellectual powers were astounding to those who knew him because he had been a poor student in the French elementary school. His teachers called him "the lazy one," and he was graduated only because his father was a respected elder in the little Vietnamese community which consisted of a cluster of straw huts huddled in a wide expanse of rice farms.

Phu So was born in 1919. He was a frail child, having been stricken with a strange disease which left him weak and pale. His father had taken him to a holy hermit in the hope the hermit could use his supposed mystical powers to cure the boy. The hermit taught Phu So the principles of self-hypnosis and patiently tutored him—perhaps planting in his mind the ideas that later emerged as Phu So's own.

After the death of his teacher, Phu So returned to his village. A short time after his return he fell into a hypnotic sleep, and when he awoke, he announced he was an apostle of Nguyen Van Huyen, a nineteenth-century prophet. Word of the young man's strange teachings and impressive mental powers spread throughout the countryside. Superstitious and curious natives began to make pilgrimages to the village from miles around to listen to the "new prophet."

Phu So gained quite a reputation as a faith healer. The lame, the sick, the blind and the troubled walked across rugged mountain trails, waded the swamps, and traveled the tributary streams of the Mekong to sit at Phu So's feet. He doctored the ill with incantations and potions brewed from shredded flowers and herbs. He was credited with miraculous cures and soon

his admirers were calling him Buddha Vivant—the living
Buddha.

Phu So's religious teachings were based on Buddhism, but he
preached that a Buddhist could have a pagoda shrine in his
home and "adore" Buddha without going to the temples which
were the traditional centers of worship. In effect, Phu So's teaching was to bring the worship of Buddha into the homes and
away from the temples. He advocated the simple virtues of
obedience of sons to parents, justice by administrators, and
marital fidelity. He denounced all alcoholic drinks, eating of
beef and water buffalo meat, gambling and opium smoking.

Around Phu So grew the Hoa Hao sect, which, at the height
of its power, was estimated to have at least a million followers.
By 1940, the French colonial administrators began to fear that
Phu So was becoming a political problem. A doctor examined
Phu So and declared him mentally unstable because he insisted
he was related to Buddha. The French interned him in Saigon,
but the internment only made Phu So a martyr to his followers
and more of a hero than ever.

When the Japanese invaded Vietnam, they sought to use Phu
So to undermine French influence and gain support from the
Vietnamese. They sent Phu So on speaking trips around the
country, displaying him as a friend of the occupation forces. But
Phu So secretly sent runners ahead to the villages to warn the
villagers not to believe the words he would speak. The runners
told the villagers, "If Phu So says white, he means black. If he
tells you to do something, then do the opposite."

At the end of 1943, Phu So eluded the Japanese and went into
hiding with members of his sect. He had decided to organize
an armed force of his own to oppose both the French and the
Japanese. To dramatize the creation of his army, he sent word
throughout the countryside that on December 2, 1944, in the
village of Cantho, there would be a human sacrifice.

Hundreds of men and women came from miles around by
foot and sampan to the meeting place outside the town. They
squatted on the river bank or sat in sampans at the water's
edge, tense with excitement. After a while an aged beggar,
known to most of the people because he had wandered from village to village for many years, was dragged before Phu So and

thirty of his Hoa Hao leaders who sat beside an improvised altar.

And then one of Phu So's disciples announced to the throng that the spirits demanded a sacrifice. The terrified old man was led to the altar and stripped of his clothes. He stood naked and quivering where all could see. Then a black-garbed Hoa Hao "priest" stepped forward. He drew a dagger from his belt and suddenly plunged the blade into the beggar's heart. There was a gasp from the crowd. Blood gushed from the dying man's breast. The blood was rubbed over his body, he was dragged along the river bank for all to see.

The people understood the real meaning of this pagan rite: a similar fate awaited any who opposed the Hoa Hao.

Among those who sat on the river bank watching the drama was a twenty-three-year-old peasant named Le Quong Vinh, who was to become known as Ba Cut. He watched the knife plunge into the old man's heart and his small eyes glittered with pleasure. Le Quong Vinh was a soldier in the Vietminh Communist Army. He knew nothing of Communist ideology or the dialectics of materialism. He was a professional fighter who found killing and looting more exciting and profitable than the back-breaking work in the rice fields.

In the guerrilla war against the French, he had won a reputation as a fighter with tremendous drive and energy. To him, the slaughter of the old beggar was nothing more than good entertainment.

After the sacrificial ceremony, Phu So joined forces with Ho-Chi-Minh, the Communist guerrilla leader, and together their armies fought against the French and the Japanese. By this time, Phu So was more interested in his army than in religion. And when the great war ended in the Pacific, and French rule was re-established in Vietnam, Phu So fell out with Ho-Chi-Minh, and their troops began fighting each other as well as the French. It was bitter civil war, and each day twenty or thirty men would be found drowned in the rivers, their hands and feet tied together, or their throats slit.

The peasant, Le Quong, did not forget the sacrificial scene on the river bank. He decided his future looked brighter with Phu So than with the Communists. He deserted his Red comrades and slipped into the headquarters of Phu So where, at last, he was brought before the "prophet."

"I wish to join your army," he told the religious leader.

Phu So stared for a long time at the thin, wide-mouthed young man and then said, "You have been fighting with Ho-Chi-Minh?"

Le Quong nodded. "Yes, but now I wish to fight with you."

Phu So said, "How am I to know you can be trusted?"

The peasant drew a razor-edged dagger from his belt. He placed his left forefinger on the table before Phu So and with one swift chopping slash cut off the finger at the second joint. He held the bloody, quivering stump of a finger in front of Phu So and said, "This is proof of my loyalty. I pledge you my body and my soul."

From that moment on, Le Quong Vinh was known as Ba Cut —Three Fingers. Phu So was so mightily impressed by the display of courage and disregard of pain that he made Ba Cut a squad leader in the Hoa Hao army commanded by General Le Van Soai.

Ba Cut was one of the most tenacious and skilled fighters in the Hoa Hao sect's army, but he brooded over his lowly rank. He looked with envy on General Soai and secretly dreamed of the day when he, too, would have the title of general with power to extort tribute from the villages.

Ba Cut's first chance for advancement came in 1947 when the Vietminh captured Phu So and, it is believed, executed him. Soon afterward General Soai made a deal with the French and brought his troops into the French camp. But Ba Cut did not immediately go along with his general. He waited for two months before he marched into the nearest French military headquarters with his squad and their arms—and only after he had made his own deal with the French commander. During the formalities of his "honorable surrender," the French commander bestowed on Ba Cut the rank of lieutenant.

This surrender ceremony was in June, 1947. In October, Ba Cut and his men deserted the French. They went into the swamps and began to prey on the countryside, as tough and well-disciplined a little band of cutthroats as Vietnam had ever seen.

At this time, the French were desperately trying to keep their hold in Indochina. Not only were they fighting the Vietminh Communist forces but also a strong nationalist movement which was rallying Vietnamese to its cause. In a desperate effort to hold onto their waning power, the French made a fatal mistake. They made a deal with the Binh Xuyen Society, which was nothing more than a powerful and wealthy crime syndicate. In return for the society's support in suppressing anti-French outbreaks, they gave the society complete police powers, control of the waterways and highways, and a monopoly over gambling, prostitution and other underworld rights in Saigon.

The Binh Xuyen exacted tribute on every commodity that moved over the roads and rivers from the farms, mines, and factories of South Vietnam. The society received a tax on every pound of cargo that entered or left the ports, and their power was backed by an army of hired guns.

Ba Cut prospered in this atmosphere of political, social and moral corruption, using the double cross with peasant cunning. In January, 1948, he marched his guerrillas to the side of the French and again pledged his allegiance. He was made a captain. In May, he deserted. In June, he returned again and was promoted to the rank of major. In October he deserted. In August, 1950, he returned to the French and at full-dress ceremonies became a lieutenant colonel. And then he betrayed them again. The enraged French commanders sent an armed column in pursuit of Ba Cut, but the Hoa Hao guerrillas trapped the column in an ambush and cut them down with automatic-weapons fire.

Each time Ba Cut deserted more recruits flocked to him. When he rallied to the government's side for the last time in 1953, he brought 3,000 men with him. This time the puppet ex-Emperor and Chief of State, Bao Dai, personally bestowed on Ba Cut the rank of major general—and the little peasant's prestige with the Hoa Hao sect reached its peak. His men admired him not only because he had outsmarted and outfought the French but because he had made the Emperor look like a fool. For almost a year, Ba Cut remained with the French Army while his troops were equipped with American-made rifles, machine guns, mortars, trucks and jeeps, supplied from the American military aid program.

But after the French defeat at Dien Bien Phu and the parti-
tion of Vietnam giving the Communists control of North Vietnam, Ba Cut called his officers to a secret meeting and ordered
them to prepare for a return to the jungles and mountains. A
few days later, the deserters set fire to fifty automobiles, trucks,
and jeeps and all other equipment they could not take with
them. As the smoke of the burning vehicles rose in the sky, Ba
Cut and his men slipped away once more into the area he regarded as his domain, the provinces of Long Xuyen and Rach
Gia near Cambodia. Here he was a virtual king, ruling by
terrorism and wielding more actual power than the royal Bao
Dai. The peasant at last had achieved the pinnacle he dreamed
of when he stood before the "prophet," Phu So, and chopped
off his finger.

Once Ba Cut came back to Saigon to revel in the fleshpots. He
had let his hair grow long and he wore the ragged garments of a
peasant so that none recognized him. Walking the streets, he
saw a nineteen-year-old girl whose beauty made his heart
pound—and he desired her as he never had desired any woman.
He learned her name was Cao Thi Nguiet—a name which means
"the moon"—and that her father, once wealthy, had lost his
money and turned for solace to opium smoking.

Ba Cut did not bother to pay court to the maiden. He went
directly to her father and paid the old man 500,000 piasters for
permission to marry the girl. When she learned of the bargain,
she ran to friends weeping, horrified that her father had
pledged her to marry an ignorant peasant and to live in the
jungle.

But she could not bring herself to disobey her father. She and
Ba Cut were married and she followed him into hiding. A few
months later a friend implored her to return to Saigon—but she
refused.

"I'm happy," she said, "because I am in love." It did not matter that Ba Cut had three other wives.

In the political upheavals that shook Vietnam after the Communists won control of North Vietnam, the puppet Bao Dai was
ousted and South Vietnam was proclaimed a republic. Ngo
Dinh Diem was elected President.

Diem was incorruptible. He knew that if South Vietnam ever
was to be truly independent and strong there could not be a

state within a state such as the Binh Xuyen Society. He ordered his army against the society and in a short, vicious war the Binh Xuyen gangsters' army was defeated.

In the summer of 1955, Diem decided to move against Ba Cut and his Hoa Hao army. The young Nationalist army—with many betting against them—went into action. They waded through the rice paddies, cut their way through the jungles and forded streams to maintain steady pressure on the guerrillas. At the end of twenty-five days of bitter fighting, the Hoa Hao army was destroyed although Ba Cut escaped with his headquarters command.

Six months later, Ba Cut sent an emissary to Saigon. With brazen insolence, he offered to support Diem on condition that he retain his rank of general and control over the provinces where he had built his empire.

President Diem retorted by ordering the beginning of "Operation Ba Cut." And once again the government's forces moved into action. Their intelligence agents reported that Ba Cut was in the lowlands, but was heading toward Nui Sap (Flattop Mountain) to set up headquarters and reorganize his battered army.

During the night of April 11 and the morning of April 12, Ba Cut and eleven of his aides traveled in sampans down the Mekong to the small village where Ba Cut was born. Next day they slipped along the streams and canals, working their way toward the mountains. At dawn, the bandit group left their sampans and cut across country on foot through the rice fields. A heavy mist hung over the fields and almost obscured the village of Chac Ca Cao, where Ba Cut planned to get food before pushing on.

Unknown to Ba Cut, a squad of fifteen Nationalist soldiers, commanded by a major, was waiting in hiding. They saw the bandits approaching with their automatic weapons cradled in their arms. They opened fire and there in the mist and fog they fought it out. Finally, Ba Cut and his men threw up their hands in surrender.

When his captors approached, Ba Cut saluted the major and said, "My luck is gone . . . you are the lucky one."

At his trial, Ba Cut appeared barefooted, wearing a black cotton garment which had become the "uniform" of the Hoa Hao sect. He was sentenced to death for armed rebellion, treason, kidnapping, and murder.

At dawn on July 13, 1956, Ba Cut was led to a cemetery on the bank of the muddy Cantho River where a guillotine had been set up. He kneeled and placed his head on the chopping block and then the executioner released the weighted blade—and Ba Cut's head toppled into a basket.

He died only a short distance from the spot where he had sat almost twelve years earlier and watched with pleasure as a dagger was plunged into the heart of an old beggar.

THE PHILIPPINES

THE TIME: *1945–1949*

THE PLACE: *Manila*

THE CRIME: *Murder*

When a country's political leaders themselves become involved in crimes of smuggling, bribery, theft and pay-offs, then the stage is set for death to get into the act sooner or later.

Manila was such a stage in the years that followed the liberation from the Japanese. Among the players were Americans who moved in to get their share of the spoils. The stakes were huge and men who knew the right people in government could walk away with fortunes made in smuggling and black-market operations.

But some didn't walk away. They were carried to the nearest cemetery. Not all of them died because they made the wrong move in their crimes. Some died because they mixed love with

232

crime, and not too wisely, as did an American named George C. Murray.

During this period of corruption in the Philippines, there was born an organization known as the Philippine Bureau of Investigation. It is a small police investigative force modeled after the United States' own Federal Bureau of Investigation—and headed by men who dreamed of making it an incorruptible force for good law enforcement.

The PBI still exists. It is like a small flame in a dark, gusty night. Perhaps the flame one day will spread. Then the Philippines will be freed of its tainted politicians and men such as George C. Murray.

18. Love Can Be Murder

At 10:25 P.M. on August 12, 1949, handsome George C. Murray of Kansas City gave a last look at himself in the bedroom mirror of his home in San Juan, Rizal—a suburb of Manila. He smoothed his dark brown hair, straightened his tie, and gave a little tug to the dark handkerchief peeping from the breast pocket of his gray suit.

Satisfied with what he saw, he turned to his pretty Filipino wife, Esther, who was watching him with the intensity of a woman very deeply in love. Murray grinned. "Let's dance one more," he said.

Murray turned up the radio and took the dark-haired woman in his arms and they swayed together to the tempo of the orchestra's slow beat. When the number ended, Murray glanced at his wrist watch.

Mrs. Murray said, "I wish you weren't going into town tonight, George."

"I've got to go," Murray said, "Tom is back and this is the only chance we'll have to talk business. Tomorrow he may be in Hong Kong." Murray glanced around the room and said, "Where is my pistol?"

Mrs. Murray shook her head. "I haven't seen it."

Murray shrugged. "I suppose I left it in the car." He kissed his wife good-bye and hurried downstairs, while Mrs. Murray peeped into the nearby bedrooms to check on her four children. The children were sleeping soundly and the maid-nurse, Maria Naral, was preparing for bed.

Murray hurried to the garage and climbed into the big black Cadillac. His chauffeur, José Tagle, appeared and asked if Murray wished him to drive the automobile. "Go back to bed, José," Murray said. "I won't need you tonight." He drove the car into the night. The headlights of the Cadillac bored into the darkness and the car swung onto the highway leading into Manila. Rain pelted the windshield and the lights of on-coming cars glistened on the wet asphalt.

Behind the wheel of the Cadillac, George C. Murray, aged

thirty, was a model of a young, successful businessman. Not many ex-soldiers could boast, three years after the end of World War II, that they were nearing the millionaire class. But Murray was on his way. And he moved in business and political circles where a man's success was judged by his connections and his shrewdness.

During the war, Murray had been in the U. S. Army's criminal investigation division. He had worked in Europe but near the end of the European war, he had been sent to the Philippines, where he helped in breaking up some of the huge black-market rings dealing in materials stolen from the American military supplies. He learned a great deal about the sharp operators and where they made their mistakes. He distinguished himself in one big case by breaking up a ring dealing in smuggled narcotics.

When the war ended, Murray took his Army discharge in Manila and became treasurer and half-owner of the Equipment Trading Company, known as ETRACO, an import-export firm trading in surplus goods. Within two years he had a half interest in a $200,000 yacht called the *Mistress*—a converted, Diesel-powered Navy vessel big enough to carry passengers and freight. While automobiles were extremely difficult to obtain at that time, Murray managed to have a Cadillac and also a Buick. He was frequently racing around the waterfront in high-powered speedboats. And he was well known at Manila's night spots.

In 1947, the year in which he bought half interest in the yacht, he met and married Esther del Rosario, who was as pretty as Murray was handsome. She was a widow with four children by a previous marriage.

Murray was a striking figure whether on his yacht, at the wheel of a speedboat, or behind the wheel of his Cadillac. He was over six feet tall and had the shoulders of an athlete. His suits, tailored in Hong Kong from the best British woolens and cottons, fitted well. He looked and lived like a successful man. Murray's story was not particularly unusual in the Manila of postwar days. After the Islands' liberation from the Japanese, there was political, economic and moral chaos. Fortunes were waiting to be made by men who took advantage of the situation.

The sharpshooters came from all over the world to move into the lucrative smuggling and black-market operations. And also many came to take advantage of legitimate business opportunities in a country rich in resources and ripe for development. No one asked too many questions about where a man's money came from.

Murray must have looked back on his brief postwar career with a great deal of satisfaction as he guided the Cadillac into Manila and parked it outside the Riviera night club. He entered the night club and was led to a secluded table occupied by a beautiful dark-haired girl. Her big brown eyes looked at him as lovingly as had the eyes of his wife a short while before. The girl, whose beauty drew admiring glances from others in the club, was Carol Varga, the Philippines' popular twenty-year-old movie star.

Carol Varga and Murray made a handsome couple as they sat with their heads close together in the dimly lit club. They had met aboard Murray's yacht when the boat was being used for some of the scenes in the movie *Sagur* in which Varga was starred. The yacht had become, along the Manila waterfront, almost as much of a mystery ship as Murray was a mystery man. It was seen in Hong Kong, Singapore, and other Southeast Asia ports almost as often as it was seen in Manila Bay.

As the couple sat at the night-club table (Carol told friends later), Murray asked her to marry him and she told him that she would. Carol also said that Murray held her close and whispered, "If I should die, Carol, I want you in my arms."

It was 4 A.M. when Murray drove his Cadillac into the garage at his home. Quietly he made his way into the two-story stucco house and to the bedroom. He undressed and lay on the bed wearing only his shorts.

Had Murray opened his eyes for a moment he would have seen the pistol's muzzle a few inches away. The first blast from the gun drove a bullet squarely between his wide-set eyes. The second shot tore through the lower right side of his mouth shattering his teeth. The third shot smashed into his neck just to one side of the jugular vein. And the fourth shot went directly through his heart.

A hand opened the French door beside the bed and a rain-washed breeze stirred the curtains. Then a woman's scream broke the stillness and the Murrays' three German boxer dogs in the pen beside the house began to bark.

Five minutes later a police car screamed to a halt outside the Murray home. Red-eyed, Mrs. Murray sat with the children huddled against her, their eyes big with fright, and told police that someone had slipped into the bedroom by climbing onto the balcony, and had shot Murray. Mrs. Murray said she was having a cup of coffee in the downstairs kitchen when she heard the shots. She ran upstairs and found her husband dead, the door to the balcony open.

Between hysterical sobs, she said, "When George went to bed, he told me not to wake him before ten o'clock . . . I wasn't able to sleep . . . I went downstairs to make a pot of coffee . . . I was sipping the coffee when I heard the shots . . . I ran upstairs and met our maid coming downstairs . . . I looked in the children's room to see if they were all right and then I ran into the bedroom and saw George . . . I screamed 'George, what happened?' But he was dead . . . I sent my oldest daughter to wake up the chauffeur and have him get a doctor . . . That's all I know."

Police asked Mrs. Murray if she knew of any enemies who might have killed Murray.

"George had enemies," she said, "because he had been threatened on several occasions. That's why he carried a pistol."

Police could not find a murder weapon but they took pictures of the bedroom and told Mrs. Murray to let no one disturb the bedroom until they made a more thorough search for clues. In Murray's desk they found telegrams, letters, and business papers which they took with them for study. When police examined these papers, they found a sensation that was to jar all of Manila. They found that the yacht, the *Mistress,* was in reality a gun-running vessel which had been smuggling arms, ammunition, jeeps, and war materials to rebel groups in Indonesia, Malaya, and other Southeast Asia countries.

This was the secret of Murray's spectacular success as a young businessman. One letter from a man named Stewart, written from Hong Kong eleven days before Murray's death, asked him to send immediately 12,000 rounds of .30-caliber M-1 ammunition. Another letter, from a mysterious "Captain Johnson," acknowledged receipt of arms and ammunition shipped to Malaya.

Johnson's letter said, "The Singapore police have been trailing me the last few days. From Bob came the information that an agent of your local militia has been asking questions about me, my business, etc. I would advise you to be more careful. Try to arrange another shipment soon. Bob says he can manage to get better prices and I think he can."

From other papers, police pieced together this story: Soon after his discharge from the U. S. Army, Murray had begun buying up huge stocks of army-surplus equipment. His backer was an international gambler. Murray obviously had political pull in high places, because he was successful in buying three depots of surplus materials.

And then in early 1948, the U. S. Army turned over to the Philippine government its great Base R in Calatagan, in the province of Batangas. This was a huge supply depot sprawling over hundreds of acres. It was one of the great bases used in supplying the U. S. armed forces in the final drive against Japan. The army had stock-piled tremendous amounts of equipment and matériel in these bases, including millions upon millions of dollars worth of jeeps, armored cars, tanks, field guns, crates of M-1 rifles, Tommy guns and machine guns, thousands of Garand rifles, and tons of ammunition still in the original crates.

But with the end of the war, these mountains of supplies became "surplus." In some fashion, Murray managed to get the government contract to haul material from Base R to the other points in the Philippines designated by the government. Strange things happened to the truck shipments. Somewhere along the route between bases, the new rifles, Tommy guns, machine guns, and ammunition were removed from their cases and replaced with worn old Enfield rifles, battered pistols, useless equipment and even rocks. No one bothered to check the contents of the cases before they were stored in warehouses. The thefts were not discovered until months later.

The profits in graft and smuggling were almost unbelievable and Murray was one of the "big-time operators." When the story of Murray's connection with the graft broke in the Manila papers, the *Philippine Herald* said: "Stunned by the discovery of the prominent names involved, names that held influence in the sacred precincts of the government, investigators were immediately advised by their superiors to move with utmost caution and care . . ." There were strong hints, too, that high government officials were involved in the smuggling and had been getting a rake-off on the surplus deals. The stench of corruption ran throughout the government but there were many Americans who had aided and abetted in the gigantic frauds.

As police studied Murray's background, they realized that he might have been killed by any one of a hundred enemies, or by one of his "friends" who had reason to cut him out of the lucrative trade.

Some were inclined to write off Murray's murder as just one of those things—just another of the postwar tragedies that had become so very common. But the Philippine Bureau of Investigation (PBI), a struggling young agency which was trying desperately to emulate the American FBI and remain above corruption, was not willing to write off the case. There were several questions that needed answering, questions which disturbed the officers as they reviewed the case.

Some of these questions were: If a stranger climbed onto the balcony near the dogs' pen, why didn't the boxers bark? No one heard the dogs until after the shots were fired. Why had police found no footprints in the muddy front yard? Why were there no mud smears on the white stucco wall below the balcony? And where was the maid of the Murray household whom Mrs. Murray said she passed on the staircase as she rushed to her husband's room after hearing the shots?

When PBI agents and police returned to question Mrs. Murray, they found a freshly laundered nightgown hanging in a closet. The police picture of the murder scene had shown two white gloves lying on the bedroom floor but the right-hand glove was now missing.

Acting on a hunch, PBI Agent Faustos looked over the Murray premises and found a pathway leading to a gate opening onto an adjacent yard. In a neighbor's home, he found the terrified maid, Maria Naral, who told him she had been brought there by Mrs. Murray immediately after the shooting.

At PBI headquarters the maid told police that she was awakened about 4:30 A.M. when Mrs. Murray came into her room with the youngest child, Eddie. "She told me Eddie couldn't sleep and the child wanted to sleep with me. Then Mrs. Murray left the room and closed the door behind her. About thirty seconds later I heard some explosions, I thought they were a car backfiring. After a few moments I opened the door to go to the toilet on the first floor. I saw Mrs. Murray come out of her bedroom. She started downstairs but then she turned and I passed her on the steps. When I came back upstairs I looked in the Murrays' bedroom and saw Mrs. Murray standing there with the children. Mr. Murray was lying in bed, bleeding.

"Mrs. Murray grabbed me by the arm and took me into the hall and said: 'If anybody asks you any questions, tell them the shots you heard were the backfiring of a car and that you also heard the dogs bark. Tell them I was in the kitchen and that we met on the stairs as you were going down.'"

"Did you hear the dogs bark before the shooting?" she was asked.

"I didn't hear them."

"Was the door to the balcony open that evening?"

"I closed the door myself and locked it before I went to bed."

Asked if she knew what had happened to Murray's revolver, the maid replied, "I heard Mr. Murray ask Mrs. Murray for his pistol before he left that night. He usually kept it under his pillow or at the bedside. Mrs. Murray said she didn't know where it was—but I had seen her put it in her sewing bag."

At first, the chauffeur was reluctant to tell the police anything. But finally he told them that he was awakened by the shots and stepped outside his room in the garage to see what was wrong. He said he was standing on the pavement looking toward the balcony of the Murray home when a figure of a woman emerged from the bedroom. He saw her throw something in the direction of the dogs' pen.

In the dogs' pen, police found Murray's revolver. Ballistics tests showed that it was the murder weapon. After repeated questioning Mrs. Murray produced the missing glove. Laboratory tests showed traces of nitrate on the back of the glove, none on the palm.

Mrs. Murray insisted that she had used the glove in handling fertilizers which contained nitrates and also that she wore these gloves while lighting matches to burn insects from her flowers. But police had a different idea as to the source of the nitrate— since such telltale traces often are left by a pistol's explosion.

The beauteous Carol Varga told police she had heard from some people that Murray was a married man but she preferred to believe such talk "the idle talk of jealous women." She admitted a girl friend had told her "George's wife has a pistol and might go after you or George."

She said, "He was always a gentleman—generous, kind. He never forced himself on me. Slowly but surely I was falling for him. I made up my mind that I would do my best to become a great star and perhaps someday be in a position to become George's wife."

Mrs. Esther del Rosario Murray insisted that her husband had been killed by an enemy who slipped through the balcony window. But police were convinced Murray was the victim of a jealous wife who preferred to see him dead rather than lose him to Carol Varga.

Mrs. Murray was charged with murder. The evidence against her was entirely circumstantial, but in summing up the case, Judge Ceferino de Los Santos said, "The theory of the defense, that the late George C. Murray was killed by an outsider who must have been a paid agent or hireling . . . is fanciful and therefore incredible . . . the court finds the accused guilty." Mrs. Murray began serving a life sentence on October 26, 1950, after the supreme court denied her appeal.

One thing was certain: George C. Murray knew a great deal about smuggling, but he knew very little about a woman in love.

JAPAN

THE TIME: *1948*

THE PLACE: *Tokyo*

THE CRIME: *Murder*

The Japanese people, during the occupation headed by General Douglas MacArthur, were incredibly submissive to orders from the Supreme Commander's headquarters. At one moment they were ready to fight to the death in defending the homeland as they had been in defending caves on Pacific islands, in futile banzai charges, and in kamikaze attacks on the American fleet. In almost the next moment, they were willing to obey without question the orders issued by the victor—because the Emperor asked them to obey.

Strangely enough, this obey-without-question attitude gave a murderer precisely the psychological situation he needed to carry out his fantastic scheme of robbery by murder. How the Japanese police solved this case stands as one of the best examples of detective work in modern crime.

The democratic processes adopted by Japan in the aftermath

242

of the war brought many changes to the Japanese police. Prior to the war, they had become puppets of the war lords who had used them to harass and to crush opposition to their plans for expansion. Like the police of Germany, Italy, and Soviet Russia, they were used as a means of forcing conformity to government policy.

With Japan's adoption of a constitution and a democratic form of government, the police powers were curbed enormously. In fact, the pendulum swung so violently that the police found themselves harassed to the point that normal police work became difficult. Often the harassment took the form of organized opposition by the Communist-controlled labor unions.

Nevertheless, the Japanese police are one of the most efficient anticrime organizations in the world.

19. Death in a Teacup

At 3:20 P.M. on January 26, 1948, Manager Takejiro Yoshida signaled an employee to lock the doors of the suburban Shiinamaki branch of Tokyo's Teikoku (Imperial) Bank. The last customer had departed and tellers were closing their cash drawers and checking their figures on the day's business.

Before the lock snapped, a visitor pushed through the door. He wore a loose-fitting white cotton coat over his brown suit. An arm band indicated that he was a Welfare Department health officer. He carried a small leather case which resembled a medical kit.

The visitor bowed politely to Manager Yoshida and introduced himself as Dr. Jiro Yamaguchi. He asked if he might speak to Mr. Yoshida on a matter of urgency.

The bank manager led the visitor to his private office and invited him to sit down. "What can I do for you?" Mr. Yoshida asked.

The doctor explained he had come to the bank on orders from Lieutenant Honet at General Douglas MacArthur's headquarters. The Americans, he went on, were deeply concerned over the fact that there had been a severe outbreak of amebic dysentery in the vicinity of the bank, caused by people in the neighborhood drinking water from a polluted public well. In addition, health officers feared there was danger of a typhoid epidemic.

"As you know," Dr. Yamaguchi said, "the occupation authorities are most particular when contagious diseases are concerned. I came directly here from headquarters in advance of the sanitation squad and police. It will be necessary for me to give you and all your employees a preventive medicine."

Manager Yoshida nodded. "I understand, Doctor," he said. He was not surprised at the dysentery epidemic report because only that morning he had learned that one of his customers was ill with dysentery. He also knew the Americans insisted on stern enforcement of health and sanitation regulations wherever the welfare of the city was concerned. Sometimes, it seemed to him, this concern went to absurd lengths.

"What do you wish us to do?" Mr. Yoshida asked.

Dr. Yamaguchi explained that everyone in the bank, to protect himself and others, would be required to take a dose of the medicine he had brought with him. He said every man, woman and child in the neighborhood was being given the preventive medicine.

Mr. Yoshida called his fourteen employees into the office. The doctor explained to them the grave danger to the community and the decision reached at General MacArthur's headquarters. He told them to bring their teacups into the room so that he could give them a preventive drug which was in liquid form. Some of the employees showed surprise at the peremptory request, but the group returned to their desks for their cups. At that time, the orders of the American Occupation Forces were being obeyed by the Japanese virtually without question and this one seemed no stranger to them than some of the others.

When they trooped back into the room with their teacups, one of the employees said he had never heard of a drug that prevented dysentery. He asked the name of the drug.

One of his fellow workers laughed. "Oh, what do we care," he said. "All we have to do is drink it."

Dr. Yamaguchi said, "Is everyone present?"

"Yes," Mr. Yoshida said, holding his own cup in his hand.

The doctor said, "You must take two medicines. The second must be taken immediately after the first. You will swallow the first dose quickly and then I'll pour the second dose into your cups."

He added, "This drug is very potent. Be careful not to let it touch the enamel of your teeth. Just stick out your tongue a little and cover your lower teeth as you swallow." He showed them how to toss the solution down their throats in one swift movement. Then he took a large bottle from his case and carefully poured the cups about one-third full of a liquid which he mixed with a little tea. The group held their cups in readiness and when the doctor gave the command "Dozo!"—they quickly gulped the liquid.

Some of them gasped and began coughing. One said, "It burns like whiskey."

The doctor said, "You'll feel better after the second dose." He poured more of the liquid into the cups. Again the employees drank it down.

Someone said, "My throat is burning terribly. May we gargle some water?"

"Of course," the doctor said calmly.

The group hurried into the main office to a water fountain and began to drink the cool water. Suddenly Hidehiko Nishimura, an accountant, collapsed on the floor. He sprawled on his back with his eyes open and glazed. His breath rattled in his throat as he gasped for air. Mrs. Masako Takeuchi ran toward the manager's office screaming in terror. She collapsed and fell headlong. Around her, others were sinking to the floor with moans and choking noises, writhing in an agony of pain.

The visitor wearing the white coat stood and watched his victims dying. Quickly he scooped up 164,400 yen in cash and a check for 17,400 yen—the equivalent of about $600 American money, but a substantial amount to most Japanese. Then he walked out of the bank, closed the door behind him, and disappeared into the gloom of the cold night.

Mrs. Takeuchi lay unconscious for several minutes. Slowly she fought back to consciousness and a world of fear and pain. She dragged herself across the lifeless bodies of her friends. Somehow she managed to open the door and crawl out into the dark street, crying for help. Her voice was little more than an incoherent babble. Passers-by ran to her and finally she made herself understood. One of the group was a policeman. He pushed his way into the bank into a scene of horror that resembled a battlefield. Twelve men and women lay dead. Of the fifteen who drank the doctor's "medicine," only Mrs. Takeuchi, the bank manager and one other were alive.

A hasty analysis of the dregs in the teacups clutched in the hands of the dead revealed traces of the deadly poison, potassium cyanide.

This was the most chilling and sensational bank robbery and mass murder in the history of Tokyo. It sent police on a nationwide manhunt that would continue for more than two hundred days and nights before the killer was tracked down.

The report of the mass slaughter was relayed immediately to Inspector Ohori, in charge of the Tokyo police department's criminal investigation division, and he took charge of the case.

The three survivors were rushed to a hospital where their stomachs were pumped and other measures taken to counter-act the effects of the poison. Almost miraculously, they lived. Police tried to keep the trio isolated from newspaper reporters until their stories of the crime could be checked. But editors of the Japanese press—enjoying a freedom they had never known in the prewar days—sent squads of reporters to try to obtain interviews. Some reporters posed as doctors, others as hospital workers. One placed a ladder against the wall of the hospital and broke through a window into the patients' room to demand an interview. The American press in its wildest days never saw anything quite like this.

When Inspector Ohori dug into the case, he was shocked to find that a man representing himself as a doctor had, on two previous occasions, entered suburban banks and used the same story in an effort to induce employees to drink the "medicine" which he carried with him.

The first case had occurred three months before the mass murders, at the Ebara branch of the Yasuda Bank. The sup-posed "doctor" had introduced himself to the bank manager and given him a personal card bearing the name of Dr. Shigeru Matsui of the Japanese Welfare Ministry. This "Dr. Matsui" had persuaded eighteen bank clerks and the manager to drink the solution he gave them. All became ill, but none of them died because the mixture was too weak. The mystery man fled from the bank without attempting a robbery—but the bank manager kept his card. The second case had occurred only nine days before the murders. A man representing himself to be "Dr. Jiro Yamaguchi," handed a card to the bank manager and demanded that the manager and the clerks take the medi-cine he offered as a preventive against typhoid and dysentery. But the manager became suspicious and the visitor ran away.

Ohori was horrified that neither of these cases was reported by the precinct police to Tokyo's central police headquarters. The police involved explained lamely that since no robbery had actually taken place, they did not think it necessary to bother central headquarters with a report. Besides, they said, the motive of the man involved was not clear to them at the time.

The day after the robbery-murder, the police lost a chance to capture the killer when a careless bank teller cashed the 17,400-yen check stolen from the Teikoku Bank. By the time the bank manager spotted the check with its forged endorsement, the man who had cashed it was gone.

Descriptions of the killer given to police by witnesses left no doubt that "Dr. Matsui" and "Dr. Yamaguchi" were the same person. He was a man past middle age with a mole on his left cheek and a scar under his chin.

The card bearing the name "Dr. Jiro Yamaguchi" was found to have been printed in a small shop near the Ginza. But no one could be found with that name. As for "Dr. Matsui," an investigation disclosed there was a physician by that name who lived in Sendai. Police found the real Dr. Matsui had an impeccable reputation and he had been far from Tokyo at the time the killer was giving potassium cyanide to his victims.

As Ohori studied the case, the most promising clue seemed to lie in the fact that the robber had used one of the real Dr. Matsui's cards in the robbery-murder attempt at the Ebara Bank. Ohori's men compared the card used by the robber with Dr. Matsui's personal cards. They found that the card was one of a lot of one hundred cards which Dr. Matsui had obtained in March, 1947, at Sendai, prior to attending a medical meeting.

Dr. Matsui had given ninety-six of the cards to persons he had met at the medical meeting and other places. He had only four of the cards left in his possession. Like all Japanese business and professional men, Dr. Matsui was a liberal giver of personal cards. In Japan, the exchanging of cards, even with the most casual of introductions, was (and still is) considered an act of courtesy and respect. Many Japanese keep carefully indexed files of the cards they receive. Some have serial numbers printed on their cards for cross-indexing and for quick reference to the names and business connections of persons with whom they have exchanged cards.

While Dr. Matsui had no indexed file, he had kept the cards of all of those with whom he had exchanged greetings. Listing these names, police began a painstaking search for the ninety-six persons to whom Dr. Matsui had given his cards. Inspector Ohori was convinced that the killer would be found among them.

In a remarkable investigation that lasted for many weeks, police searched among Japan's millions. It appeared even to the police to be a hopeless task at times and there were some who grumbled that Inspector Ohori had embarked on the wildest of wild goose chases.

But, incredible as it seems, the police accounted for all ninety-five of the remaining cards and checked on the stories of those who held them. They questioned 7,300 persons in verifying that each person was where he claimed to be at the time of the mass murder. One by one they eliminated from their suspect list ninety-five of those who had received cards from Dr. Matsui. The single name that remained on the list was that of Sadimacha Hirasawa, an artist whose paintings had won some favorable attention at art shows from time to time.

Dr. Matsui had among his cards one bearing the name of Hirasawa. The card described him as president of several art societies and head of a national art research association. According to his own description, Hirasawa was one of Japan's leading figures in the art world. Dr. Matsui told police he remembered meeting Hirasawa aboard a ferry while making a trip to Hokkaido and, naturally, they had exchanged cards. He recalled that the artist was carrying a painting of his own, titled "Spring Is Near," which he said he was to present to the Crown Prince. Dr. Matsui was impressed by Hirasawa's position in the world of art and the fact that his picture was to hang in the Crown Prince's collection.

Ohori could find no police record on Hirasawa except that his name was mentioned in two suspected arson cases. The artist's home in Tokyo had caught fire twice under mysterious circumstances—and fires in flimsily built Tokyo are as dreaded as a plague. The cause of the fires had never been determined. It seemed that when firemen arrived at the scene of the first fire, Hirasawa was directing the fighting of the fire and had become something of a hero in the neighborhood. An insurance company had paid Hirasawa's claim for damages after he was praised by the fire chief for his firefighting effort. In both cases, Hirasawa had gone to the police station for questioning about the cause of the fires, but he had so charmed the police captain with his story of fighting the fires and his experiences in overcoming a bandit who attacked him that they never got around to discussing the cause of the fires.

There was some truth to Hirasawa's claim to importance in the art world even though many of his critics thought his work was second rate. He seemed an unlikely suspect in the mass murder. But Inspector Ohori ordered a secret investigation into his background and movements.

The press was in full cry on the murder story and was shadowing the police on every move they made in the case. In the prewar days, the Japanese police would not have bothered themselves with public opinion or the question of civil rights. But under the new democratic constitution protecting individual rights, the police had become sensitive to pointing a finger of suspicion without solid evidence behind them.

Ohori sent one of his men to interview Hirasawa at his home in Tokyo but Mrs. Hirasawa said her husband had gone to Otaru City in Hokkaido because his parents were very ill. Police found Hirasawa at the home of his parents in Otaru City and were struck by the fact that the artist's parents looked remarkably healthy. Hirasawa seemed to be quite willing to discuss anything the police wished to ask him about his whereabouts on the day of the robbery-murders. He told them that on January 26 he had gone to the Mitsubishi Exhibition Grounds to meet President Oshima of the Oshima Land Company—and that in fact he had sold Mr. Oshima one of his paintings. He added that when he returned home late in the day, he had learned of the bank robbery from radio news broadcasts.

Asked about his meeting with Dr. Matsui, Hirasawa said, "Of course I remember Dr. Matsui. We exchanged cards while on the ferry going to Hokkaido." He recalled that the doctor had taken a fountain pen from his pocket and written an address on the card.

A police inspector said, "Would you let me see the card?"

The inspector had noted that Hirasawa had a mole on his left cheek and a scar under his chin.

"I'm sorry," Hirasawa said, "but my wallet was stolen by a pickpocket soon afterward and Dr. Matsui's card was among those I lost." In addition to losing the cards, he said he had lost about 11,000 yen.

When Hirasawa's story was checked with Dr. Matsui, the doctor was puzzled about the story that he had written on the card with his fountain pen. "I never carry a fountain pen with me," he said.

Detectives were assigned to watch Hirasawa's home near the scene of the bank robbery. Some posed as deliverymen, as repairmen and bill collectors in questioning members of Hirasawa's family and their neighbors. They obtained samples of Hirasawa's handwriting from postcards and letters. A handwriting expert compared this handwriting with the signature on the check cashed the day following the robbery. He said they were written by the same person.

The police discovered that shortly after the robbery Hirasawa had given his wife 80,000 yen and that his bank account showed deposits of 44,500 yen although a few days earlier he and his wife had been trying to borrow money from friends. In fact, Hirasawa had been so short of funds that he had not been able to meet his dues to an art society.

Questioned about his income, Hirasawa said the money came from the sale of paintings and from gifts of money made to him by wealthy art patrons. But police could find no one who admitted he was a patron of Hirasawa and no evidence that he had sold pictures amounting to more than 100,000 yen. Hirasawa said that Oshima, the industrialist, had bought one of his paintings and was among his patrons. But Oshima denied he was a patron although he had paid 2,000 yen for one painting. He recalled that once he had joked with Hirasawa about the fact that the artist fitted the description of the murderer which had been broadcast by the police.

By mid-August, 1948, almost eight months after the crime, Ohori had no doubt that he had found the murderer. He sent a detail of police to Ebara and Hirasawa was arrested. He protested his innocence violently and declared he was being persecuted. Detectives tried to bring Hirasawa back to Tokyo in secrecy but the story of the arrest had leaked to the newspapers and hundreds of people turned out at the railroad station in Tokyo to get a glimpse of the accused man.

People then began to take sides, for and against Hirasawa. Some newspapers charged he was the victim of a gross miscarriage of justice and that police were railroading him in total disregard of his civil rights. Stories were written that "so gentle a man" could not possibly have been involved in such a fiendish scheme.

When Hirasawa was arrested, the police obtained a search warrant. In his home they found a brown suit similar to that worn by the robber, a loose-fitting white coat such as the murderer had worn, and a leather case resembling the one carried by the "doctor." Two of the survivors of the massacre positively identified Hirasawa as the killer. But confusion was compounded when some employees at the other banks first identified Hirasawa—and then said they weren't sure he was the man.

At police headquarters, Hirasawa continued to deny he was guilty. An inspector pressed him to explain the source of the money he had given his wife and deposited to his account at his bank. This time Hirasawa said he received the funds from President Hanada of the Iino Marine Transportation Company in October, 1947—three months before the robbery. The inspector pointed out that President Hanada had died prior to October.

Hirasawa could not explain the discrepancy in his story. Finally he shrugged and said, "You are right. No one can obtain money from a dead man. I am the man."

Five months later, the artist repudiated his confession and claimed it had been extorted from him by police brutality. His trial was one of the legal sensations of postwar Japan. Hirasawa appeared in court dressed in ceremonial Japanese robes and sat impassively until the day he heard the judgment that he had been found guilty and the judge sentenced him to death.

Hirasawa's face twitched and he cried, "A great wrong has been done."

But Hirasawa still lives. His death warrant—for reasons never explained—remains unsigned by the Minister of Justice.

Some say it is because the case became too much of a political issue. Whatever the reason, Hirasawa continues to paint as he sits in his prison cell. He told a reporter that if he ever is released, he will sell his paintings to finance a campaign for election to public office.

"My purpose in running," he said, "will be to save those convicted of false charges."

But Inspector Ohori says quietly, "There was no mistake."

THE UNITED STATES

THE TIME: *1957*

THE PLACE: *Campton, Kentucky*

THE CRIME: *Bank robbery*

Fast cars, good highways, easy paroles for criminals, and a big, rich country in which to operate have combined to give a broader dimension to crime in the United States than in any other country.

A few months ago, Director J. Edgar Hoover of the Federal Bureau of Investigation issued a statement in which he cautioned against the Federal government's being given domination over the investigation and prosecution of racketeers. He said that "what is needed is co-operative law enforcement with no city, county, state or federal agency standing alone."

Mr. Hoover's statement was, in effect, a plea against any action by Congress which would place such heavy responsibility

254

upon one agency that it would become a national police force with powers overshadowing local law enforcement.

Within the Anglo-American system of law, the basic responsibility for law enforcement lies with the local police. The reason for this is that the framers of this system wisely decided against a national police force which could become an oppressive political force. And Mr. Hoover's plea is to keep this system as it is.

Since World War II, bank robberies have been increasing in the United States. This is one of the many areas of crime in which the most effective work is done by close co-operation between the FBI and local police.

20. A Crude Case of Robbery

Highway 15 writhes like a serpent through the hills of southeast Kentucky, past a town known as Viper, on through the narrow streets of Hazard, and into mountain passes whose beauty is breath-taking when the laurel and rhododendron bloom in the spring and wild flowers scent the air. Descending the mountain highlands, the strip of asphalt winds in a northwesterly direction alongside the tumbling waters of Troublesome Creek before flattening out on its way through Campton and Pine Ridge into the rich Bluegrass region of central Kentucky.

Highway 15 and the little tobacco-farm town of Campton (pop. 450) are only a squiggle and a dot on the map of the nation's highway system, but they became important to Kentucky State Police and the FBI exactly at midnight on Saturday, January 5, 1957. The first hint of this came at 8:30 that evening on a lonely stretch of road near Lexington, about sixty-eight miles from Campton, when two officers in a cruising Fayette County patrol car spotted an automobile parked on the roadside. "Let's see if anything is wrong," the sergeant said, and the patrolman behind the wheel eased on the brakes. He noticed that the car had Oklahoma license plates.

In the parked car, two ex-convicts watched the lights of the approaching vehicle. Earl Morris' hands gripped the wheel until the knuckles were white when he saw the red dome light on top of the slowing car. "They're cops," he whispered. Paul Scott dropped the acetylene and oxygen tanks he'd been testing and his fingers closed around the barrel of a machine gun.

The patrol car stopped parallel with the parked car and the sergeant rolled down the window. "Can we give you any help?" he asked.

"No, thanks," Morris said. "We had a flat tire—but everything's all right now. No sweat."

Something in the tone of the voice tripped a wire of suspicion. The sergeant decided to take a closer look at the two men. "Hold it a minute," he said to his companion. He opened the car door and stepped toward the other car.

But Paul Scott was moving, too. He came around the car and

shoved the snub nose of the machine gun within a foot of the officer's belly. "Get back in that car, damn you—or I'll kill you," Scott snarled. "Get goin'!"

The sergeant had no choice. Slowly he backed toward the patrol car. He was no more than five feet away when Scott fired a burst of ten rounds—over the sergeant's head.

"Next time," Scott said, "I'll aim at your gut." And then he leveled the gun at the patrol car as the sergeant slammed the door and the car shot away into the darkness.

Bluegrass police, alerted by a radio warning from the sergeant, threw up roadblocks on the main highways leading like wheel spokes from Lexington into Georgetown, Paris, Winchester, Richmond and Nicolasville. But Morris and Scott, driving over back roads, by-passed the Winchester barricade and headed up Highway 15 toward Campton. There was no sign of pursuit.

It was nearing midnight when their car rolled slowly down Campton's deserted main street toward a 1956 Chevrolet parked at the curb. "There he is," Paul Scott said. He leaned out the window and motioned the driver of the Chevrolet to follow. The driver was his brother, Don, also an ex-convict.

The two cars moved back down Highway 15 about six miles to a point near Pine Ridge where they swung behind a screen of trees which hid them from the view of any late travelers.

"Where in hell you two been?" Don Scott said. "I was beginning to think you'd backed out or the cops had grabbed you."

Paul told him about the brush with the law and how they dodged the police trap they figured had been set for them on the main roads.

"You should have seen them cops light out when Paul cut loose with that machine gun," Morris said. "Like a bat outa hell."

Paul Scott interrupted, "That's over with. Now let's get busy. We'll go over the plan one more time. First thing, we stash the guns and torch in the hiding place in the alley. Earl, you drive on past the bank and park. Then you come back and stand guard. Don, you climb up on the bank roof and keep watch. I go in through that washroom window. I figure I can get to the money in about an hour, maybe less."

Morris said, "If they haven't moved it out. You think they could have?"

"No. I figure there's maybe $130,000 in there. There always is when the tobacco season is over. After we get the money, we'll drive back here in Earl's car, switch over to Don's car, and then hightail it out of here."

The three men drove back into the sleeping town and their plan of operations began smoothly. Don Scott climbed to the roof of the two-story Farmers and Traders Bank and found a vantage point from which he could sweep the street with machine-gun fire if necessary. Earl Morris parked the car and slipped back into the shadows of the alley to stand guard while Paul Scott, using a wrecking bar, jimmied open an unbarred window which opened on the alley. He slipped inside, dragging his machine gun and the acetylene torch with him. Then he set to work prying open the washroom door, which led to the main room of the bank.

Inside the bank, a man rose slowly from a cot in a small room beside the bank vault. He listened to the sound of the iron bar biting into wood and his hand reached for the pistol beside the bed. Barefoot, he crept to the doorway and crouched there with the pistol aimed at the washroom doorway twenty feet away.

This was the surprise waiting for Paul Scott. He didn't know that bank officials, nervous about a previous robbery attempt and heavy tobacco sales deposits, had hired tough, straight-shooting, ex-paratrooper, Daniel Boone Stone, to guard the bank at night. And now, twenty-two-year-old Dan Stone was going to earn his pay.

Paul Scott worked on the washroom door with a flashlight held in his mouth. The wrecking bar tore the door from its lock, and Paul reached down to pick up the machine gun. He pushed open the door, the flashlight still held in his mouth.

Dan Stone leaned against the door frame and took steady aim. Flame spurted from the barrel of his P-38 automatic. He fired twice. One bullet smashed into the side of the flashlight, drove the flashlight battery spring deep into Paul Scott's tongue, and ripped through the bandit's mouth and out the side of his neck. Scott fell to the floor, blood gushing from his mouth and

neck. He thrashed around with stunned desperation, groping
for the machine gun and mouthing animal-like sounds.

Dan Stone stood for a moment, then hurriedly sprinted for
the door to summon help. He didn't know how many men were
out there in the darkness. He unbolted the door and raced to
call Wolfe County Sheriff George D. Little whose office was
only a few doors from the bank. He found the sheriff talking
with his deputy, Frank Adams, and Commonwealth Attorney
Ed Graham. Adams grabbed up a shotgun and the four men
ran to surround the bank.

Earl Morris had heard the crack of the pistol inside the bank.
He ran for the getaway car. Inside the bank, Paul Scott dragged
himself back to the washroom window. Desperately, he tried to
lift the heavy window but it was stuck and he was too weak
from shock to budge it. Savagely, he kicked out the glass and
rolled through the window into the alley, still clutching the
machine gun.

From the rooftop, Don Scott watched as his brother stag-
gered to his feet. "Head up this way, Paul," he cried. "Get to the
car." And quickly, he climbed down to help his brother. They
ran stumbling toward the automobile where Morris was starting
the engine.

Behind them sounded the pounding of feet. Don Scott
wheeled suddenly and the machine gun spit fire in a shattering
burst. Two of the thirty shots smashed into Sheriff Little's knees.
The impact of the bullets slapped his mangled legs from under
him and his pistol fell from his hand. Deputy Adams cut loose
with a shotgun blast and young Dan Stone emptied his pistol—
but this time he missed.

Stone dived for the fallen sheriff. "Give me your gun, Sheriff,"
he said, groping for the gun. But before his hand closed on it,
Paul Scott leaped on him, and, using his machine gun as a club,
crashed the butt against Stone's head, ripping open a gash and
stunning him. Deputy Adams swung his empty shotgun like a
baseball bat at Paul Scott but then he had to retreat.

The Scotts leaped into the car. Morris raced through the town
and up Highway 15 before the excitement in them died and
they realized they were headed away from Pine Ridge and Don
Scott's getaway car.

"Stop the car," Don said. "We've got to get back to my car—even if we have to shoot our way back. This car is too hot."

Morris slammed on the brakes to swing the car about, but it skidded into a ditch and crashed against a tree. The wheels spun and all their cursing and heaving wouldn't budge the machine.

"We've got to walk," Don Scott said. "But let's see how bad Paul is hurt." In the beam of the headlights, he saw the spring driven deep into Paul's tongue. "It'll have to come out," he said. "Get the pliers, Earl, and hold his tongue."

Paul gurgled curses and groans of anger and pain, but finally the battlefield emergency operation was done. Morris switched off the car's lights, and the armed fugitives began hiking across the frozen fields toward Pine Ridge, twelve miles away.

It was 8:30 A.M. when Taylor Booth, Wolfe County School Superintendent, drove into the parking lot of the County High School at Campton to make an inspection of the school buses. He opened the rear door of a bus and looked down the muzzle of a .38-caliber revolver. The red-eyed, unshaven man behind the gun growled, "Mister, you're in a peck of trouble."

The startled superintendent stammered, "Why . . . what have I done?"

"Because you're here, that's why. We're going to get away even if we have to kill you. In this game, mister, it's best not to leave witnesses."

Booth argued with the men that it would be useless to kill him. Finally he said, "You don't have to shoot me. I'll stand right here. I'm not armed."

Finally, the two men—one with a bloody bandage around his neck—climbed into Booth's Chevrolet after warning him not to move or sound an alarm. And they drove away. These two were Earl Morris and Paul Scott. They had slipped back to the Campton school yard with Don Scott before daybreak. They had hidden in the bus while Don went after his car at Pine Ridge. He was to return and pick them up.

The trio managed to elude Kentucky State Police who converged on Campton. The police were joined later in the day by a squad of eight FBI agents headed by Special Agent in Charge Ray L. Faisst of Louisville. The State Police and FBI agents combined forces and set up a joint command post in Campton. A citizens' posse was organized and deputized to help in the search.

Clues to the men's identity began to pile up. A bloody shirt was found in the school bus with the name "Scott" stenciled inside the collar. Morris' abandoned Chrysler was found and soon his identity and background were being established through the FBI's Washington headquarters. Don Scott's car was found at Pine Ridge.

The FBI agents, police and deputized citizens spread a warning by telephone throughout the area for farmers to be on guard against these men who were armed, desperate and dangerous. As the hours passed, the identity of the hunted men came into focus, and later information was added to tell this story:

On May 11, 1951, thirty-one-year-old Earl Morris of Antlers, Oklahoma, robbed the state bank at Collinsville, Texas, of $4,009 in cash. He was captured an hour later after a gun battle with police.

A few weeks later, Texas State Police gave chase to a speeding car whose occupants turned out to be Paul Scott, thirty, and his twenty-nine-year-old brother, Don, of Springfield, Kentucky. Police searched their car and found $10,000 in cash which had been stolen in a safe robbery at the Sheppard Air Force Base at Wichita Falls, Texas. While they were being questioned, the sullen Scotts tried a break for freedom by grabbing an officer's service revolver—but they were subdued after a wild shooting battle.

All three were convicted and sentenced to Texas State Prison at Huntsville, the Scotts to five years each and Morris to ten years. They became fast friends while serving their time. And when they could talk freely they discussed their crimes and where it was they had made their mistakes.

Morris said, "I should have killed that guy at Collinsville— and then they never would have caught me."

Paul Scott said, "I figure if we'd had machine guns, we wouldn't be here. Next time, we'll have machine guns and nobody is going to stop us . . . nobody."

Don Scott nodded agreement. "If we had had one machine

gun, we'd still have that $10,000 and we'd be having ourselves a time."

Morris served only two years of his term before he was released on parole and the Scotts were free after three years. Morris went to work in Ponca City, Oklahoma, as a painter for a contracting firm. The Scotts found jobs as hospital laboratory technicians back in Kentucky. But the trio's paths were to cross again.

In March, 1956, Paul Scott drove to Ponca City and sought out Morris. They talked over old times and then Paul told Morris about a little bank in Campton, Kentucky, that would be a pushover. The town had no police force—only a sheriff and a deputy—and they could break into the bank easily.

"Earl," Paul said, "when the tobacco season is over, there'll be over a hundred thousand dollars in that bank waiting for you and me and Don. How about it?"

Morris told Scott to count him in. And Scott said, "This time, Earl, we won't make the same mistake. We'll have machine guns."

Early in December, Morris received a letter from Paul Scott urging him to come to Leitchfield, where he was working. The tobacco auctions were under way and farmers were banking the receipts from the crops. It was time to make plans.

Morris drove to Leitchfield and moved in with Paul. Don drove over from a nearby town. They agreed on Sunday evening, December 16, as the target date but they postponed their move because they had no ammunition for the machine guns they had stolen from the Danville National Guard armory.

On January 5, they were ready. Morris had bought three hundred rounds of ammunition for the machine guns and he and Paul Scott had stolen acetylene and oxygen tanks and a torch from an equipment-company truck in Lexington. The torch completed their equipment for the robbery.

Morris and Paul Scott drove out of Lexington toward Winchester after the theft of the torch. About a mile from the city, Paul said, "Pull over and stop, Earl. I want to test the pressure in these tanks." The car rolled to a halt on the shoulder of the road. And then it was that the patrol car drove up and a voice said, "Can we give you any help?"

Now, less than twenty-four hours later, Earl Morris and the Scotts were hiding out in the cold, hostile foothills, with the FBI, police and a posse on their trail. Paul was badly wounded. Earl Morris had frostbitten feet. And Don was miserably cold, hungry and frightened. The bank job had been botched. So far as they knew, the sheriff was dead. They knew that by this time a posse was after them.

The search went on through Sunday night. On Monday morning, Don Scott was found by Kentucky police in a farm house near Pine Ridge where he had been given food and shelter by a kindly couple. He surrendered meekly—whimpering that he knew his brother was dead.

The hunt for Paul Scott and Morris suddenly narrowed on Tuesday to a lonely area near Pine Ridge when a worker discovered the car which had been stolen at gun point from Superintendent Booth. There were bloodstains on the seat.

The call to Campton brought FBI agents, police and possemen hurrying to the area where they fanned out into the fields and woods.

Walking across a corn field, Posseman Harold Alexander saw a movement in one of the corn shocks. "Come out of there or I'll kill you," he shouted.

His shouts brought FBI agents and police running to surround the corn shock. Crouching low, an agent approached the shock and said, "We're FBI agents . . . There are ten guns surrounding you . . . Come out peacefully if you know what's good for you . . . and keep your hands in front of you."

After a moment, there was a rustling of dry corn stalks and Paul Scott came crawling out. "Don't shoot, for God's sake. I surrender. I'm hurt."

"Who else is in there?" an agent asked.

"Morris is in there but watch him."

And then Morris crawled out to have his hands shackled. The corn shock was overturned and officers found a machine gun, a clip of ammunition, and a .38-caliber pistol. Nearby Morris pointed out the hiding place of a .22-caliber pistol, and admitted it belonged to them.

Morris said later, "When that farmer shouted at us, I thought the sheriff was dead and that guy was going to kill us. I picked up the machine gun and was ready to use it . . . No one is going to hurt me while I have a machine gun . . . Then I heard somebody say it was the FBI out there. I told Scott to go out first and I'd cover him with the machine gun and if anybody hurt him, I'd use it. But if nobody hurt him, I'd come out and give up."

Scott had another version: "When the first guy started shouting, Morris picked up the machine gun. He wanted to start firing, but I told him he'd hurt enough people and I didn't want anybody else hurt. When I heard you people say you were FBI, I figured that even if the sheriff was dead, you'd protect us. I told Morris to put that gun down, that I was going out."

Both men were taken to a Lexington hospital, Morris to be treated for frostbitten feet and Scott to have a fragment of bullet removed from his inner throat.

It's an ironical footnote that the hospital was The Good Samaritan, a fact all three of the bandits could ponder while serving thirty-year prison terms.

THE TIME: *1957*

THE PLACE: *California*

THE CRIME: Bank Robbery

Bank robberies have become so popular with professional criminals and amateurs alike that they constitute one of the gravest crime problems throughout the United States. And often the amateur's methods are more baffling than the professional's.

On December 3, 1958, a slender, gray-haired woman in her late fifties walked into the crowded lobby of the First National Bank of New York during the noon-hour rush. She carried a brown paper bag and looked like a gentle grandmother as she took her place in a slow-moving line of customers.

When she reached the No. 5 teller's window, she shoved the paper bag and a hand-printed note across the counter. The note said: "Put all your $5, $10 and $20 bills in this bag—there are two men guarding me with guns—I have acid in this glass— if you make an attempt to alert anyone there will be shooting and you will get this acid in your face. Give me 5 minutes to get out of here—you wouldn't want to see any of your associates get shot or acid in eyes. HURRY."

The young teller saw a glass of clear liquid in the woman's hand. He stuffed $3,420 into the sack and the woman walked through the Seventh Avenue exit and disappeared in the crowds. She was caught a month later trying the same trick at another bank. The glass of clear liquid proved to be nothing more than water. But the case is an example of the type of crime which bedevils the police and the FBI in increasing numbers.

During 1959, the FBI was involved in the investigation of 782 burglaries, robberies and larcenies of banks. There were hundreds of other cases handled by state authorities. In ten years, this type of crime has increased by 246 percent, with most of the increase in the past two years.

Prior to 1934, a bank robber could—and often did—rob a bank, commit murder, and escape with thousands of dollars without violating a Federal law because such crimes were only in violation of state laws. Congress has changed the laws since then to make such acts a Federal offense. Now the FBI and local police work as a team against the criminals.

21. The Handsome Fraud of Fairfax

The handsome home nestled in a fashionable section of Fairfax near San Francisco was the residence of William Liebscher, Jr., thirty-nine, university-educated, well-mannered, and handsome. Liebscher was proud of his home with its landscaped garden and the balcony where you could stand at dusk and look at the lights winking on across a prosperous community. All of it was evidence of the achievement and success of an automobile broker who had the respect of his neighbors.

Liebscher's first marriage had been a failure, but now he was happily married. He and his young wife, Jan, enjoyed doing things together and Liebscher, particularly, enjoyed the nights of play-acting with the community's Little Theater group. As an actor, Liebscher admitted to himself, he wasn't bad at all— not bad at all. He was aware that he made an impressive stage appearance with his broad shoulders and his height of six feet, one.

Liebscher's business friends accepted him for what he appeared to be, an aggressive, home-loving, successful automobile broker. Once when he was dining with a friend at Fisherman's Wharf in San Francisco, the friend said, "Bill, you're obviously doing all right. What do you think is the most important part of building a sound business?"

Liebscher replied without hesitation, "A good credit rating. You've got to have good credit. It means everything. You can't go places without credit . . ."

"Okay, okay," the friend laughed. "Don't get so excited about it."

"I'm not excited," Liebscher said. "I'm just telling you."

Occasionally a shadow of foreboding passed across Liebscher's mind with the thought that someday he might lose the house on the hill—the shining, solid symbol of his standing in the community . . . The shadow came with the thought that *they* might be closing in, that he had, somewhere, somehow, made a mistake since that first job he had pulled off so easily on . . . when was it? . . . on February 3, 1956.

But Liebscher had pushed such thoughts out of his head on the sunny Friday morning of June 14, 1957, when he kissed his pretty wife good-bye. "I've got a busy day ahead, sweetie," he said. "I'll call you if I'm going to be late."

During the morning Liebscher sold a couple of cars and then, after a quick lunch, headed his car for Fairfield, about fifty miles northeast of San Francisco. He drove into a parking lot just off the main street, shut off the ignition, and then looked around to be sure no one was near. Quickly, he took a make-up pencil and mirror from the glove compartment and skillfully drew a small mustache. He added crow's feet to the corners of his eyes and deftly deepened the age lines around his mouth. Satisfied with what he saw in the mirror, he put on green-tinted glasses, changed hats, and reached under the front seat to pull out a realistic-looking plastic pistol. He shoved it into a gray sock until the barrel protruded from a hole cut in the toe. He transferred a money order from his wallet to his coat pocket into which he also stuffed the pistol.

Liebscher, who had aged himself ten years in two minutes, stepped from his car and strolled toward the main street. He turned the corner and walked to the nearby First Western Bank.

The young woman teller at the window near the door reached up automatically for the money order being tendered by the towering man wearing dark glasses. But suddenly he turned the money order over and in a glance she saw printed on a small card: "Be calm and I won't shoot. Give me your 20s, 10s and 5s." Then she saw the muzzle of a revolver pointing at her, sticking from a hole cut in a piece of material.

Terrified, the woman quietly handed over $2,555 in cash and watched the robber walk from the bank before she recovered and screamed an alarm. But when a guard and officials rushed to the street, the mystery robber had disappeared.

Liebscher had simply walked from the bank, run quickly across the street, turned the corner, and walked into the parking lot. Then, swiftly, he wiped away the make-up lines with a piece of tissue daubed with cleansing cream. He put the gun and sock back under the seat, and shoved the money beneath the floor mat into the compartment housing the car battery. Then he drove from the lot and headed for Fairfax.

There was a tense minute outside Napa City when he was stopped at a police roadblock and questioned briefly about his business and destination. But the police waved him on after making a routine notation of his automobile registration and license. It was close but he was sure they hadn't suspected him and he heaved a breath of relief as he headed toward the home in the hills and his wife who was waiting—a wife who never dreamed that her husband was returning calmly from his thirteenth bank robbery in seventeen months.

"What kind of a day did you have?" she asked.

"Not bad, sweetie, not bad." He pulled her into his arms. "Business is getting better. What's for dinner?"

Monday morning, en route to work, he visited his bank and paid off $1,500 of the loan about which the bank had been nagging him lately.

He felt better after the visit to the bank. A man couldn't afford to get a bad credit rating, not if he was going to move ahead. He could see the time coming soon when he wouldn't owe anybody a dime—except for the mortgage on the house. And, hell, everybody had a mortgage. Some pretty sharp guys argued it wasn't smart to pay off a mortgage, not when you could charge off the mortgage interest against income taxes.

He felt better, too, when he read the Sunday and Monday morning papers and saw that the Fairfield police didn't have a clue to the identity of the bank robber. Best of all, no one had seen the getaway car. He wasn't surprised by this news of a lack of clues. Before he started the bank robberies he had worked for a time as a bank teller. He noticed in the newspaper stories about robberies that witnesses usually gave a scrambled description of the robber and hardly ever was anyone able to recall the license number or make of a getaway car. That's why he always used his own car on the jobs he pulled.

He remembered that in bull sessions with bank employees, they often discussed what they would do if suddenly faced by a robber pointing a pistol at them. Without exception, the line had been: "It's not my money and the bank is insured. If they point a gun at me, I'll give them the money." Liebscher was the only one who had said, given a chance, that he would try to grab the robber and disarm him. But then most of the tellers were women and the men weren't as big as he was, nor had they been boxers as he had been while in the Army Air Corps from 1941 to 1945.

Liebscher had reason to feel safe. His theory, that a simple robbery was the best system, had worked without a hitch thirteen times and netted him $27,765 of untaxed income. The reactions of the bank tellers and witnesses had been precisely as he had expected they would be.

He felt so confident that on July 10, 1957—using the same technique as in the past—he walked into a branch of the American Trust Company in San Francisco, presented his demand card for the fourteenth time, backed by the toy pistol, and walked away with $700. But Liebscher would not have felt so smugly safe had he known how swiftly the circle was being closed by the police and the FBI.

For months FBI agents had studied photographs and backgrounds of scores of hoodlums and former bank robbers and checked out their alibis. Stolen car reports were screened for any possible connection with the robberies. Witnesses were interviewed again and again for a better description of the robber whose modus operandi had become painfully familiar. But even though banks were issued warnings after each robbery, the phantom bandit came back again and again, and then walked away with little left behind to single him out from millions of men in the San Francisco area.

But Liebscher had left telltale clues behind him that slowly began to accumulate, piece by piece, as they were supplied by local police. None alone was much help, but when put together in the FBI's central file, they became more and more important.

The first major clue was left behind by Liebscher when he robbed the Westlake Branch of the Bank of America at Daly City, near San Francisco, on July 18, 1956. At that time he walked out with $1,750—but he failed to retrieve the money order used to camouflage the demand note. The money order was signed with a fictitious name, but it gave the FBI a sample of the robber's handwriting.

Bank employees, when asked to give their impression of the robber's profession, agreed generally that he probably was a salesman—and some even guessed that he was an automobile

salesman. One witness, a young Chinese optometrist, came up
with an unusual bit of information. He recalled seeing a man
of the robber's description standing at a table near a teller who
was robbed.

"This man wore glasses with Shuron frames and Calobar D
lenses," the Chinese said. "They were prescription glasses in my
opinion because the frames were too expensive for ordinary sun
glasses."

"How can you be so positive?" he was asked.

The young optometrist grinned. "You may think it's odd, but
even when I see an attractive young lady wearing glasses, I
notice the glasses first—and then her legs."

The FBI sought to trace their man through professional men
who prescribed glasses in Northern California. They came to a
dead end as they did with so many efforts which took hundreds
of man hours of work. But every possibility had to be checked
out.

A scrambled clue—but an important clue—turned up after
Liebscher got $2,555 from the Bank of America at Napa City
on May 10, 1957. After reading about the robbery in the newspapers, a Vallejo school teacher informed Napa City police he
believed he had seen the robber in his getaway car. This witness
said he had been driving through Napa City about the time of
the robbery. He saw a well-dressed man run across the street
and disappear around a corner near the bank.

"I thought something might be wrong," he said, "so I circled
the block. I saw an automobile drive out of a parking lot and as
it passed me I got a glimpse of the driver, a big man."

When the teacher heard no sirens and saw no indication of
unusual excitement in the street, he drove on toward his home
in Vallejo and forgot about the incident until he read news
stories about the robbery.

Napa City police passed on this information to the FBI.
Agents also talked to the teacher and added these bits to the
file: the suspect car was a tan sedan and the teacher thought it
looked like the pictures of the 1951 Packard which agents
showed him. The car carried a California plate and the license
numbers, as he remembered, were prefixed by the letters EPC.

The Department of Motor Vehicles at Sacramento supplied

the FBI with all EPC Packard registrations in Northern California. Agents located the owners, one by one, through successive ownerships and changes of address. They made sure none of these cars had been in the vicinity of Napa City on May 10. When this avenue produced no results, the search was expanded to all tan automobiles with an EPC license.

And then, unexpectedly, came the clue which pulled the pieces together. The Napa City police handed over to the FBI in San Francisco the list of vehicle registrations and license numbers jotted down by the officers who threw up the roadblock after the Fairfield robbery. From Sacramento, FBI agents obtained physical descriptions of the registered owners of the cars. And agents studying the list noted that one car which passed the road block was a 1953 tan Lincoln Capri carrying license CPC 874.

One agent said, "You know, all this time, we've been looking for the letters EPC. Maybe that teacher at Vallejo saw the letters CPC. That's close."

The driver's name, the agents noted, was William Liebscher, Jr., whose business address was a used-car lot in Fairfax. Also, Liebscher was a big man and his description tallied with that of the robber except for the age.

This thing looked hot. Liebscher's car was tan and could have been mistaken for a Packard. The letters CPC were close to EPC. He was an automobile salesman—and he had been in the vicinity of Fairfield at the time of the robbery.

A squad of agents drove to Fairfax and compared the handwriting on the now dog-eared money order, used in the 1956 robbery, with the handwriting on automobile sales transactions known to have been written by Liebscher. The writing appeared to be identical.

It was late in the afternoon when Liebscher came back to the used car lot where he conducted his business. When confronted by the FBI agents, he hesitated only a moment before admitting his guilt. He confessed to all eighteen robberies and he wasn't coy about it. He knew his little world of fraud and deceit had come tumbling down.

"I'm sorry, gentlemen," he said quietly, "for all the trouble I've caused you." He explained how he had gone deeper and deeper into debt because of his first marriage and some bad automobile deals—and how he tried to pay off his debts with the robberies to protect his credit rating.

Liebscher made one telephone call before he went to jail. He called home and when his wife answered he said, "Sweetie, I won't be home for a long time . . . I'm in trouble . . . I'm with the FBI . . . I hate to tell you this, but I've been robbing banks for a year and a half—and they've got me."

In the big house on the hill in Fairfax, a stricken young wife said through her tears: "It's strange. It's strange that you can live with a man for three years and not know . . . I must talk to him before I can believe anything."

On September 11, 1957, Liebscher was sentenced in U. S. Federal Court to fifteen years' imprisonment.

And, incidentally, the glove compartment of his car yielded the green-tinted glasses. Just as the young Chinese optometrist said, they had Shuron frames and Calobar D lenses.

 **ABOUT THE AUTHOR**

DON WHITEHEAD, author of the 1956 best seller, *The FBI Story,* has been a reporter and writer for thirty-two years and twice has been awarded the Pulitzer Prize. The first prize, for international reporting, was given in 1951 for his combat stories written during the early months of the Korean War. In 1952 he was one of three newspaper reporters who accompanied President Eisenhower on his post-election trip to Korea. His account of this journey won him his second Pulitzer Prize, for national reporting.

Born in Inman, Virginia in 1908, Don Whitehead attended the University of Kentucky. He was a reporter for the Associated Press for twenty-three years. During World War II he saw as much front-line combat as most soldiers, and was awarded the United States' Medal of Freedom for his wartime reporting. He left the AP to write *The FBI Story* and then joined the New York *Herald Tribune* as chief of the paper's Washington Bureau. He resigned this position in 1957 to do independent writing and in 1958 made an eight months tour around the world to collect material for JOURNEY INTO CRIME.

Don Whitehead and his wife live in Knoxville, Tennessee, where he plans to continue writing books while turning out a local column for The Knoxville *News-Sentinel.*